ORIGINS OF SACRIFICE

ORIGINS
OF SACRIFICE

A Study in Comparative Religion

By

E. O. JAMES

KENNIKAT PRESS
Port Washington, N. Y./London

ORIGINS OF SACRIFICE

First published in 1933
Reissued in 1971 by Kennikat Press
Library of Congress Catalog Card No: 75-118530
ISBN 0-8046-1153-X

Manufactured by Taylor Publishing Company   Dallas, Texas

TO

ROBERT RANULPH MARETT

D.Sc., LL.D., F.B.A.

*Rector of Exeter College, Oxford; University Reader
in Social Anthropology*

PREFACE

Notwithstanding the unique position occupied by the ritual of sacrifice in the history of religion, no volume exists, I think, which deals exclusively with the institution from the standpoint of anthropological research. Innumerable works, of course, treat adequately the various historical, philosophical, doctrinal and devotional questions involved in the evaluation of sacrificial worship in terms of validity and ultimate reality, of which mention may be made of Dr. Hicks's recent investigation of the part played by the concept in the formative period of the Christian religion, and the gradual departure therefrom, as he believes, with disastrous results. Again, from an entirely different angle, an interesting attempt has been made by Dr. Money-Kyrle to explain the meaning of certain varieties of sacrifice, and the unconscious impulses invoked by them, by the aid of the methods of psycho-analysis. Anthropologists, too, have not been slow to produce theories to account for the original conscious motives which called the ritual into being, and to put on record countless instances of the rite from all parts of the world and in all states of culture. But, so far as I am aware, no one has yet undertaken a systematic scientific investigation of the material as a whole.

Of modern regional studies perhaps the most notable is the admirable course of lectures on *Sacrifice in*

the Old Testament delivered before the University of
Oxford by my learned friend the late George Buchanan
Gray, in the capacity of Speaker-Lecturer. We can
never be too thankful that this manuscript was discovered by Dr. D. C. Simpson in Gray's study after his
sudden death in 1922, and that this invaluable piece of
research has been made accessible to scholars through
the labours of Dr. T. H. Robinson and his collabora-
tors in the work of preparing the volume for the
Press. It is to be hoped that its publication will
stimulate others with a similar intimate knowledge of
particular cultures to produce detailed investigations
of the institution in their own regions.

In the meantime I have ventured to step into the
breach with a wider survey of the numerous rites
comprehended under the name of Sacrifice, or belonging to the complex of ideas out of which, as it seems
to me, the institution arose. In the anthropological
treatment of a ritual of this character which has persisted throughout the ages, and undergone a complete
metamorphosis in the long course of its complex
history, there is a danger of interpreting the final
products in terms of crude beginnings by the simple
method of overleaping the intervening series of changes
in thought and expression. As Professor Percy
Gardner has pointed out, it is all too easy to assume,
for example, that the notion of a ceremonial eating of
a divine victim persisted from savage orgiastic rites
not only into the more civilized pagan mysteries, but
even into early Christianity. A certain school of
anthropologists, he says, " take ancient religion at its
lowest, not at its highest levels," regardless of the fact

that " while magic and materialism no doubt persisted, all the noble spirits warred against them." [1]

To counteract this source of error, I have carried the investigation through its successive stages to the higher ethical manifestations of the ritual in the hope of discovering the fundamental principles inherent in the institution as a whole, and of determining the chief phases of its expression. In so doing, however, I am very conscious of the pitfalls awaiting those who stray outside their own domain. In these days of specialization it is only possible normally for one man to speak with anything approaching a voice of authority on one subject, and unfortunately the rite of sacrifice as a universal phenomenon belongs to many departments of research, in most of which I can lay no sort of claim to first-hand knowledge. For instance, I am neither an Egyptologist nor an Assyriologist, and if I move rather more freely in Biblical studies, there are many technical critical questions here about which I should be very loath to pass an opinion, since any conclusions I might reach would be based on insufficient knowledge. Clearly, then, a work of this character demands some co-operation with specialists in their several departments.

In securing this all-important assistance I have been singularly fortunate. The advantages of living in Oxford are manifold, and not least among them are the unique opportunities afforded for consultation with experts in almost any subject. Furthermore, our scholars are quite the most generous people in the world, who unstintingly give of their time and know-

[1] *E.R.E.,* ix, p. 82.

ledge to any serious student, even on matters which must sometimes appear somewhat trivial; a quality which incidentally is not confined to this University, as I have good reason to know. Thus, if I am more indebted than I can say to my friend Dr. A. M. Blackman for the amazing amount of trouble he has taken in discussing with me the Egyptian sections of the book, it was Mr. Herbert Loewe, until recently University Lecturer in Rabbinic Hebrew at Oxford, and now Reader in Rabbinics in the University of Cambridge (his Alma Mater), who, at the end of a very busy term, and while within the throes of a removal, ungrudgingly devoted several mornings to a discussion of the later Jewish material. Dr. G. H. Box, Professor Emeritus of Rabbinical Hebrew, King's College, London, also made several valuable suggestions in this connexion. Professor Percy Gardner willingly bestowed upon me his unrivalled knowledge of the Greek mystery cults, and I have also consulted Dr. J. G. Milne, of the Ashmolean Museum, Oxford, concerning this aspect of the subject.

In the discussion of Babylonian conceptions of sin and atonement, Professor Langdon's advice and help have been invaluable, and he most kindly allowed me to see the proofs of his volume on Semitic Mythology which was then in the Press. Dr. T. H. Robinson, Professor of Semitic Languages, University College, Cardiff, who happened to be lecturing in Germany when I consulted him on certain questions arising out of the Old Testament evidence, did not hesitate to place his immense learning at my disposal on his return to England, despite many pressing claims on his time and attention. On the Christian aspect of the problem, the Oriel Professor of the Philosophy of the Christian Religion, Dr. L. W. Grensted, has supplied references and given me additional information with regard to the doctrine of the Atonement; the Rev. J. S. Bezzant, Fellow of Exeter College, made several valuable suggestions concerning New Testament interpretation, and Dr. Darwell Stone gave me his help and advice in Patristic matters. For the main thesis, however, and any errors which may appear in it, I am alone responsible.

Finally, it should be pointed out that this volume could never have been written if that splendid army of field-workers had not recorded faithfully the actual state of things as they have found it in operation to-day, or revealed by the spade or the text the hidden secrets of the past. To trace origins and determine fundamental principles are generally better reserved for subsequent and separate treatment in the study, but those who engage in these tasks should not be unmindful of their obligations to the producers of the raw material. In the arduous task of proof-reading, once again, I have to thank my friend the Rev. A. Mallinson, and my ever-devoted wife.

The dedication is the expression of a debt that a pupil owes to a master capable of kindling within him an ever-increasing enthusiasm for his own department of research which has endured from youth to middle age.

E. O. James.

Oxford, 1932.

ABBREVIATIONS

A.A.	.	American Anthropologist.
E.R.E.	.	Encyclopædia of Religion and Ethics (Hastings).
G.B.	.	The Golden Bough (Frazer).
J.H.S.	.	Journal of Hellenic Studies.
J.R.A.I.	.	Journal of the Royal Anthropological Institute.
J.T.S.	.	Journal of Theological Studies.
R.B.A.E.	.	Reports of the Bureau of American Ethnology (Washington).

CONTENTS

INTRODUCTION

CHAPTER I

THE BLOOD OFFERING

CHAPTER II

VEGETATION RITUAL

CHAPTER III

HUMAN SACRIFICE

with the growth of the maize—The purpose of the ritual—Human sacrifice characteristic of relatively advanced cultures—The distribution of the custom—Its place in the Inca Empire—Human sacrifice for the crops in West Africa and among the Pawnee—The offering of the " Meriah " among the Khonds in Bengal—These sanguinary rites connected with the revivification of the gods responsible for the well-being of society.

CHAPTER IV

HEAD-HUNTING AND CANNIBALISM

The head a seat of soul-substance—The potency of the head in promoting the growth of the crops—Head-hunting in Borneo and Assam associated with the productivity of the soil—Planting and reaping the principal occasions of these escapades—The eschatological interpretation of the ritual—The sacramental eating of the head of the victim prompted by a desire to imbibe the qualities of the deceased by consuming his soul-substance—Ritual cannibalism—The motive of vengeance a later phase of anthropophagy—The cannibal banquet and the blood-covenant.

CHAPTER V

MYSTERY CULTS

Social solidarity and the covenant idea deeply laid in human society— Initiation into the ceremonial life of the tribe—The rites usually involve tests of endurance, a ritual combat, a death and rebirth symbolism, instruction, lustrations, and sometimes a sacred meal—The relation of initiation rites to the coronation ceremony—Secret Societies in North America— The Grand Medicine Society of the Ojibwa and the Pawnee Hako ceremony —The growth of mystery cults in the Græco-Roman world—The quest for immortality—The Eleusinia—The preparation of the votaries—A sacred marriage and the reaping of an ear of corn may have occurred at the supreme moment in the initiation—The evidence does not warrant the conclusion that Demeter was a corn totem with whom the neophytes entered into mystic relations in a sacramental meal—An orgiastic communion may have been part of the Thraco-Phrygian worship of Dionysos in early times—The mystic character of the later Orphic rites—The fusion of the mortal with the divinity in the Attis-Cybele ritual—The *Taurobolium*—The union of the novice with the deity in the Isis mysteries—Syncretism and the highly artificial character of the evidence make it impossible to disentangle the original elements in the Greek mystery religions—Mithraism and the Early Christian Fathers . . . .

CONTENTS

CHAPTER VI

SACRAMENT AND SACRIFICE IN CHRISTIANITY

The mystery significance of initiation into the Christian Church—The Pauline theology of baptism and Græco-Roman parallels—The Church essentially the New Israel, and the immediate antecedents of the Christian sacrament are to be sought in Judaism-Jewish proselyte baptism, and the ritual of lustrations—The Rabbinical evidence of the Tannaitic period—The Johannine baptism in Jordan not a Levitical purificatory lustration, or regenerative bath—The theory of Josephus and the Marcan evidence—The earliest Christian authority (Q) seems to represent the mission of the Baptist as apocalyptic and Messianic—The relation of John to the Essenes—Essenism a movement probably Jewish in origin but having incorporated various elements from extraneous sources—Foreign influences in Judaism at the beginning of the Christian era—Hellenic culture in Palestine, and its relation to proselyte baptism, and the Essene and Johannine rites—The nature of Galilean Judaism—Christ and His early environment—The baptism of Jesus—Its Messianic significance as a seal for entrance into the kingdom of God—The Pauline doctrine, and the complex personality of the Apostle—Paulinized Christianity a new synthesis—Its development as a spiritualized mystery religion—The relation of the Eucharist to mystery sacramentalism—The origin of the rite—An established institution by about A.D. 55—The Last Supper probably occurred on Nisan 14—The character of the meal—The possibility of it having been a new *Kiddûsh* introducing a new division of time—The equation of Jesus with the Paschal lamb—The sacrificial significance of " the Blood of the Covenant "—The development of the Eucharist as a sacramental drama in the mystery of the *opus redemptionis*—The Agape—" Do this in remembrance of Me "—The Eucharistic sacrifice in the Early Church—The bloodless oblation—The development of the liturgical Eucharistic drama as a repetition of the initial sacrifice . . . .

CHAPTER VII

PROPITIATION AND ATONEMENT

The primitive conception of good and evil—The anger of mortal gods—Ritual defilement and its removal—The idea of propitiation and the offering of life to preserve life—The Paschal ritual—Atonement in the cuneiform texts—A Sumerian penitent—Ritual holiness and the prayer to Ishtar—The " curse of Eridu "—*Kuppuru*—The transference of evil and the ritual of the scapegoat—The Hebrew *kipper*—The goat assigned to Azazel in the Day of Atonement rites—The identification of *Azazel*—The origin and significance of the Day of Atonement ritual—The *Asham* and *Hattath*—The primitive background of the post-Exilic sacrificial system—The Mishnaic

CHAPTER VIII

PRIESTHOOD AND THE ALTAR

Sacerdotal intervention deeply rooted in the institution of sacrifice—An organized mediatorial priesthood belongs to the later stages of the ritual—The priest and the magician—Magic and religion different psychological approaches to the sacred—In primitive society the worker of magic is normally a private practitioner engaged in uttering spells and mystic formulæ—The notion of *mana*—No evidence of a godless age in which the magician alone held sway—Public ritual directed to powers superior to man to secure abundance and prosperity—Rain-making a religious ceremony—The term " magico-religious "—The transmission of the priestly office—The conception of *baraka* in Morocco and its relation to the Sultan and his community—*Baraka* and *mana*, though more or less impersonal in character, are closely related to a personal being—The transmission of this quality gives efficacy to priestly ministrations—The king, like the priest, is not the lineal successor of the magician, being himself divine—The royal priesthood exercising its functions by virtue of its peculiar relationship with the gods—Divine potency and soul-substance—The special relation of the priest to the supernatural order may involve ecstatic intercourse with the spirit world—Shamanism—Sacerdotal and psychic powers often intimately connected—Divination and Prophetism—In Babylonia the *barû*, or soothsaying priest, sought the aid of the sun-god by means of the liver, an organ rich in soul-substance—The Hebrew *kōhēn* the pre-Exilic equivalent of the *barû*—The priesthood in Israel developed round the sacred ark which was probably regarded as charged with divine soul-substance, and therefore an instrument of divination—The development of the carefully regulated centralized hierarchy at Jerusalem from a loose system of guardians of local shrines—The sons of Zadok and the Aaronic order—The Levitical priesthood—The place and function of Moses in the hierarchy—The royal

CONTENTS

CHAPTER IX

THE INSTITUTION OF SACRIFICE

INTRODUCTION

In undertaking a scientific investigation of the ritual and belief comprehended in the term " sacrifice " the initial problem centres in the evaluation and classification of the vast and varied data now available as a result of anthropological inquiry on the one hand, and of the systematic study of the archæological and literary sources on the other. Moreover, the issue is complicated, especially in the case of the more primitive material, by the nature of the evidence. Thus, the very word " primitive " is purely a relative expression, for what the study of modern savage races yields is not a history so much as " a number of pictures of given peoples each taken as it were by an instantaneous photograph at a given time." [1] Since this material is descriptive rather than historical, before it can be used to reconstruct the past it has to be broken up into its component parts, and each element analysed in relation to its complex cultural history. No classification or comparison of rites, beliefs and customs can be satisfactory which does not take into account the internal lines of development, and external influences which each strand in a culture pattern has undergone, any more than an examination of existing rocks is sufficient to determine the essential nature and history of the strata. Human culture is not a simple straightforward

[1] Hobhouse, Wheeler, Ginsberg, *The Material and Social Institutions of the Simpler Peoples* (Lond., 1930), p. 2.

I

process of evolution with gradations as clearly defined as those exhibited by the geological record of the earth.

Most anthropologists have now wisely given up the fascinating but futile search for ultimate origins, but, nevertheless, something in the nature of a time sequence is an integral part of ethnological inquiry. In the skilful hands of the late Edward Tylor, and more especially of Sir James Frazer, the comparative method, it is true, has been made the instrument for the collection and classification of enormous quantities of invaluable material so that the pioneer volumes entitled *Primitive Culture* are likely to remain the Bible of this aspect of the science, while *The Golden Bough*, as a storehouse of facts, will never be superseded, however much the theories and inferences may be abandoned or modified with the increase of knowledge. But the method fails, so far as the determination of historical sequence is concerned, because customs and beliefs manifesting a superficial resemblance to one another are frequently brought together regardless of the non-comparability of the actual occurrences. Before it is possible to compare any institution, custom or belief in a given area with corresponding phenomena elsewhere, it is necessary to take into consideration all the factors that have led to the precise course of the development.

As F. W. Maitland pointed out in the last century, " Our Anglo-Saxon ancestors did not arrive at the alphabet or the Nicene Creed by traversing a long series of ' stages,' they leapt to the one and to the other." [1]

[1] " The Body Politic," in *Collected Papers* (Camb., 1911), iii, pp. 285 ff.

It is, of course, often possible to establish a regular cultural sequence, but with a religio-social structure like sacrifice the various strands of the original pattern persist in such a changed form that we can only identify them as parts of the whole in relation to the fundamental design. Institutions survive because they are capable of adapting themselves to changed conditions through an increasing differentiation of form in accordance with increasingly definite functions. The new circumstances produce changes no less vital than those exhibited by organisms in the biological sphere. Frequently, indeed, it is a case of dying to live, for unless customs and beliefs can acquire a new functional value by undergoing a radical change and taking on a new existence through the impact of extraneous cultural influences, they tend to disappear. The most fundamental human institutions, therefore, are those which are based on some central expression of a permanent need which may become the accumulation of thought and character in the midst of the ebb and flow of circumstances.

The intensest emotions of a community are discharged in representative ritual which thus becomes the revelation of the inmost desires, strivings and necessities of the group mind; the expression in action of thoughts that cannot be uttered adequately in words. When perception does not find an immediate outlet in some form of activity an emotional tension is produced creating an unsatisfied desire. By way of relief, a sort of pantomimic rehearsal of the situation is performed, the pent-up desire to act discharging itself on the symbol of the object. Thus

3

ritual becomes the outward and visible signs of an inward and emotional experience.

To the cultured observer a sacred dance or complicated sacrificial rite may suggest many underlying motives and conceptions, but to the primitive performers and worshippers it appears probably as one indivisible whole—the expression of a single desire and purpose. Therefore, to understand the meaning and function of the ritual the emotional content must be recognized, just as the soul of a musical composition is only to be found in the blending of all the separate sounds.

To catch the inner significance of a fundamental institution like sacrifice, the ritual should be studied anthropologically, historically and psychologically as an attitude to life and a conception of reality. In its rudimentary aspects the symbols set forth a certain magico-religious outlook which, with the development of conceptual thinking, becomes intellectualized and sytematized into a definite cultus. Since the primitive mind deals in feelings rather than concepts, the desire to awaken an awareness of the mystery of life as an abstract principle, and to identify the worshipper with the vital forces in nature, finds concrete expression in forms that can only be represented with difficulty in our conceptual language. Moreover, the interpretation of this ritual of realization varies as the vision of reality changes, for, as Professor Malinowski has pointed out, " studied alive, myth is not symbolic, but a direct expression of its subject-matter ; it is not an explanation in satisfaction of a scientific interest, but a narrative resurrection of a primeval reality, told in satisfaction

4

of deep religious wants, moral cravings, social submissions, assertions, even practical requirements." [1]

Myth, therefore, as well as ritual fulfils in primitive
culture an indispensable function since it " expresses,
enhances, and codifies belief," and vouches for the
efficiency of the sacred actions performed. The translation of emotional reactions into ceremonial representations gives them a stability they would not
otherwise acquire since rituals tend to be protected by
supernatural authority and sanctions, and thus become
rigidly-observed and time-honoured conventions.
In the attempts to explain and justify established customs in the form of a pragmatic charter of primitive
faith and moral wisdom, the mythological setting may
vary as new revelations of reality become explicit, and
receive tribal sanction. Thus the ancient rites are given
a new significance and made to fulfil a new function.

This process of transformation, however, creates a
host of difficulties for those engaged in reducing the
material to any intelligible order in an historical sequence. The anthropological evidence, as we have
seen, is mainly descriptive, and while it serves a very
useful purpose in clothing with flesh the dry bones of
archæology, it is subject to its limitations. Similarly,
the literary sources of our knowledge of the early
civilizations can hardly claim uncritical reliance. Thus,
in Ancient Egypt the Pyramid Texts incorporate all
classes of ancient lore available for the purpose of
giving life to the king, and setting forth in ever new

[1] *Myth in Primitive Psychology* (Lond., 1926), p. 23 ; cf. *Argonauts of the Western Pacific* (1922) and article " Culture " in *Encyclopædia of the Social Sciences* (Lond., 1931), vol. iv, pp. 640 ff., for a fuller account of the function of myth in relation to social structure.

and different pictures the royal blessedness in the celestial realms of Re. The period occupied by these complex rituals extends over a thousand years, and such order as exists is due to the priests. Since their chief concern was to maintain and elaborate the State fiction, their efforts made confusion worse confounded. As Dr. Breasted says, " their imagination flits from figure to figure, and picture to picture, and, allowed to run like some wild tropical plant without control or guidance, weaves a complex fabric of a thousand hues which refuses to merge into one harmonious or coherent whole." [1]

In Babylonia the chief written sources for the history of the early periods are the lists of kings, certain legends, references to events in omen-texts, and, later, the royal inscriptions and the year-names of the kings. Recent excavations at Kish and Ur, and a number of other well-known sites, are throwing a flood of light on this literary evidence, but the documentary records of the Sumerian scribes only survive in excerpts embodied in Babylonian chronicles of much later date. There remain, however, copies of schematic lists of kings which there is reason to believe the scribes of Larsa and Nippur copied from earlier documents, the earliest versions at their disposal being probably original or contemporary accounts of the earlier dynasties. These lists, or the earlier part of them, must have been recopied time after time, however, thus perpetuating errors that crept in at a remote date, and rendering them of uncertain value as historical statements. The same applies to the *History of*

[1] Breasted, *Religion and Thought in Ancient Egypt* (Lond., 1912), pp. 135 f.

Babylonia compiled in Greek by the Chaldean priest Berossus, which, like the corresponding work of Manetho in Egypt, has perished, and is known to us only by fragmentary quotations from Alexander Polyhistor and Apollodorus, preserved by Eusebius and George the Syncellus.

It is upon these records that we depend for our knowledge of the early developments of Babylonian religion. Towards the end of the third millennium B.C. definitely religious inscriptions occur in considerable numbers, either in the original Sumerian text, or in translations, or both, until about the third century B.C. In the later tablets, such as those from the library of Assur-bani-pal, and the later Temple archives, there is much information concerning the gods and their worship, but the complex character of the texts, due to an intermingling not only of Sumerian and Semitic, but also of foreign elements, makes it exceedingly difficult to acquire a clear understanding of the fundamental principles and historical development of Babylonian religion.

If in many respects we are better equipped when we pass from the valley of the Euphrates to the Ægean, yet even the Greek literary sources would remain vague and uncertain unless they were supplemented by the evidence from the innumerable public inscriptions brought to light by recent archæological research. Being civil documents, however, they are mainly concerned with the State-organization, and while they throw much light on the minutiæ of sacrificial ritual, they do not reveal the heart of the Mystery religions, which remain an enigma.

The late writers on whom we have to rely for the most part for our information of these secret cults did not in the least understand the phenomena with which they had to deal, and even those who might have given us reliable information were not concerned to present an unbiased survey of the mysteries. The material from the earlier sources is therefore very largely uncritical in regard to origins. Thus, for instance, when Hesiod refers to the rich fields of Crete in connexion with Demeter,[1] he reveals ignorance of the fact that there are no such fields in the island, where arable land is scarce and the production of corn negligible. It was not, in fact, until the post-Aristotelian period that definite treatises in prose were written describing the various aspects of Greek religion. Thus, the chapter on sacrifice by Theophrastus is mainly preserved for us by Porphyry; Philochoros, a third-century writer, has described the festivals, sacred days and the Attic rites; and Istros, the slave of Kallimachos, deals with the Cretan sacrifices. But of most of this literature only fragments survive in quotations by later writers, lexicographers and scholiasts, whose accuracy is not beyond suspicion, as, for example, in the case of Pliny, who maintains that an African tribe had no heads, and the mouth and eyes were in the middle of the chest.[2] Their statements, therefore, like those of the Christian Fathers, must be used with cautious criticism, and even philosophers like Plato are prone to idealize the cult-phenomena. Pausanias is a more reliable guide, both as regards his own observations and in respect

---

[1] *Theogony*, ii, pp. 969 ff.   [2] *Historia naturalis*, v, 8.

of his use of the earlier literature, while Herodotus has been described by Farnell as " the intellectual ancestor of the modern anthropologist and student of comparative religion." [1] Passing to Judaism, the literature ranges from every stage of the historic past but the very earliest period. The bulk of the documentary evidence, however, comes from the ninth century B.C. onwards, and is derived from sources of various ages and characteristics. This complex material was enlarged, revised and woven together by later editors to produce consecutive narratives in which were combined ancient folk-lore and legend, primitive ritual and belief, oral tradition, sacred drama, poetry and lofty prophetic utterance, together with the germ of philosophy in the form of theodicies and apocalypses, extending over a lengthy and important period in human history, and representing the thought and knowledge of a great variety of writers.

The earliest sources of the Pentateuch were the work respectively of a Judæan historian (commonly called J) living about the middle of the ninth century B.C. (i.e. c. 850), and of an Ephraimite scribe (known as E) who wrote in the Northern Kingdom about 780 B.C. These narratives were subsequently combined, in some cases in rather a clumsy manner, and brought into relation with a third source (P) which had been produced by the priestly school during the Exile in Babylonia, though it was probably not until just before the return of Ezra (600–450 B.C.) that the Pentateuch assumed its present form. The Book of Deuteronomy represents a separate section based on the Book of the

[1] *E.R.E.*, vi, p. 393.

Law found by Hilkiah in 621 B.C., but the Deuteronomic tendency lasted well into the fifth century B.C.,
if not later, and the original roll must have been
re-edited and considerably enlarged after the Exile.[1]

In the so-called " historical books " of the Old
Testament the primary aim is religious rather than historical, with the result that themes are developed into
Midrashim for purposes of religious instruction in
accordance with the thought and practice of later times.
If real history is often contained in these picturesque
narratives, it is not until we come to the prophet Amos
in the year 760 B.C. that we find the actual words of
a living writer.   From henceforth the literary sources
are the records of contemporary events, however much
they may be idealized and made to serve theological
motives.   About 200 B.C. and later a new intellectual
movement made its way into Judaism as Hellenic
influences moulded Jewish life.   It was at this time that
a Jewish philosophy concerning the problems of human
life developed in the " Wisdom Literature," and in the
Maccabæan age a special type of eschatological literature
suddenly grew up in Palestine and continued into the
Christian era, describing in cataclysmic language the
supposed approaching end of the epoch.

While Christianity and Islam have a literature of
their own, each admits the validity of the Jewish
scriptures, and bases its doctrines largely upon them.
The Church, in fact, represented itself as a kind of new
Israel, Judaism, in the words of St. Athanasius, being

[1] Embedded in these documents is much earlier material, e.g. the " Book
of the Covenant " in Ex. xx. 22—xxiii. 33 ; cf. xxiv. 7—the oldest known
collection of Hebrew laws, and bearing a resemblance to the Code of
Hammurabi.

" the sacred school of the knowledge of God, and of the spiritual life for all mankind." The New Testament differs from the earlier Hebrew narratives in that it represents an account of events which occurred within the living memory of the authors, or in the lifetime of their immediate predecessors. Therefore, as documentary data it is more reliable than the records of oral tradition. But, even so, since we are dealing with several accounts of the same story derived from various sources, critical study is necessary to determine the different elements in the narratives, and to arrive at a correct estimate of the Figure whose personality and teaching dominate the whole collection of writings and give it its inherent unity.

The four canonical accounts of the life of Jesus present a common picture, though the Fourth Gospel preserves certain characteristics of its own. Hitherto it has been generally thought that the First and Third Evangelists based their narratives substantially on the Marcan material, which belongs probably to the days of the Neronian persecution between the years A.D. 65 and 67.[1] To this they added large additions from their own sources, drawn mainly from a document commonly designated Q, which was more a record of the teaching of Christ than a biographical account of His life. Thus the non-Marcan matter in Luke has been analysed into Q, and the writer's own material obtained from a variety of sources (L). It is now urged by Streeter that Mark was the earliest of the written Gospels, but that St. Luke had written his

[1] A. E. J. Rawlinson, *St. Mark* (Westminster Commentary), Lond., 1925, p. xxix.

narrative, based on Q and L, years before he encountered Mark. He thereupon incorporated large extracts from the Marcan material into his own account. Similarly, the First Gospel, which was written rather later, probably some time between A.D. 80 and 102,[1] was composed from numerous sources, including Matthew's own material (M) collected with a view to setting forth Jesus as the true Messiah and Lord of the New Israel, and supplemented from Mark and Q.

This " four document hypothesis," while open to objections, unquestionably broadens the basis of the evidence for the authentic Christian tradition, since behind the First and Third Gospels are the teaching of the Churches of Antioch (Q) about A.D. 50, Rome (Mark) about A.D. 60, Cæsarea (L) also about A.D. 60, and Jerusalem (M) about A.D. 65.[2]

This may be represented in tabular form as follows :

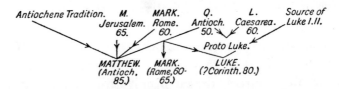

The Fourth Gospel, whoever the author may have been, must have been written between A.D. 90 and 120, and it unquestionably reflects the thought and belief of the Ephesian Church at the beginning of the second century. Yet while there is unmistakable evidence of a Hellenic strain in the narratives, the appeal is to the Jewish Scriptures and the Synoptists,

---

[1] C. H. Turner, *J.T.S.*, x, p. 172.

[2] Streeter, *The Four Gospels* (Lond., 1926), pp. 150, 214, 489.

interpreted in terms familiar to the semi-Greek, semi-Oriental population of Asia Minor. The writer's purpose being theological rather than biographical, he makes no attempt to reproduce the actual words of Christ, and omits many of the incidents recorded elsewhere, selecting episodes illustrating the doctrines he desires to teach (cf. St. John xx. 30 f.). There can be little doubt that he was acquainted with Mark,[1] and it is now becoming apparent that he also knew Luke or Proto-Luke.[2] It may be, as Taylor suggests, that Proto-Luke and John independently reflect common traditions, even if the Fourth Evangelist was acquainted with St. Luke.[3]

In the Pauline literature, the epistles unquestionably written by the Apostle are 1 and 2 Corinthians, Romans and Galatians. The evidence for the authenticity of Colossians, Philemon, Philippians, and Ephesians is less convincing, though not to be lightly set aside. The Pastoral Epistles (1 and 2 Timothy and Titus) constitute a more serious problem in Pauline authorship, and while expert opinion is very much divided, they may turn out to be " much edited fragments " of genuine letters. The ancient problem of Hebrews seems to be solved best by attributing the epistle to an unknown author of the second generation of the Church, while in the case of the shorter epistles (James, Jude, 1 and 2 Peter) it is impossible to arrive at any satisfactory conclusions, regarding date and authorship. The Johannine literature is part of the

---

[1] B. W. Bacon, *The Fourth Gospel in Research and Debate* (New Haven, 1926), pp. 366 ff.

[2] Streeter, *op. cit.*, p. 402 ; Bacon, *op. cit.*, p. 368.

[3] Taylor, *Behind the Third Gospel* (Oxford, 1926), p. 225.

complex problem of the Fourth Gospel, and the Apocalypse may have been compiled from various eschatological sources during the Domitian persecution at the end of the first century A.D. by a Palestinian seer of the Johannine school who had lived in Asia.

With the rise of Gnosticism in the second century it became necessary to safeguard the original Christian tradition, and to this end Apostolic authorship was made an indispensable condition for the admission of a document into the Canon, so that even the Second and Third Gospels came to be attributed to Petrine and Pauline influences.[1]   This practice has caused considerable confusion of dates and authorships, and incidentally led to a false and quasi-magical conception of inspiration, which has had the effect of retarding the scientific analysis of the literature.   In the light of modern critical methods, however, the books are now assuming their true positions in the historical sequence of events at the beginning of our era.

The Canon was well-established before the Qur'an made its appearance, though Muhammed was better acquainted with the Old than with the New Testament. It was chiefly the earlier narratives connected with Adam, Noah, Abraham, Lot, and Moses, and the otherwise unknown prophets Hud, Salib, and Shu'aib, that occur in the sacred scriptures of Islam.   Elijah and Jonah are the only Old Testament prophets mentioned, and these are supplemented by accounts of David and Job.   It would seem that the sources of information were for the most part oral tradition, Rabbinic Midrash, and the later apocalyptic writings.

[1] Tertullian, *Adv. Marc.*, iv, p. 5.

Monotheism is steadfastly maintained throughout, but the sacrificial system belongs to the earliest type of Hebrew ritual.

The Qur'an as it now stands is a collection of *suras*, or chapters, of very mixed character, containing a series of " revelations " alleged to have been made to the Prophet, dictated from an original code, " the Mother of the Book," which is preserved in Heaven as a " well-guarded tablet," and brought to earth by an angelic being, later identified with Gabriel. It is probable that Muhammed did not himself write down his speeches, the revelations having been recorded by his followers from memory and odd notes.[1] Hence the numerous obscurities in the received text, which have been further complicated by the imperfect character of the Arabic script, and the dialectical peculiarities in the speech of the original recorders. Moreover, the thought of the prophet was far from clear. Nevertheless, if his " messages " were largely the product of confused thinking, they convinced him, and ultimately his followers, of their divine origin.

Among the great polytheistic systems of the East, Hinduism alone lays claim to a revelation vouchsafed and preserved in an ancient sacred literature which forms the basis of the religion. The *Rig-Veda*, the earliest version of which may date from about 1200 B.C., consists of hymns arranged in ten books containing over ten thousand verses, addressed to the gods during sacrifice, and regarded as the source of all Hindu theology and practice. Six of them (II–VII) —the " family-books "—form the nucleus of the

[1] R. A. Nicholson, *Literary History of the Arabs*, 2nd ed. (Camb., 1930).

collection ; the eighth book and the fifty hymns of the first book are ascribed to the family of Kanva, while those of the ninth book are addressed to the deified plant, *soma*, the juice of which is offered to the gods. The remainder of the first book, and the whole of the tenth, are of later date.

This literature is held to be eternally pre-existent, but revealed to the different poets (*Rishis*) in whose families the hymns were sung ; but of their real origin nothing is definitely known. Their composition probably extends over many generations, but it is fundamentally primitive in character, reflecting a time when Aryan territories were still limited southward by the physical barriers of Rajputana and eastward by the Upper Ganges. Archaic words and phrases for forest life and culture suggest an earlier phase when the Indo-European invaders were making their way into the Punjab from the Eurasian grasslands ; an event that seems to have occupied a place in the Hindu sacred literature comparable to that of the Exodus in the Hebrew scriptures. Thus the " Way " became a symbol of moral progress, and the good land into which the Aryan-speaking immigrants had come found representation in the description of the Lotus of the world with its seed-vessel in the sacred lake Manasarowar, the mystic reservoir of life, and source of the Sutlej River, with the Indus and Brahmaputra rising near by ; its inner petals upturned from the Himalayan ranges, and its outer row, reverted, are sections of the foothills and plain between the greater rivers.

Upon this foundation the most complicated and

abstract religious literature in the world arose, each generation adding fresh treasures to the sacred text, together with methods of pronunciation, rules of grammar, and principles of metre, all elaborated with the utmost minuteness into different branches of Vedic lore. By comparison with classical Sanskrit literature these writings are crude and primitive in character, resembling in some respects the Jewish Talmud, yet lacking neither in higher philosophical thought, nor in ethical rules of right conduct.

In addition to the *Rig-Veda*, there are the *Samvedas* for the second order of priests, the " praise-singers," and the *Yajurvedas*, consisting of *Vedas* containing the sacrificial liturgical stanzas and formulæ connected with the " forest " rituals. Later the *Yajurvedas* were separated into two, " Black " and " White," the former being composed of the sacrificial verses only, the latter of the whole text. With the development of the schools of Hindu philosophy, about the middle of the ninth century B.C., the *Brahmanas* appeared as comments and explanations of the *Vedas*, and elaborations of the sacrificial ceremonial. Several centuries later the Canon was completed by the philosophical treatises—the *Upanishads*—drawn up by the priestly schools between 700 and 500 B.C. These scriptures were supplemented by many legal codes, or *Dharmasastra*, of which the most notable is the *Manava Dharmasastra*, or Code of Manu, a work similar in character to Deuteronomy, but in its present form belonging to about A.D. 200.

It is in this treatise that the hierarchical system is set forth. " The Lord created the king for the protection of this world, having taken immortal particles from Indra, the Wind, Yama, the Sun, and Fire, and Varuna, the Moon, and the Lord of Wealth. Inasmuch as the king is formed of these particles of these chiefs of the gods, he surpasses all beings in brightness."[1] How far this conception of the divine kingship prevailed in the times of the earlier records it is very difficult to determine. The majority of Vedic scholars are of the opinion that no such notion is to be found in the hymns, but Hocart contends that " in the age of those ritual treatises known as the *Brahmanas* the king was already divine, and as these treatises revolve round the Vedic hymns it seems most likely that kings were already divine when those hymns were written."[2]

Similarly in the Iranian *Avestan* literature, while no reference is made to the great Persian monarchs of the Achæmenid dynasty, the exploits of semi-divine royal heroes occur, and their names suggest Vedic or Indo-Iranian prototypes. Moreover, the Persian poet Firdausi, in his epic, the *Shah-namah*, co-ordinates all these various dynasties from the earliest hero-kings through the Achæmenid era down to Alexander the Great.

The literary evidence in the old Indian writings is obscure, and so far as the kingship and sacrifice are concerned, the issue is further complicated by the fact that the king did not himself perform priestly functions, so that the priestly caste came to rank above the royal, and eventually became divine (Brahmin). Thus the Law of Manu declares : " This universe is the

[1] Manu, *Law Treatise*, vii, 3.   [2] *Kingship* (Oxford, 1927), p. 11.

Brahman's, whatever comes into this world; for the Brahman is entitled to this universe by his superiority and his birth."[1] Moreover, with the rise of Buddhism, though Buddha himself was an heir apparent (*yuvaraja*), as the son of Suddhodana, king of the Sakya clan of Kapilavastu, all external ritual was at a discount, the emperor being essentially a moralist in the Buddhist scriptures.

The Pali literature comprises collections of poems and rules—the " Three Baskets " or *Tripitaka*—the first of which, the *Vinaya Pitaka*, dealing with monastic discipline. The second, or *Sutta Pitaka*, is the chief source of our knowledge of the *Dhamma*, or religion of Gautama and his earliest disciples, and of the most important products of Buddhist literature grouped under five sections (*nikayas*). The " Third Basket " is the *Abhidhamma Pitaka* of higher religion, sub-divided into seven groups of catechetical doctrinal explanations. These scriptures, however, are not of any very great importance for our present purpose inasmuch as it was not until the rise of the new school of *Mahāyāna* that the Buddha was raised to the position of a salvation god with a highly developed polytheistic ritual theology.

From this rapid survey of the character of the material available for a scientific study of the institution of sacrifice, it is apparent that, even if the investigation be confined to the evidence of civilized antiquity, the sources are not without their difficulties, while the interpretation thereof by specialists in each and every

---

[1] Manu, i, 100.

department is chaotic in its fundamental contradictions. Moreover, in point of fact, although our ritual, and its associated myth, belong essentially to the cult of the divine king, the antecedents go back to a very much more remote period, when in Palæolithic times man began to speculate about the mystery of life in its various manifestations.

If we leave out of consideration altogether modern races in a primitive state of culture, there is still the archæological evidence which reveals long before the belief in the divinity of kings is likely to have arisen—and certainly ages before written history began—a magico-religious attitude towards the very problems with which the kingship and sacrifice were mainly concerned. For behind all the manifold and varied ramifications of the higher ritual lie the elementary facts of life, such as the food supply, the fertility of man and beast, and protection from the evils of famine, disease and death. Therefore, to determine the fundamental character of the institution, some attempt must be made to analyse and evaluate in historical sequence the concepts which in the complex sacrificial pattern have found expression in the blood offering and the bloodless oblation.

CHAPTER I

THE BLOOD OFFERING

WITHOUT prejudicing the issue at the outset of the investigation by attempting anything in the nature of precise definition of the institution of sacrifice, the broad distinction between blood offerings and the bloodless oblation, familiar through the story of Cain and Abel, and similar interpretations of the ritual, suggests a line of approach which takes us at once to the earliest strivings of the human race after things unseen, and at the same time opens the way for the exploration of the rudimentary aspects of sacrificial cultus.

It seems clear that the Hebrew legend turns on two rival theories of sacrifice which were current and possibly hotly contested when the narrative took shape, the dispositions of the two brothers being later explanations of the incident. That Yahweh should show preference for blood offerings is in accordance with Hebrew ritual, in which the oblation of blood is considered to be more efficacious than the bloodless sacrifice, in contradistinction to the vegetation theory maintained by Greek philosophers like Porphyry in the fifth century B.C.[1] Behind both these speculations, however, there lies a long and complex history, in which the blood and the vegetation offering each plays its part.

That in actual historical sequence the concept which

[1] Porphyry, *De Abstinentia*, ii, 56.

found expression in the oblation of blood was the earlier may be deduced from the archæological evidence, since, before the invention of agriculture, as far back as the Aurignacian culture phase in the Palæolithic, it appears to have been recognized that the blood is the life of man and beast alike, the going out of which constitutes death. As Professor Elliot Smith says, " In delving into the remotely distant history of our species we cannot fail to be impressed with the persistence with which, throughout the whole of his career, man (of the species *sapiens*) has been seeking for an elixir of life, to give added ' vitality ' to the dead (whose existence was not consciously regarded as ended), to prolong his own life from all assaults, not merely of time, but also of circumstance. In other words, the elixir he sought was something that would bring ' good luck ' in all the events of his life and its continuation. Most of the amulets, even of modern times, the lucky trinkets, the averters of the ' Evil Eye,' the practices and devices for securing good luck in love and sport, in curing bodily ills and mental distress, in attaining material prosperity, or a continuation of existence after death, are survivals of this ancient and persistent striving after those objects which our earliest fore-fathers called collectively the ' givers of life.' " [1]

Now the blood was regarded as the life-stream *par excellence*, the seat of vitality being the heart. The same kind of animating principle, called by Kruijt, *zielestof*, or soul-substance,[2] came to be associated with certain

[1] *Evolution of the Dragon* (Manchester, 1919), p. 145.
[2] E.R.E., vii, p. 232. Rivers, *Folk-lore*, xxxi, 1920, pp. 46 f. James *Folk-lore*, xxxviii, 1928, pp. 338 ff.

parts of the body and its secretions. Thus the extremities, such as the nails, are thought to be impregnated with the vital energy, and therefore great care has to be taken in coming into contact with the parings. Certain internal organs, notably the liver and the intestines, are also liberally endowed with the essence, as are the teeth, the saliva, the placenta and umbilical cord, the bones and the skin.

Animals and plants, and certain inanimate objects, similarly possess soul-substance, but only in the case of those animals and plants which are of particular importance to man does it take the more personal forms. But the possession of a common vitality establishes a mystic vital bond between all who share the same life-essence, and since this potency is capable of transmission from one person or object to another, renewed health and strength can be secured by a ritual transference of soul-substance. Similarly, the extraction of the life from a body entails death unless it can be restored speedily and renewed by the aid of objects richly endowed with vitality.

It is this fundamental principle which underlies blood ritual in its various manifestations, and it constitutes the motive apparently of those Palæolithic cave paintings which portray scenes of wounded animals. Thus, for example, in the inner recesses of the cavern called Niaux, near Tarascon-en-Ariège, three hollows on the ground have been utilized as wounds by drawing around them the outline of a bison, and annexing to the cups little arrows painted in red. It is now generally admitted that designs of this character, which are numerous in the Franco-

Cantabrian region,[1] together with the mutilated clay models of animals having spear thrusts upon them, recently discovered by M. Casteret at Montespan,[2] can only be explained satisfactorily in terms of hunting magic. Nothing less than a strong supernatural reason is likely to have led Magdalenian man into a cave which to-day necessitates swimming nearly a mile up a subterranean stream, and passing through the neck of a syphon—if these conditions prevailed in Palæolithic times.

Probably no single interpretation accounts for all the impulses which lie behind these paintings, engravings and sculptures, but, nevertheless, those which occur in the dark and remote regions in the heart of the mountains, as in the case of Niaux, Pasiega, or Castillo, or in an inaccessible spot like Montespan, can hardly represent " art for art's sake," since this motive alone would not have lured successive groups of people—at Pasiega from Aurignacian times to the end of the Magdalenian—into these treacherous paths, difficult enough for us moderns to traverse with our powerful acetylene lamps, but incredibly more so when only flickering lights were available.

Moreover, the occurrence of masked dancers among the designs, such as the figure called " The Sorcerer " at Trois Frères,[3] and similar representations at Lourdes, Abri Mège, Marsoulas, Mas d'Azul, and Cogul, points to a definitely established control of the chase

[1] Cf. Burkitt, *Prehistory* (Camb., 1925), pp. 192 ff. ; Luquet, *The Art and Religion of Fossil Man* (Oxford, 1930), pp. 96 ff.

[2] Bégouen and Casteret, *Revue Anthropologique*, 1923, pp. 533 ff.

[3] *C. R. Acad. des Inscriptions*, 1920 ; Mainage, *Les Religions de la Préhistoire* (Paris, 1921), p. 314 ; Burkitt, *Our Forerunners* (Lond., 1924), pp. 208 f.

by a properly constituted ritual. The primitive mind being incapable of drawing sharp distinctions between the symbol and the person or object symbolised, to act upon one produces a corresponding effect on the other. These masked dancers, therefore, do not merely represent animals ; they are the animals themselves in substantial reality inasmuch as they possess a common soul-substance.

Ritual is essentially an attempt to control the unpredictable element in human experience, and the means whereby the body corporate preserves its integrity and health. The rite is felt to be effective in some mystic way in bringing about the desired result, and giving collective expression to the most fundamental of all instincts, that of the preservation of life. In hunting magic this centres in the contol of the chase, and the renewal of vitality, and there can be little doubt that the numerous Magdalenian designs depicting dances and disguised individuals constitute the earliest emotional reactions towards the food supply. This is confirmed by the evidence from the North American Indians.

Thus, the Apache medicine-man causes large and elaborate pictures to be made in caverns, and on the floor of lodges, representing mythological animal scenes. Around these designs ceremonies are held in which masked dancers often participate in order to control the chase, promote fertility among the flocks and herds, and ward off evil.[1] Similarly, each member of the Zuni Bow Priesthood places a carved effigy of

---

[1] J. G. Bourke, *Folk-lore*, ii, 1891, p. 438 ; cf. *9th* R.B.A.E. (Wash., 1892), pp. xliii f.

his animal ally in the " House of the Deer Medicine," and before hunting selects a "fetish," and breathes upon it to stiffen the legs of his prey.   When it is caught, he dips the image in the blood from the heart, sips it himself, and devours a part of the liver.   Once a year —at the New Year Festival, or " Day of the Council of the Fetishes "—the sacred images are taken from their houses and arranged in rows in front of an altar in a sacred chamber.   Prayer for the maintenance of the food supply is then made to them, and after they have been sprinkled with prayer-meal, and appropriate dances duly performed, in which the cries of the animals are reproduced, the rites conclude with a great invocation round the altar.   In this way the images become re-charged with magical power.[1]

The Ojibwa Indians solicit the services of the medicine-man, or Midē, before setting out for the chase.   Having sung a magic song, he draws on a piece of birch bark, with a sharp-pointed bone or nail, the outline of the animal desired by the applicant.   The heart is indicated by a puncture, upon which a small quantity of vermilion is carefully rubbed ; this colour being very efficacious in effecting the capture of the animal, while a line is drawn to the heart from the mouth along which the magic is destined to pass to the vital spot.[2]   Here, as in the Palæolithic paintings, the heart is regarded as the centre of life, injury to which causes death through loss of blood.   Moreover, since the blood is the life, designs painted with it become more potent inasmuch as they are charged with its

---

[1] F. H. Cushing, *2nd R.B.A.E.* (1883), pp. 11 ff.
[2] Hoffman, *7th R.B.A.E.* (1891), pp. 222 ff., 247.

vitality. Red pigment is the next best thing to blood by way of substitute, and it has the advantage of being more durable and therefore of rendering the spell more lasting.[1] Hence, doubtless, the use of vermilion in the Ojibwa drawing, and the prevalence of red ochre in the Palæolithic paintings.

It is a matter of common knowledge that blood is frequently employed by primitive people in the decoration of sacred objects, and, if Bégouen is correct in his conjecture that the reason why it is now almost impossible to disentangle the outlines of the palimpsests, executed one upon another in the most sacred spots in the Palæolithic caves, is because the artists first smeared the walls with blood before beginning their work, a similar practice would seem to have been in vogue in prehistoric times. Be this as it may, that blood, and certain substances resembling it in colour, are regarded in primitive society as vitalizing agents is well established. Thus, just as the Carib father, lying in couvade, draws blood from his own body to nourish a delicate child, or mothers on the Orinoco prick their tongues to strengthen sickly babies,[2] so the red seeds of the roucou plant (*bixa orellana*) are mixed with oil to form a thick dye with which the head and hair (both being important seats of soul-substance) are smeared at critical junctures.[3]

The Revivification of the Dead

It is this belief that lies behind the widespread use

[1] Cf. Elliot Smith, *The Evolution of the Dragon* (Manchester, 1919), p. 149.
[2] C. D. Dance, *Chapters from a Guianese Log-Book* (Demerara, 1881), p. 250; J. Gumilla, *Historia natural, civil y geografica de las naciones del Rio. Orinoco.* (Barcelona, 1791), i, p. 164.
[3] Joest, *Inter. Archiv. für Ethnol.*, v (Leyden, 1893), p. 80;

of blood and its surrogates in the cult of the dead. In South-east Australia, for example, the men of the Dieri open a vein in the arm and pour the blood over a sandhill in which a mythical ancestor is thought to be buried,[1] while among the tribes of the Darling River several men, having cut each others heads with a boomerang, cause the blood to drip on the corpse lying in the grave before them.[2] In the Central region the Arunta women who have not taken part in the dance during the interment, approach and cut their heads until the blood flows on the grave.[3] Since the sick and aged are frequently smeared with blood to renew their vitality and restore them to health,[4] it would seem that the funerary ritual had a similar significance in relation to the dead. Thus Smythe maintains that the object of letting blood drip over a corpse is to strengthen the deceased in the grave, and to assist him to rise to another country.[5]

In the classical mythology of Greece and Rome it is this belief which finds expression in the story of the visit of Odysseus to the underworld by way of the land of the Kimmerians. Here he dug a trench and poured into it the blood of black victims, and soon the shades gathered round clamouring for the blood.

[1] Howitt, *Natives Tribes of S.E. Austral.* (Lond., 1904), p. 798.
[2] F. Bourney, *J.A.I.*, xiv, 1884, pp. 134 f.
[3] Spencer and Gillen, *Native Tribes of Central Austral.* (Lond., 1899, pp. 507 ff.
[4] *Op. cit.*, pp. 382, 461, 464 ; Howitt, p. 380.
[5] R. E. Smyth, *The Aborigines of Victoria* (Melbourne, 1878), ii, p. 274. For similar evidence from other regions, see Haddon, *Camb. Exped. to Torres Straits* (Camb., 1908), vi, pp. 135, 154; Turner, *Samoa* (Lond., 1884), p. 144 ; Ellis, *Polynesian Researches* (Lond., 1861), p. 150 ; Pritchard, *Polynesian Reminiscences* (Lond., 1866), pp. 125 ff. ; Yarrow, *1st R.B.A.E.* (1881), pp. 72, 90.

When their requests were granted, their memories of the upper world and the power of speech returned to them. Thus revived, they told him, one by one, the sorry story of their latter days, and from Teiresias he learnt the vicissitudes that were to mark the remainder of his life.[1] A reminiscence of the same practice may perhaps be detected in the alleged custom of the lads of Peloponnese lashing themselves annually at Olympia on the grave of the legendary hero, Pelops, till the blood streamed from their backs as a libation to the god.[2] Similarly at Roman funerals the women scratched their faces till they bled to please the ghosts with the sight of the blood.[3]

In the light of this widespread evidence the presence of red ochre in the Palæolithic ceremonial interments at Grimaldi on the Italian Riviera is suggestive of an Aurignacian cult of the dead conceived in similar terms. Thus the body of a man of Crô-Magnon type in La Grotte du Cavillon, the fourth cave of the series, was covered with red ochreous powder which had stained the bones, as was also the case at Paviland on the Gower coast of South Wales where the feature was so marked that the skeleton is commonly called the " Red Lady," although actually it is probably that of a man.[4] One of the skulls found at Barma Grande (Grimaldi) was in " a bed of red earth," and " had a thick coating of red ochre comparable to a skull cap,"[5] while in Grotte des Enfants red powder surrounded

[1] *Od.* xi, 34 f.

[2] Scholiast on Pindar, *Olymp.*, i, 146.

[3] Servius on Vergil, *Æn.* iii, 67.

[4] R. Verneau, *Les Grottes de Grimaldi* (Monaco, 1906), ii, p. 298 ; W. J. Sollas, *J.A.I.*, 1913 ; xliii, pp. 325 ff.

[5] *Grim.*, ii, p. 299.

the head of one of the "negroids," and traces of the pigment occurred on the other interments.[1] At Brünn[2] and at Crô-Magnon[3] the remains were partially coloured with red, and at Chancelade a layer of iron peroxide spread over the whole body and the surrounding strata.[4] The same phenomena recurred at Hoteaux[5] and Obercassel.[6]

It is impossible to consider as accidental such a wide distribution of a practice connected with the cult of the dead both in ancient and modern times, and since there is reason to believe that early man connected the shedding of blood with loss of vitality, it is reasonable to suppose that he likewise associated the offering of blood, or its equivalent, with the renewal of life and strength. Thus Professor Macalister seems justified in concluding that " the purpose of the rite is perfectly clear. Red is the colour of living health. The dead man was to live again in his own body, of which the bones were the framework. To paint it with the colour of life was the nearest thing to mummification that the Palæolithic people knew ; it was an attempt to make the body again serviceable for its owner's use." [7]

Intichiuma and the Blood-Covenant

This vitalizing power of blood, and of substances charged with its potency, is further illustrated by

[1] *Op. cit.*, pp. 41, 260 f.
[2] Boule, *Les Hommes Fossiles* (Paris, 1921), p. 268.
[3] *Grim.*, ii, 304.
[4] Hardy, *La Station quaternaire de Raymonden* (Paris, Leroux, 1891), pp. 50 ff.
[5] Tournier and Guillon, *Les Hommes Préhistoriques dans l'Ain* (Bourg, 1895), p. 61.
[6] Boule, *op. cit.*, p. 274.
[7] *Textbook of European Archæology* (Camb., 1921), p. 502.

certain ceremonies performed by the Australian aborigines to maintain and increase the food supply. Thus
among the Dieri the *mura-mura* Minkani is thought to
be hidden in his cave in a sandhill, and in order to
bring forth the young carpet-snakes and iguanas
concealed therein, the men wound themselves and
pour the blood on the sacred spot.[1] In the Central
region, the men of the Undiaro kangaroo totem assemble at the foot of a hill supposed to be full of
kangaroos, on the slope of which two blocks of stone
project, one above the other. One of these stones
represents a male, the other a female kangaroo. The
headman of the clan with a man who is in the relation
of mother's uncle to him climbs up to the two blocks
and rubs them with a stone. They then repair to a
rocky ledge, thought to be haunted by the spirits of
ancestral kangaroos, and paint it with stripes of red
and white to indicate, it is alleged, the red fur and white
bones of the kangaroo. When this has been done, a
number of young men sit on the top of the ledge, while
the men below sing of the *increase* of the kangaroos.
Blood-letting follows. " The men open veins in their
arms and allow the blood to stream out on to and
over the ledge of the sacred ceremonial stone, which
represents the spot where a celebrated kangaroo of
the Alcheringa went down into the earth, its spirit part
remaining in the stone which arose to mark the place."[2]
The young men then go and hunt the kangaroo,
bringing their spoils back to the camp, when what
appears to be a quasi-sacred meal on the flesh of the

[1] Howitt, *Native Tribes of S.E. Austral.*, p. 798.
[2] Spencer and Gillen, *Native Tribes of Central Austral.*, pp. 193 ff., 199 ff.,
206 ff.

animal is eaten.   The rites are brought to a conclusion
with a totemic dance, after which the species may be
eaten sparingly.[1]

When the Emu clan desires to perform intichiuma
ceremonies, several men open veins in their arms and
allow the blood to stream on the ground till it is
saturated.   When the serum has coagulated, they
trace designs in it in white, yellow and black, representing different parts of the body of the emu.   A song is
chanted to this figure during the totemic dance that
follows, the effect of the rite being to prevent the
sacred species from disappearing by quickening the
embryos of the new generation.[2]   Similarly, in the
Unjiamba, or Hakea-flower totem, a young man opens
a vein in his arm during the intichiuma ceremony,
and allows the blood to sprinkle on a stone representing a mass of hakea-flowers, in the centre of the oval-
shaped pit where the rite is performed.   The stone is
thus made a *churinga*, and the spot henceforth becomes tabu to women, children and the uninitiated.[3]

In these primitive and prehistoric rites the fundamental concept is that of the blood as the life charged
with potency efficacious alike to the living and the
dead, to supernatural beings and to men.   The origin
of this notion may reasonably be sought in the fact
that loss of blood is directly connected with weakness
and death.   From this primary observation other
deductions would easily follow : (*a*) that blood was the
essence of life ; and (*b*) by the primitive law of
association, any substance resembling blood, like red
ochre, had a similar significance and potency.   There-

[1] *Op. cit.*, p. 204.   [2] *Op. cit.*, p. 181.   [3] Pp. 184 ff.

fore (*c*) blood, or its equivalent, being the vehicle of life and consciousness, was employed as a revivifying agent. Hence the custom of burying ochreous powder with the dead. Finally, (*d*) if blood, and its surrogates, were regarded as life-giving agents in this sense, they would readily become the means of establishing a vital alliance of soul-substance between those thus united in a blood-bond with one another. This explains why blood became one of the most important and potent vehicles in effecting intercommunion between the sacred and human order, and of consolidating tribal relationships.

In this cycle of primitive ideas and practices it is possible to detect the beginnings of a method of approach to magico-religious phenomena which in due course found its ultimate expression in the sacrificial system. In the ritual shedding of blood it is not the taking of life but the giving of life that really is fundamental, for blood is not death but life. The outpouring of the vital fluid in actuality, or by substitute, is the sacred act whereby life is given to promote and preserve life, and to establish thereby a bond of union with the supernatural order. This seems to have been the primitive conception out of which an elaboration of ritual and belief has emerged involving notions of the reanimation of human gods by the immolation of animal and human quasi-divine victims, and vegetation offerings, on the one hand, and on the other hand, lofty ethical ideals of surrender, renunciation and self-sacrifice.

It is not suggested, however, that the institution in any of its more developed aspects belongs to the primeval stage of human evolution in the sense required by Robertson Smith's theory of the theanthropic animal at once god and kinsman, still less by the Freudian application of this hypothesis. So far as the historical sequence of these concepts is concerned, it is unlikely that the Palæolithic hunters got beyond the awareness of a vital relationship existing between themselves and certain animal species on which they depended for their food supply. From the notion of blood as a kind of soul-substance responsible for the phenomenon of life, a sense of kinship doubtless developed at a very early period between man and the creatures upon whom he depended for his sustenance, and with whom he was united by the possession of a common vital principle. In other words, he was conscious of a unity of life uniting him in a mystic and irrational manner to the source of his food supply.

The Relation of Men and Animals

Thus we are told on the authority of Sir Everard Im Thurn that among the Indians of Guiana there is no " sharp line of distinction such as we see between man and other animals, between one kind of animal and another, or between animals—man included—and inanimate objects. . . . According to the view of the Indians, other animals differ from men only in bodily form, and in their various degrees of strength. And they differ in spirit not at all ; for just as the Indian sees in the separation which takes place at death or in dreams proofs of the existence of a spirit—all other qualities being in his view much the same in men and other animals—he sees proof of the existence

in every animal of a spirit similar to that of man." [1]
That is to say, men and animals are animated by a
common soul-substance which may take up its abode in
particular objects, and is capable of projection from
one species to another.

These general conclusions are supported by a long
array of facts, and admitted by subsequent investiga-
tors. Among the Caribs, for instance, we are told that
" animals, and plants, and lifeless beings live and act
like man. In the morning the animals go to ' their
work,' like the Indians do. The tiger and the snake
and all other animals go out hunting, having ' to look
after their family ' like the Indian has." [2] Or, again,
Von den Steinen says, " the Indian did not know that
he was separated from the animal world by a gulf.
He merely perceived that all created beings conducted
themselves as he did in essentials : they had their
family life, they understood each other by means of a
language of their own, they had habitations, fought
each other, lived upon what they caught or upon
fruits ; in short, he felt himself to be *primus inter pares*,
but not above them." [3]

It was this mystic relationship which found expression in the notion of animal guardians received
through a dream or revelation in times of fasting and
during initiation rites. Thus among the Omaha
" the ceremony of initiation rests on the assumption
that man's powers and activities can be supplemented

[1] E. F. Im Thurn, *Among the Indians of Guiana* (Lond., 1883), pp. 350 f.,
352.
[2] *Reports of Twenty-First Congress of Americanists* (1924), p. 221.
[3] K. von Steinen, *Unter den Naturvolkern Zentral-Brasiliens* (Berlin, 1894),
p. 201.

by the elements and the animals, only through the grace of *Wakonda*, obtained by the rite of vision, consisting of ritualistic acts and a fervent prayer of humility explaining a longing for something not possessed, a consciousness of insufficiency of self, and an abiding desire for something capable of bringing welfare and prosperity to the suppliant." [1]

So closely is the existence of a man bound up with that of his *nagual*, or animal chosen to be his tutelary divinity, that the life of the one depends on that of the other. Among the Omaha the individual is supposed to acquire the qualities of the creature assigned to him as his guardian at puberty. If in the vision which determines his tutelary genius, he sees an eagle, he will have a keen and piercing foresight ; if, on the other hand, it is a bear that appears to him, he will be slow and clumsy, and therefore likely to be killed in battle.[2] Similarly, the Thompson Indians of British Columbia think that every man partakes of the nature of his animal guardian spirit. Thus a man who has a grisly bear for his protector will be much more warlike than one who has a cow, a coyote, or a fox for his ally.[3]

At the age of puberty Algonquin youths are sent to a solitary place to undergo a period of fasting. The first thing that appears in a dream to the novice is regarded as his guardian spirit to whom he looks in after life for guidance and protection. The man destined to be a warrior will have a vision of an eagle or a bear, a serpent will appear to the future

[1] Hewitt, *Handbook of Amer. Indians North of Mexico*, ii, p. 790.
[2] *Op. cit.*
[3] J. Teit, *Memoirs Amer. Mus. Nat. Hist. Jesup, N. Pacific Exped.*, i, pt. iv (New Haven, 1900), p. 356.

medicine-man, a wolf to the hunter. To complete the bond, a portion of the nagual is worn about his person as an embodiment of its soul-substance.[1] The Blackfeet associate the "medicine-bag" with the guardian spirit, a description of the roots and herbs to be gathered to prepare it having been vouchsafed in a revelation to the novice when he received his tutelary animal.[2]

Since the tutelary spirit is the link which connects man with the invisible world, in a hunting state of culture, where human beings depend largely on the creatures around them for their food supply, this mystic union with the animal creation raises a serious problem. To kill and eat a species so closely akin to a man's own nature, and in many respects superior to him in strength and wisdom, is an anomaly calling forth an emotional situation to be approached by an appropriate ritual. Thus, for example, when a dead bear was brought into a Tlingit camp in Alaska," its head was carried indoors and eagle down and red paint put upon it. Then one talked to it as if to a human being, saying, 'I am your friend, I am poor and come to you.' Before the entrails were burned he talked to them, saying, 'I am poor, that is why I am hunting you.' When one came to a bear, he said, ' My father's brother-in-law, have pity upon me, let me be in luck.' "[3]

Among the Koryaks of North-eastern Siberia, a sacred dance is held after the killing of a bear during which a woman puts on the skin of the slain animal

[1] F. Parkman, *The Jesuits in N. America* (Boston, 1870), pp. lxix ff.
[2] E. F. Wilson, *Report Brit. Assoc.*, 1887, p. 187.
[3] J. R. Swanton, 26th *R.B.A.E.* (Wash. 1908), p. 455.

and dances in it, entreating the owner not to be angry but to be kind to his people. Food is offered to him on a wooden plate, and then a ceremony is performed with the object of sending the spirit back to his home in the neighbourhood of the rising sun, equipped with adequate provision for his physical sustenance on the way.[1] To the east the Gilyaks, on the Ameer, who have a great devotion for the bear, suckle a cub, and when he is old enough they take him in December or January to the bank of the river to ensure an abundance of fish. After leading him into every house in the village, as in the case of the Meriah among the Khonds,[2] he is tied to a peg and shot dead with arrows. His head is then cut off, decked with shavings, and placed on a table where a feast is prepared. Apologies are offered to the sacred species for his death, and his flesh is cooked and eaten in special vessels. The brain and entrails are consumed last, and the skull laid in a tree near the house. A bear dance by the women follows.[3]

Among the Ainu, although the bear is the chief divinity, it is killed whenever possible. In fact, " in bygone years they considered bear-hunting the most manly and useful way in which a person could possibly spend his time."[4] But having killed it they " sit down and admire it, make their salaams to it, worship it, and offer presents of *inao*." When it has been skinned " the head is decorated with *inao*, and thanks are

[1] W. Jochelson, *Memoirs Amer. Mus. Nat. Hist.*, x, 1905–8, pp. 88 ff.
[2] Cf. chap. iv, p. 97.
[3] L. von Schrenck, *Reisen und Forschungen im Amur-Lande* (St. Petersburg, 1891), iii, pp. 696 ff.
[4] J. Batchelor, *The Ainu and their Folk-lore* (Lond., 1901), p. 471.

offered first to the bear itself, and then to the gods for protecting them and rendering them successful."[1] This veneration reaches its climax in the well-known Bear Festival when the cub that has been caught, and if possible suckled by a woman, is killed after due apology. Care is usually taken to avoid the shedding of blood in the process, but occasionally it is drunk warm by the men in order that they may imbibe the courage and other qualities of the species, and to deepen and express their consciousness of their identity with it. Both share a common life, and therefore when animals are eaten it must be with respect and reverence, and with due apology.

Mr. Batchelor regards the bear as the Ainu totem,[2] but this conclusion is not justified inasmuch as it is by no means the only animal venerated in this manner. Thus the skulls of foxes, for instance, are set up on sacred posts outside the huts and addressed as "precious divinities."[3] In fact, an animal is seldom, if ever, killed without some apology, and if the bear is singled out for special respect, the Ainu do not speak of themselves as belonging to any particular animal or vegetable clan. Almost any creature that is killed in hunting, or offered in sacrifice, is the subject of sacred rites by reason of its supernatural qualities.

Behind this paradoxical situation, in short, is the belief that animals share with human beings a common life. As Mr. Mooney says, speaking of Cherokee mythology in particular and of primitive thought in general, " in the primal genesis period they seem to be

[1] *Op. cit.*, p. 477.   [2] *Op. cit.*, pp. 8 ff.
[3] B. Scheube, *Die Ainos*. Reprinted from *Mittheilungen der Deutschen Gesellschaft bei Sud-und Sud-Ostasiens*, Yokohama, p. 15.

completely undifferentiated, and we find all creatures
alike living and working together in harmony and
mutual helpfulness until man, by his aggressiveness and
disregard for the rights of the others, provokes their
hostility, when insects, birds, fishes, reptiles and four-
footed beasts join forces against him. Henceforth
their lives are apart, but the difference is always one of
degree only. The animals, like the people, are organized
into tribes and have, like them, their chiefs and town
houses, their counsels and ballplays, and the same
hereafter in the Darkening land of Usunhiji. Man is
still the paramount power, and hunts and slaughters
the others as his own necessities compel, but is
obliged to satisfy the animal tribes in every instance,
very much as a murder is compounded for, according
to the Indian system, by ' covering the bones of the
dead ' with presents for the bereaved relatives." [1]

Sometimes the species is too sacred, however, to
eat at all for food, as in the case of the totem and the
tutelary spirit, and then it is often sacrificed once a
year, and the holy flesh, or certain parts or attributes
especially impregnated with soul-substance, consumed ceremonially to imbibe the inherent vitality.
Thus among the Todas the sacred cow buffalo is
strictly tabu except once a year when all the adult
males of the village join in the solemn slaying of the
animal and roasting of its flesh on a fire made of
certain trees. It is then eaten by the men alone. [2] In
Central Australia the members of the witchetty grub
totem are forbidden to eat their sacred species out of

[1] J. Mooney, 19th R.B.A.E. (Wash., 1900), i, p. 261.
[2] Frazer, Golden Bough, pt. viii (Spirits of Corn, ii), p. 314.

camp like ordinary food; otherwise the supply of
grubs would fail. When these creatures become
plentiful after intichiuma (i.e. at the period analogous
to harvest time among agricultural people) large
supplies are gathered which are brought into camp,
cooked and stored away in *pitchis*. In due course
they are taken to the men's quarters, where all the
initiated males assemble. The alatunja grinds up the
contents of the *pitchis* between two stones. Then he
and the other men of the totem eat a little and distribute what remains to those who do not belong to the
totem; after which the grub may be eaten sparingly
by the group.[1]

This last example is typical of the Australian attitude
towards the sacred species. " A man will only eat
very sparingly of his totem, and even if he does eat a
little of it, which is allowable to him, he is careful, in
the case, for instance, of an emu man, not to eat the
best part, such as the fat," and only very rarely does he
venture to consume the eggs,[2] presumably because
they are especially rich in soul-substance. In a rather
higher state of culture, where more developed conceptions of the soul obtain, the fundamental reason
for the tabu becomes more apparent. Thus, the
Bororo in South America believe that " every tapir
and every wild pig, and every alligator, and possibly
every member of some other family of animals
shelters the shade of one or another of their departed
tribesmen. They never kill one of these creatures
unless a sorcerer is within reach to exorcise the soul,

[1] Spencer and Gillen, *Native Tribes of Central Austral.*, p. 203.
[2] *Op. cit.*, p. 202.

41

for they dare not in any circumstances eat the flesh of such a creature until the sorcerer has cast out the soul. They believe that if they should eat it, they would surely die."[1]

Here the notion of a common life shared by men and animals has become specialized into that of the soul-animal, and the tabu explained accordingly. In Australia it is an impersonal vital essence that creates the mystic union between the group and its ally, thereby rendering the species sacred and tabu. Therefore, by consuming portions of the flesh, or anointing the body with the fat or the blood, the bond is strengthened. One life runs through the group, human and animal, and this substantial unity may be consolidated by the totemite imbibing the soul-substance of the totem. But the evidence does not warrant the further deduction that these rites represent an act of sacramental communion with a slain god, as Robertson Smith and Jevons have supposed.[2]

Totemism

Totemism has every appearance of being a very specialized expression of the primitive control of the food supply by magico-religious sanctions. In certain communities any article of diet may become a totem, and in the process of socialization collect a ritual calculated to consolidate the group in an ally mainly responsible for the maintenance of life. Even in Palæolithic times, as we have seen, it seems that the control of the chase centred in a cult in which dancers

[1] W. A. Cook, *Through the Wilderness of Brazil* (Lond., 1911), p. 408.
[2] *Religion of Semites*, new ed., by S. A. Cook (Lond., 1927), pp. 409, 412 f.; Jevons, *Introduction to the History of Religion* (Lond., 1896), pp. 101 ff.

sought to identify themselves with certain animal species by means of disguises, gestures and actions, very much as the Indians of South America believe that in the mask and the associated rites there reside the vital potency which passes into the dancer, "makes him himself a potent demon and renders him capable of driving out demons, or rendering them favourable. In particular, the demons of growth, the spirits of animals which play a part in it, and the animal-spirits of hunting and fishing must by mimetic gestures be conjured up within the reach of human-power."[1]

This, however, is not totemism, and we have no evidence of anything in the nature of a totemic organization of Palæolithic society. If such had prevailed, it is highly improbable that in one cave so many different varieties of animals would be depicted, as each totem presumably would have had its own sanctuary for the performance of its particular rites. Moreover, although the institution is widespread to-day, it is unknown among such very primitive people as the Andamanese, the Semang and the Paviotso, while in North America the exogamous totemic folk in the South-west region, and along the North-west Pacific coast, have a higher general culture than the clanless non-totemic tribes isolated from the focus of civilization.

The elaboration of ritual and social organization in a typical totemic community is hardly suggestive of the institution being genuinely primitive, especially as in its most characteristic form it is connected with

---

[1] T. Koch-Grunberg, *Zwei Jähre unter den Indianern* (Stuttgart, 1908–10), Bde. 11, p. 196.

culture heroes and the theory of metempsychosis. Thus, in Australia each member of the tribe is regarded as a " reincarnation of the never-dying spirit of one of the semi-animal ancestors, and, therefore, when born he, or she, bears of necessity the name of the animal or plant of which the Alcheringa ancestor was a transformation or a descendant." [1] That is to say, in the Alcheringa there were only totemic beings, half animal in form and half human. It was these who made the stock of the souls which have ever since been located in certain centres, whence they enter women of the right totem when their time for reincarnation has come.

The original Alcheringa ancestors were not distinctly human, animal or vegetable, and it is from this stock that the clans are thought to be derived since the spirit individuals left behind have been continuously undergoing rebirth by entering the bodies of women. Thus each person is the living incarnation of an original *mai-aurli* who emanated from a totemic ancestor. " Every individual goes back after death in spirit form to the spot at which it was left in the Alcheringa by the ancestor of the totem. If, for example, it were originally a pigeon spirit, then it will go into the rocks at the spot where the pigeon ancestor performed ceremonies in the Alcheringa and left spirits behind. In the course of ages any single individual can run the whole gamut of the totems, but always returning at death to its original home." [2] So the clan reproduces itself *ad infinitum*, the soul-

---

[1] *Native Tribes of Central Austral.*, p. 128.
[2] *Northern Tribes of Central Austral.*, pp. 145, 174.

substance continually undergoing reincarnation in a ceaseless circle of transformations. Therefore, the clan totem consists of a group of individuals sharing with a certain animal or vegetable species, or other sacred object, a common ancestral life which is capable of assuming any form according to the requirements of the moment.

Behind these elaborations the fundamental conception is that of the culture heroes making human embryos through a process of reincarnation in which women are the vessels for the germination of the soul-substance. This notion, however, is far too specialized to be regarded as genuinely primitive in the sense required by the Palæolithic evidence. Therefore, to erect an elaborate reconstruction of the theory of sacrifice on the basis of totemism is to build on very insecure foundations. Even more precarious is it to postulate with Freud a " primal state of society " when man lived in small communities of an adult male and a number of females and their children, since this condition can be observed nowhere. Even more improbable is the supposed slaying and eating of the father by the jealous and expelled sons, who thus put an end to the father horde. On this unverifiable hypothesis the totem feast becomes the repetition and commemoration of the criminal act with which began social organization, moral tabus and religion.[1]

To avoid the difficulty of finding an adequate motive for the repetition of the alleged primeval parricide, and a racial memory of the drama, Dr. Money-Kyrle

---

[1] Freud, *Totem and Taboo*, Eng. trans. by A. A. Brill (New York, 1918), pp. 235 f.

has modified the Freudian theory by making sacrifice
the symbolic representation of an unconscious desire
to kill the father, which each individual is supposed to
have acquired for himself. During the long period of
infancy the predilection for incest in the unconscious
has been conditioned, it is contended, and variations
in the institution of sacrifice are correlated with
various solutions of the central complex.[1] But the
totemic sacramental meal is still a fundamental feature
in the analysis, and however much the theory be
modified and restated, it rests upon a purely hypothetical situation without parallel in any known culture.

Thus, for example, the evidence for the existence of
a " father horde " in contrast to a " son horde " of
expelled bachelors has yet to be produced, and even if
the Darwinian-Atkinson guess concerning the alleged
gorilla-type of human society could be substantiated,
it would not follow that the practice of ritual cannibalism was a characteristic feature of the organization,
since the diet of this species would be presumably
mainly edible fruits. Moreover, as Prof. Malinowski
has pointed out, the theory tries " to explain the
origins of culture and hence involves a circular
argument," since the " pre-cultural animals " must
have had a " substantial store of cultural goods and
implements " if " the use of a new weapon " was the
cause of the momentous discovery.[2] " No material
culture is imaginable," in fact, " without the con-
comitant existence of organization, morality and
religion." [3]

[1] A. Money-Kyrle, *The Meaning of Sacrifice* (Lond., 1930), pp. 193 ff., 213 ff.
[2] *Sex and Repression in Savage Society* (Lond., 1927), p. 153.
[3] *Op. cit.*

Leaving on one side the probability that primitive society was matriarchal in character, which Freud does not dispute,[1] the hypothesis breaks down with the Robertson Smith theory of sacrifice. If totemism is a specialized form of the doctrine of metempsychosis in which Alcheringa ancestors play the part of Creators, it is scarcely likely to be an aspect of primeval society, as we have endeavoured to show. There is no reason to suppose that the practice was known in Palæolithic times notwithstanding the existence of a developed life ritual. Moreover, it is not by any means of universal application in the higher states of culture. Thus, it has yet to be proved that the Hebrews passed through a totemic stage in the evolution of their highly complex sacrificial system. Be this as it may, it certainly cannot now be maintained that " originally all sacrifices were eaten by the worshippers," and, " in the oldest sacrifice the blood was drunk by the worshippers, and after it ceased to be it was poured out upon the altar." [2]

Therefore, even if the psycho-analytical theory were accurate in itself, it would not throw light on the origins of sacrifice. It is not until we reach the stage in which the hypothetical parricides, or their descendants, treated their totem as they are alleged to have treated their sire, killing him, eating him, and mourning for him, that we come to bed rock ; and then the causal relation between deicide and parricide is not very convincing. No adequate reason is given to explain why a blind, unconscious urge should have led the primeval murderers to repeat their crime in the form of a totemic sacramental communion, or how it came

[1] *Totem and Taboo*, p. 235.   [2] *Religion of the Semites*, p. 389.

to be extended to widely separated races. It might have been expected that the sublimation would have taken a very different form, and in divers modes of expression, in successive generations, but these are questions for psychologists to determine.

Excluding totemism and its derivatives, real and supposed, as inadequate explanations of the origin of sacrifice, an analysis of the ritual of the blood offering in its rudimentary modes of expression takes us back to an early stage in the food quest long before the institution as a culture pattern emerged. From time immemorial blood has been regarded as the restorer of life to the dead, the bestower of health and strength to the living, and the sacred bond uniting those who possessed a common soul-substance. It is this cycle of ideas which appears to lie behind the Palæolithic hunting ritual, and constitutes the fundamental concept in the blood offering in higher states of culture.

The instinctive craving for life led to a great variety of ways and means being devised to overcome the disabilities of decay and death which became woven into an elaborate culture pattern in the Near East in the third millennium B.C. It is in the same setting that the origin of sacrifice must be sought, the blood offering being a fundamental element in the institution since the blood from the beginning seems to have been looked upon as the source of life.

CHAPTER II

VEGETATION RITUAL

TURNING now to the second of the two broad distinctions in the institution of sacrifice, the vegetation offering is second only in importance and antiquity to the blood offering, and has many points in common with it. It is, in fact, the agricultural counterpart of the hunting ritual, and its developments.

In the Palæolithic cultures, when the cultivation of the soil had yet to be accomplished, any object directly associated with the female principle and generative functions seems to have been regarded as a symbol of vitality capable of transferring its fertilizing properties from one person or thing to another. Hence the numerous figures of women with the maternity organs grossly exaggerated that occur in Palæolithic sites from the Aurignacian onwards, extending from the Italian Riviera and the Dordogne to Austria and Moravia,[1] and almost identical in form with the figurines associated with the cult of the Great Mother in Crete, Malta, the Ægean, Egypt and Western Asia.

M. Luquet's contention that this interpretation is "adventurous" inasmuch as hunters would be more likely for economic reasons to resort to infanticide and abortion to keep down their numbers, is scarcely con-

---

[1] Déchelette, *Manuel d'archéologie* (Paris, 1908), pp. 217, 428 ff., 584; Obermaier, *Fossil Man in Spain* (New Haven, 1925), pp. 214 f.; Sollas, *Ancient Hunters* (Lond., 1915), pp. 374 f.

49

vincing.[1]　As Frazer has said, " to live and to cause
to live, to eat food and to beget children, these were
the primary wants of man in the past, and they will be
the primary wants of men in the future so long as the
world lasts.　Other things may be added to enrich
and beautify human life, but unless these wants are
first satisfied, humanity itself must cease to exist.
These two things, therefore, food and children, were
what men chiefly sought to procure by the performance
of magical rites for the regulation of the seasons." [2]

Whatever may have been the precise motive of the
Palæolithic female figurines, it is unthinkable either
that their human counterparts had no desire for
motherhood or that the models represent portraits of
Aurignacian women, there being no suggestion of
the abnormalities depicted on the statuettes in the
Crô-Magnon or Grimaldi skeletal remains.　Granting
that the majority of the burials known to us are those of
males, it is not usual to find a race where all the women
are fat and the men thin.　Moreover, the physiognomy
is invariably ignored in the figurines, all the emphasis
being laid upon the sexual organs, which is exactly
what would be expected in fertility charms.

To the primitive mind the figure of a woman with
her characteristic features brought into prominence
readily becomes a symbol of her functions since the
portrait, the person or thing represented, and the
attributes associated therewith are conceived as one
complete whole.　Since woman is the mother of the
race, she is essentially the life-giver, and her image is

[1] *The Art and Religion of Fossil Man* (New Haven and Lond., 1930),
pp. 109 f.
[2] *Golden Bough*, 3rd Edition, pt. iv, " Adonis," (Lond., 1914), p. 5.

endowed, like blood, with vitalizing power. In this connexion it is interesting to record that the well-known bas-relief of a woman holding the horn of a bison in her right hand, found by Dr. Lalanne among the remains of the Aurignacian occupation of the rock-shelter at Laussel (Dordogne), contains traces of red colouring matter on the figure.[1] If this was a fertility object, as seems probable, the red pigment was added doubtless to increase its vitalizing qualities, and render it more potent in causing animals to multiply.

In addition to these figures, objects resembling female attributes have a similar significance, just as ochre is the equivalent of blood. Thus certain shells such as the Red Sea cowry, shaped in the form of the portal by which a child enters the world, seem to have been connected with the female principle, and to have been employed as fertility charms.[2] If the hypothesis has been over-worked by some of its advocates, the fact remains that there is abundant evidence of shells associated with so many Palæolithic interments which appear to have an amuletic value as vitalizing agents. In the Grottes des Enfants at Grimaldi, for instance, the bodies were surrounded with a multitude of shells, and the two children were placed in a shroud composed of nearly a thousand sea-shells.[3] At La Grotte du Cavillon the body of a Crô-Magnon man, lying in the contracted position, had over two hundred pierced shells about his head, while in the original Crô-Magnon

---

[1] *L'Anthrop.*, xxii, 1912, pp. 129 f.

[2] Elliot Smith, *Evolution of the Dragon*, pp. 150 f. ; J. W. Jackson, *Shells as Evidence of the Migrations of Early Culture* (Manchester, 1917), pp. 138 ff.

[3] *L'Anthrop.*, xvii, pp. 257–320 ; R. Verneau, *Les Grottes des Grimaldi*, ii, pt. ii.

burial at Les Eyzies three hundred pierced marine shells, chiefly of the *Littorina* species, were discovered beside the skeletons.[1] These, it would appear, had been strung together to form necklaces as in the case of the later examples found at Mas d'Azil.[2] In a ceremonial interment at Laugerie-Basse cowries were arranged in pairs upon the body; two pairs on the forehead, one near each humerus, four in the region of the knees and thighs and two upon each foot.[3] Here the idea of an ornamental necklace does not seem to be at all convincing, the general circumstances suggesting a ceremonial interment fully equipped with fertility symbols calculated to give life to the deceased.

The Corn-Mothers

Taken collectively the Palæolithic data point to the existence of an established cult of the female principle in which amulets of various kinds played a prominent part in the conservation and promotion of life among man, beast and the dead. With the discovery of agriculture at the dawn of civilization, attention was directed to the cultivation of the soil with the result that the magico-religious control of the chase was transformed into an elaborate system of seasonal ritual to maintain the food supply, in which the same symbolism recurs. Thus, effigies composed of newly cut seedlings of corn, rye, maize or rice are conspicuous in agricultural ceremonial in many parts of the world.[4]

[1] Lartet, *Reliquiæ Aquitaniæ* (Lond., 1856–75), pp. 62 ff.
[2] *L'Anthrop.* vii, 1896, p. 633.
[3] *Comptes-Rendus de l'Accad. des Sciences*, lxxiv, 1872, pp. 1060–3.
[4] Cf. *Golden Bough*, pt. vii, "Spirits of the Corn and of the Wild" (Lond., 1914), pp. 131–204.

When the corn-spirit is regarded as an old woman, the image is made by one of the elder women, and, conversely, when it is thought to be a maiden, a young girl usually performs the rite. Sometimes it is believed that the growth of the crops is the counterpart of the maturing of the " mother," and therefore in the Bruck district of Styria the last sheaf is made into the shape of a woman by the oldest married woman in the village, of an age from fifty to fifty-five years. The finest ears are plucked out of it and made into a wreath, which, twined with flowers, is carried by the prettiest girl of the village. In some places the corn-mother is taken in procession by two lads who walk behind the girl to the squire's house, and while he receives the wreath and hangs it up in the hall, the corn-mother is placed on the top of a pile of wood, where it is the centre of the harvest supper and dance. It is then hung up in the barn till the threshing is over, and on the following Sunday the wreath is dedicated in Church. On Holy Saturday the grain is rubbed out of it by a seven-years old girl and scattered among the young corn. At Christmas the straw of the wreath is placed in the manger to make the cattle thrive.[1]

In these customs the fertilizing power of the image is apparent, the vitalizing influence of the " mother " extending from the newly sown corn to the cattle in the stall. In the innumerable examples of the ritual which Frazer has collected from all parts of the world, the fundamental intention is that of ensuring the continuance of the crops through the potency of the

---

[1] W. Mannhardt, *Mythologische Forschungen* (Strasburg, 1884), pp. 317 f. ; Frazer, *op. cit.*, pp. 135 f.

mother symbol, the newly reaped cereals transmitting to the earth and the crops renewed energy to produce their fruits by virtue of the life-giving qualities with which they are charged. Behind the ceremonial there stands the shadowy form of the Great Mother, whose image plays an integral part in the rites, and is sometimes actually called by this name. Thus the last sheaf to be taken home is frequently designated the " Great Mother," or " Grandmother " in Westphalia and East Prussia, and is adorned with flowers, ribbons and a woman's apron.[1] The inherent vitality of the figure is signified by its careful preservation throughout the winter to ensure fertility when the contents are mingled with the crops in the following spring, or brought into contact with the cattle.

So potent was the maize-mother in Peru that it was revered as a god because it had " the power of conceiving and giving birth to much maize." To promote fertility, sacred dances were held in connexion with it, and then it was burnt sacrificially in order to obtain an abundant crop of the cereal.[2] At Cuzco in this district when the grains were removed from their cobs, figures of sheaves were carved in wood and dressed up like human beings. These were then burnt, together with children and sheep, to revivify the maize spirits and enable them to perform their beneficent functions during the next season.[3]

In addition to this life-giving significance, there is apparently also another theme running through the

[1] W. Mannhardt, op. cit., p. 321 ; Frazer, p. 136.

[2] Karsten, Anales del Museo Nacional de Historia Natural de Buenos Aires, tomo xxiv, 1913, p. 210.

[3] Cobo, Historia del nuevo mundo (Sevilla, 1895), iv, pp. 25 ff.

ritual, viz. the fear of incurring the revenge of the slain corn-spirit, which was apparently never wholly set at rest, and therefore capable of causing the failure of the crops by withdrawing from the processes of growth.[1] Thus, in the Highlands of Scotland, for example, there was " a struggle to escape from being the last done with the shearing, and when tillage in common existed, instances were known of a ridge being left unshorn (no person would claim it) because of it being behind the rest. The fear entertained was that of having the ' famine of the farm ' in the shape of an imaginary old woman (*cailleach*) to feed till next harvest." [2] Her possession was a serious matter for the owner since she brought disaster, death and failure to the crops, so that reapers have been known to stay up all night to be well ahead with their work lest this misfortune should befall them.

Closely associated with the Cailleach lore is the practice of expelling death at Christmas by setting on fire the Yule log which was sometimes actually called *Cailleach Nollich* (Nollaig)—the Old Woman of Christmas.[3] The method usually adopted was that of the head of the household going to a wood on the night of Christmas Eve, and there cutting down a tree stump which he carved into the resemblance of an old woman. He then carried it home and placed it in the middle of a big peat fire burning in the centre of the room. While " the wife " blazed, the company cracked jokes, and when only the ashes remained, they abandoned themselves to festivities." This sacrifice was sup-

---

[1] I am indebted to Mrs. M. M. Banks for this suggestion.

[2] J. G. Campbell, *Superstitions of the Highlands* (Glasgow, 1900), pp. 243 ff.

[3] J. MacCulloch, *History of the West Highlands* (Edin., 1924), iv, p 349.

posed, in some places, to propitiate the angel of death, who was expected, because of it, to refrain from visiting the house for a year." [1]

There would seem to be two purposes, therefore, in these vegetation rites. On the one hand, the vitality embodied in the image is regarded as having a quickening and fertilizing power. On the other hand, the symbol is connected with famine and death. This apparent contradiction, however, is only the expression of the age-long dual endeavour of getting rid of evil to secure good, of expelling death to gain life. The fundamental concept is the will to live, and the negative ritual of expulsion is the means to the attainment of the positive desire. To conserve and promote life, decay and death must be first banished, and, therefore, the institution of sacrifice centres in the offering of an efficacious victim. But of this more anon.

The Ritual of the First-Fruits

Vegetation being the offspring of Mother Earth and animated by a quasi-divine soul-substance analogous to that which animals share with man, a similar paradoxical situation exists in agricultural communities as among hunting tribes. The crops are the means of subsistence, yet their sacredness renders them dangerous unless and until they are approached with due solemnity and " apology." Thus, in addition to the positive and negative ritual of impulsion and expulsion, the tabu surrounding the first-fruits and the

[1] A. Polson, *Our Highland Folk-lore Heritage* (Dingwall, 1926), p. 150; G. Henderson, *Survivals in Belief among the Celts* (Glasgow, 1911), p. 284; Rogers, *Social Life in Scotland* (Edin., 1886), iii, p. 244.

harvest has played an important part in vegetation ceremonial.

Before the new millet may be consumed among the Ainu, for example, cakes of the cereal are prepared and addressed as follows : " O thou cereal deity, we worship thee. Thou hast grown very well this year, and thy flavour will be sweet. Thou art good. The goddess of fire will be glad, and we also rejoice greatly. O thou God, O thou divine cereal, do thou nourish the people. I now partake of thee. I worship thee and give thee thanks ! After having thus prayed, they, the worshippers, take a cake and eat it, and from this time the people may all partake of the new millet." [1] A similar solemn meal is held among the Caffres of Zululand before the crops are gathered. The new fruits are boiled in a special pot reserved for the purpose, and the sacred food placed in the mouth of each man by the king. If any one were to partake of the crops before this has been done he would die.[2] Both the Matabele [3] and the Yomba enforce the same tabu until the chief has sacrificed a bull before the tomb of his grandfather, and deposited pots of fresh beer and porridge made from the first-fruits, in front of the shrine. The blood of the victim is then sprinkled on the carefully weeded and freshly ploughed soil, and on the rafters of the little hut. A feast on the carcass, the porridge and the beer follows.[4]

[1] Batchelor, *The Ainu and their Folk-lore*, pp. 204 ff.

[2] L. Grout, *Zululand* (Philad., 1864), p. 161 ; F. Speckmann, *Die Hermanns-burger Mission in Africa* (Hermannsburg, 1876), pp. 294 ff.

[3] Decle, *Three Years in Savage Africa* (Lond., 1898), p. 157.

[4] C. Gouldsbury and H. Sheane, *The Great Plateau of Northern Rhodesia* (Lond., 1911), pp. 294 f.

In North America the Natchez of Louisana were accustomed to hold a " feast of grain " in the seventh moon which consisted principally in the ceremonial eating of new corn sown expressly for the purpose with suitable ritual. The ground in which it was grown was virgin soil, dressed and prepared for the warriors alone, who were the only persons allowed to sow, tend and gather the grain. When it was nearly ripe they collected it, placed it in a round granary, and informed the Great Sun who appointed a day for the festival. On the feast the whole nation set out from the village to the sacred granary, the chief attending in State apparel. New fire was made by friction, and when everything was prepared for dressing the corn, it was solemnly cooked, and distributed sacramentally to the female Suns, and then to all the women who proceeded to prepare grain in all the huts. The great Sun, having offered a plate of it to the four quarters of the earth, then gave the command to the warriors to eat it ; the boys followed their example, and finally the women.[1]

It was in this district, in the Creek country, that the famous *Busk* festival took place. In July or August, when the corn was ripe, the preparations began with the extinguishing of all the fires in the village including that on the temple hearth, and the scouring of the cooking vessels in which the new crops would be placed. The public square was carefully swept, and only men of the rank of warriors who had not broken the law of the first-fruit offering, and that of marriage, during the year, were allowed to enter. A strict fast

---

[1] J. R. Swanton, *43rd Bull. B.A.E.* (Wash., 1911), pp. 113 f.

was then observed for two nights and a day which entailed purgings with emetics. This accomplished, the high priest made new fire by friction, and placed it on the altar, every spark of old fire having previously been thrown away in the village, with all traces of the old year's food. A basket of new fruits was then brought to the high priest, who took out a little of each kind, rubbed it with bear's oil, and offered it, together with some flesh, " to the bountiful holy spirit of fire, as first-fruit offering, and an annual oblation for sin." Next he consecrated the sacred emetics (button-snake root and cassina) by pouring a little of them into the fire. Then he addressed the people, exhorting them to continue to observe their customary rites, and announcing that the sins of the previous year had been purged by the new fire, which was subsequently set down outside the holy square to be carried home joyfully to the purified hearths. The new fruits were now ready to be eaten with the indispensable bear's oil. The festival was continued for eight days during which the warriors were clad in their martial array, danced round the sacred fire, rubbed the new corn on their hands, faces and breasts, and, together with the rest of the community, observed the strictest continence. Finally, the people smeared themselves with white clay and bathed in running water to remove the last traces of evil incurred during the year.[1]

The drastic preparations for the eating of the new crops indicate the extreme sacredness with which they

---

[1] F. G. Speck, *Ethnol. of Yuki Indians* (Philad., 1909), pp. 86 f. ; C. Mac-Cauley, *5th* R.B.A.E. (1887), pp. 522 ff. for the allied Seminole rites.

were regarded, every possible precaution having been taken to prevent the neutralization of the infusion of new life and vigour by contact with ordinary food. How far this attitude may have arisen out of primitive tabus imposed to prevent the gathering of the new fruits too soon, it is difficult to say, but probably some such practical motive played a part in the early developments of the observances. This is suggested by the permission of the chief being required before the crops might be eaten, and the extension of this custom in the holding of a solemn meal by a few selected members of the tribe, or totem group, to desacralize the food.[1]

But apart from the question of origins, the rites as they were actually practised within recent memory had acquired a magico-religious significance based on the conception of the first-fruits being animated by some mysterious vitality, sometimes, as among the Ainu and the Thompson Indians,[2] regarded as a spiritual being. Whether the indwelling entity is interpreted as a " cereal deity " or " corn spirit," or merely as a vehicle of an impersonal soul-substance, once the danger is overcome by appropriate ritual, the very act of desacralization may be employed as a renewal of life and vigour at a time in the year when such a defence is most needed. It would seem, then, that the first-fruit ceremonial is essentially neither a sacrament or communion with a deity, nor a propitiation of a powerful spirit, as Frazer suggests,[3] but mainly as a ritual

---

[1] Stow, *Native Races of South Africa* (Lond., 1905), p. 174; Kingsley, *West African Studies* (Lond., 1899), p. 456, cf. p. 174; Spencer and Gillen, *Native Tribes of Central. Austral.*

[2] J. Teit, *Jesup N. Pacific Exped.*, 1900, p. 349; cf. Batchelor, *op. cit.*

[3] *Golden Bough* (" Spirits of Corn "), ii, pp. 82 ff.

device to enable them to be consumed without injury to the recipients or to the vegetative process.

Now it was around this positive and negative impulse towards life that the complex system of myth and ritual developed which found expression in agricultural communities at the dawn of civilization. In the great death and resurrection drama impulsion and expulsion both have their appropriate rites and purposes—the riddance of evil (i.e. hunger and barrenness), and the promotion of good (food and fertility). As Miss Harrison says, it is all summed up in the old formula, " Out with famine, in with health and wealth." [1]   It is this situation which is reproduced in mumming plays, and seasonal ceremonies, such as the contest between the Old and New Year, or Winter and Summer, or between twin brothers, as in the Norse myth of Balder and Hother, or the Egyptian story of Osiris and Set.   Whatever form the hostile duality has taken, the triumph of good has been depicted by the defeat or expulsion of evil, personified as Horus and Set, Marduk and Tiamat, Yahweh and the Dragon.

In the Babylonian New Year festival the struggle was symbolized by a race between Zu and Ninurta, in which Zu was defeated and probably slain, while elsewhere rites of this character were combined with a ritual marriage, as, for example, when Winter and Spring engaged in mortal combat for the possession of a woman, in the course of which the former was slain by the latter, who married the woman.   Sometimes the play was more complicated, and Winter killed Spring, but only to cause him to be resuscitated

[1] *Epilegomena to the Study of Greek Religion* (Camb., 1921), p. 3.

or live again in the person of a young boy who promptly slew Winter. It is this motive that runs through the legend of Œdipus, who slew his father and married his mother, or of Perseus, who killed his grandfather.

Tammuz and Ishtar

Behind this ritual stands the shadowy form of the Great Mother which we have found dominating fertility and vegetation cults, probably from Palæolithic times onwards. As Prof. Langdon says, " throughout their history, from the most ancient period to the very end of their existence as a race, the unmarried goddess is a dominating figure, the persistent and unchanging influence in the vast and complex pantheon." [1] Nevertheless, the Great Mother was not the only deity concerned with fertility and vegetation in the Sumerian texts since in the cult of Ishtar and Tammuz, the son-lover of the goddess, was virtually the embodiment of the life principle, typified originally, apparently, by the vivifying waters. Thus, as Langdon has pointed out, " since in Babylonia as in Egypt the fertility of the soil depended upon irrigation, it is but natural to expect that the youthful god who represents the birth and death of nature, would represent the beneficent waters which flooded the valleys of the Tigris and Euphrates in the later winter, and which ebbed away and nearly disappeared, in the canals and rivers in the period of Summer drought." [2]

He figures in the king-lists as the antediluvian

---

[1] *Tammuz and Ishtar* (Oxford, 1914), pp. 4 f.
[2] *Op. cit.*, p. 5.

Dumuzi, " the faithful son of the fresh waters which come from the earth,"[1] The general epithet *dumu-zi* is merely the Sumerian title to designate the dying god or " faithful child of the deep," there being no particular name for the divine life-giver. When the Sumerians moved into the Euphrates valley, Tammuz became a god of the fertilizing waters, *bel girsu*, " lord of the flood." Thus, as the personification of the fertilizing waters which flooded the land in winter and which died away in summer, he was regarded as the source and controller of vegetation *par excellence*, and, therefore, the corn-spirit who dies and comes to life again every year.[2]

In this capacity, as the embodiment of the life principle, his influence was operative in all reproductive functions, and consequently during his annual descent into the Land of No-Return, and the absence of Ishtar, the Mother Goddess, in her search for her lover-son, the reproductive processes were in abeyance. It was consequently hardly surprising that in the days of Israel's exile in Babylonia women should be seen at the appropriate season " weeping for Tammuz " (Ezek. viii. 14), since no offspring of man or beast could be born till the divine heroes returned.

It would seem, then, that from the period which cannot be dated later than 3000 B.C., and may conceivably be of even greater antiquity, there existed the notion that all life depended on the reproductive activities of a divine person who was himself suffi-

---

[1] *Cuneiform Texts*, xxiv, pl. 16, i, 30 ; cf. *Expository Times*, xxvii, 1915–16, p. 519.

[2] Langdon, *Sumerian and Babylonian Psalms* (Paris, 1909), p. 160 ; i, 14, n. 9, p. 338 ; cf. *op. cit.*, p. 11.

ciently mortal in his nature to be liable to loss of virility, and even capable of death. This widespread and deeply laid belief is the theme running through vegetation ritual in its classical form everywhere, but in Babylonia the cult of Tammuz is differentiated from its counterparts elsewhere inasmuch as the worship centred in the declining energies of the hero rather than in his resurrection. It was the dying son of the virgin mother, whom " the shadows of the nether world each year claimed as a divine sacrifice for man and beast and vegetation." [1]   Therefore, the characteristic features of this worship were the annual wailings for Tammuz in midsummer and the wanderings of the sorrowing mother in the barren fields and desolate sheepfolds in search of her lost son and lover.

Possibly Tammuz was actually a prehistoric king of Erech,[2] and while he was not the recipient of adoration or sacrifice, like other Sumerian monarchs he claimed divine procreation and birth. Shortly after 3000 B.C. Sumerian rulers appear to have been worshipped and deified during their lifetime, and they may have been put to death for the life of the cities over which they presided. At any rate this is the interpretation given by Langdon to the references in the later texts to the departed shades of kings being identified with the dying god, as " a survival of an ancient idea so adapted in practice, that the king escaped actual sacrifice by some symbolic act," and incidentally at the same time attained heaven at last.[3]

[1] *Tammuz and Ishtar*, p. 3.
[2] *Op. cit.*, p. 40 ; Langdon, *Sumerian Liturgical Texts*, Univ. of Penn. Pub., Bab. Section, x, 2, 1917, p. 208, n. 1.
[3] *Tammuz and Ishtar*, pp. 27 f.

Adonis and Attis

Passing from Mesopotamia to Greece, the worship of Adonis may very likely represent another form of the Sumerian myth, the appellation " Adonis " being merely the Greek adaptation of the Syriac form of address, *Adon*, " Lord." It has been conjectured, again, that Attis is another instance of the same process, but however this may be, the two divinities were identical in their relationship to the Great Mother, and therefore to fertility and the decay and revival of nature. In all these cults, from the crude female figurines of the Palæolithic cultures, and the subsequent maize-mothers and first-fruit rituals, to the classical myths, it was the Great Mother who played the determining part in life-giving functions. But as the male element was given greater prominence, the Mother Goddess tended to occupy a subordinate position in her capacity as the wife instead of the son of the culture hero. With the development of City States, and the establishment of the divine kingship, the partnership was dissolved, and as the god and goddess pursued a separate course, the original relationship became obscured, or entirely lost, so that in some cases the divinities changed their sex as well as their attributes.

Osiris and Isis

In Egypt while Osiris is clearly the counterpart of Tammuz, he was represented as the brother-spouse of Isis and not her son. Furthermore, the living king was identified with Horus and Re, and not with the culture hero, who was always a *dead* king. So numerous were the transformations and modifications in the Egyptian cult, in fact, that Sir E. Wallis Budge has been led to assert that " had a priest of Osiris who lived at Abydos under the XVIIIth dynasty witnessed the celebration of the great festival of Isis and Osiris in any large town in the first century before Christ, it is tolerably certain that he would have regarded it as a lengthy act of worship of strange gods, in which there appeared here and there, ceremonies and phrases which reminded him of the ancient Abydos ritual." [1] Nevertheless, the fundamental features of the Plutarch myth are true to type, and throw a flood of light on the origins of death and resurrection ritual.

Thus, Osiris is represented as the inundation, and Isis the land irrigated by it,[2] while elsewhere she appears as the throne.[3] In either capacity she is related to the Great Mother. Moreover, she is described as the giver of life to the dead, " wife of the lord of the abyss," " wife of the lord of the inundation," and " creatrix of the Nile flood." As the power of the Nile she was called Sati and Sept, and, as the producer of fertility by means of water she was called Anket. She was the female counterpart of the primeval abyss from which all life sprang, and at an early period she absorbed all the characteristics of the other goddesses, very much as Re combined the functions of the gods.

The cult of Isis, however, differed from that of her husband in that it centred, at any rate in its later aspects, in the mystery of birth, whereas that of Osiris

[1] *Legends of the Gods* (Lond., 1912), p. lxxxi.
[2] *Isis et Osiris*, p. 38.
[3] Erman, *Zeits. für Ägypt. Sprache*, 1909, p. 92.

was essentially a mystery of life issuing from death. Primarily he was a culture hero who in the capacity of a beneficent king had passed through the experience of death and thereby unloosed the springs of life from the grave. Thus he was regarded as the source of immortality to the blessed dead, and in a secondary sense a god of vegetation. In the Pyramid Texts, when the dead king was identified with him, he was thought to rise in the hereafter in union with the god. " As he (Osiris) lives, this king Unis lives ; as he dies not, this king Unis dies not ; as he perishes not, this king Unis perishes not." [1] The dead king receives the throne of Osiris, and becomes, like him, king of the dead. Similarly in the Osirian Mystery as described on a *stela* dated from Senusret III (XIIth Dynasty), it was the death and passion of the god that was represented in the sacred drama at Abydos. [2]

Since the emphasis is laid on death as the gate of life it was as the dead king that Osiris was depicted, frequently with grain sprouting from his mummy, suggesting the imperishable life of the god by means of which he survived death. Furthermore, he was identified with the fertilizing waters of the Nile, so that in him was combined the life-giving power which provided the food supply in this world, and enabled the mortal body to put on immortality beyond the grave.

The connecting link between these two aspects of the Osirian ritual seems to be the Nile. The fact that his body was supposed to have been revivified at his original embalmment by lustral water poured out by

[1] Breasted, *op. cit.*, p. 146.
[2] H. Schaefer, *Die Mysterien des Osiris in Abydos* (Leipzig, 1904).

Isis and Nephthys, is an indication that the life-giving
potency of this element played a determining part in
the elaboration of the cult.   It was upon the Nile that
Egypt depended for its very existence, and in a number
of passages in the Pyramid Texts the inundation is
directly attributed to Osiris.   " The lakes fill, the
canals are inundated by the purification that came
forth from Osiris," while later Rameses IV says to the
god, " Thou art indeed the Nile, great on the fields at
the beginning of the seasons ; gods and men live by
the moisture that is in them." [1]

This is further illustrated by the libation ritual which
Dr. Blackman has shown rests on the belief that the
dead are revivified by means of " the fluid which issued
from Osiris."   " The corpse of the deceased," he says,
" is dry and shrivelled.   To revivify it the vital fluids
that have exuded from it must be restored, for not till
then will life return and the heart beat again.   This, so
these texts [2] show us, was believed to be accomplished
by offering libations to the accompaniment of in-
cantations." [3]

The first three of the libations in question (Pyramid
Text 22–23 ; 756–66 ; 868) are said to be " the actual
fluids that have issued from the corpse," while the remaining four quoted (Pyr. 2007 ; 2031 ; 1360. P. 608 ;
Pyr. 788.   P. 66) represent, " not the deceased's own
exudation that are to revive his shrunken frame, but
those of a divine body, ' the god's fluid ' that came
from the corpse of Osiris himself, the juices that dissolved from his decaying-flesh, which are communi-

---

[1] Breasted, *op. cit.*, p. 18.   [2] I.e. the Pyramid Texts.
[3] A. M. Blackman, *Zeits. für Ägypt. Sprache und Altertumskunde* (Leipzig,
1912), p. 71.

68

cated to the dead sacrament-wise under the form of these libations." [1] The water used in the rite was Nile water, drawn according to the texts from the First Cataract region where the river was supposed to come pure from its source (Pyr. 834), because the Nile was regarded as " the fluid which issued from Osiris, or the God's fluid." [2] The ritual is described as sacramental because " under the form of these offerings certain virtues and powers were supposed to be mysteriously imbibed by the recipient." [3] In this way the corpse was enabled to regain its moisture, and to become revivified since, under the form of libations, it was believed that either the actual fluids that had run from it, or those of Osiris himself, were communicated to it. Thus, the magico-religious significance of water in Ancient Egypt was analogous to that of blood in primitive thought, since it was regarded as a vital element which exuded from the body at death, and had to be restored before life could be resumed in the hereafter.

From the identification of Osiris with the life-giving waters of the Nile, and indeed of water generally, since he was also connected with the " waters of the earth and sky that he may become the sea and the ocean itself," [4] it was only a step to his equation with the life-giving function as a whole. Therefore, inasmuch as vegetation is largely the product of the action of water on the soil, and in Egypt it is the Nile that constitutes the determining feature in agriculture, it would seem that the primary fact in the Osiris cult was irrigation,

---

[1] *Op. cit.*, p. 71.
[2] *Ibid.*, p. 71, n. 3.
[3] *Ibid.*, p. 73.
[4] Pyr., 628-9.

and then the sowing and reaping of corn. His marriage with Isis, if she was a personification of the female principle, symbolizes the union of the vitalizing waters with the maternal aspect of the earth. Consequently as the annual inundation of the Nile came to be regulated by an elaborate system of irrigation distributing its life-giving waters over the fertile alluvium, the beneficent Osiris was the imperishable principle of life, who subsequently took over many other attributes and functions. The cycle of nature represented " the ever-waning and reviving life of the earth, sometimes with the fertile soil, or again discerned in vegetation itself—that was Osiris." [1]

The Solar Theology

There is, however, another integral element in vegetation ritual which plays a prominent part in Egyptian religion, and with which Osiris was also associated. If Egypt was essentially the gift of the Nile, " the all-enveloping glory and power of the Egyptian sun " was an insistent fact which could hardly be overlooked in a magico-religious interpretation of natural phenomena, especially as the rest of the river year by year was dependent in turn on the sun. Thus from the fourth dynasty a solar line of kings reigned from Heliopolis, and from this centre the temple worship appears to have derived its inspiration. It was to enhance the prestige of the Heliopolitan hierarchy that a number of local gods were identified with Re, the most general title of the sun-god, who thus became the father of the gods and men, and the patron and

[1] Breasted, *op. cit.*, p. 23.

divine ruler of the kingdom, reigning on earth in the person of his physical son, the king. Henceforth a State fiction maintained that the reigning Pharaoh was a form of manifestation of the sun-god who at death was translated to the celestial realms of his heavenly counterpart.[1]

If the king was not accorded formal worship in early times during his life, he alone is reproduced in the reliefs on the walls of the temples he was supposed to have built, in the act of making offerings to the gods as the mediator between the human and divine order. " The gods are no longer the gods of the Egyptian people, they are the gods of Pharaoh their son," [2] just as the temples were regarded as his monuments. In fact, Foucart would maintain that " as far back as we can go we find ourselves in the presence of a conception of monarchy based solely upon the assimilation of the king to the gods." [3]

The fundamental difficulty in the interpretation of the Egyptian theory of the divine kingship lies in the hopeless confusion of thought and expression concerning the various symbolizations of Re.[4] But, nevertheless, in all these syncretisms the sun-god retained his essential character as the constant source of life and sustenance whose creative powers were as manifold as they were continuous. Moreover, the king in his divine capacity was a potent agent in the process, being " the living epitome of all that is

---

[1] Sethe, *Zur altägyp. Sage vom Sonnenauge das in der Fremde war* (Leipzig, 1912), pp. 5 f.

[2] Erman, *Handbook of Egyptian Religion* (Lond., 1907), pp. 37, 52.

[3] *E.R.E.*, vii, p. 711.

[4] Cf. Introd., p. 6.

divine in the Nile valley,"[1] and therefore heir to the powers and qualities of the deities whose functions were symbolized in the ritual and regalia of the royal office. He could " make sunshine ; he was master of magic, the pupil of Thoth the great magician ; he was master of thunder, the uræus spitting fire and his voice being the thunder, he brandishes his sceptre like the thunder-bolt. As king of the harvest, he turns over the earth, and presides over the sowing. Sickle in hand, he cuts the grain."[2] Thus, as Dr. Blackman has pointed out, the official worship as represented in the temple reliefs centred in obtaining the favour of the divinities for the Pharaoh who received the promise of health, stability, good fortune, abundance and immortality in return for the life-giving offerings he presented to the gods.[3] His duties, in fact, were as numerous and vital as his personality was complex, and prominent among them was the control of the processes of Nature by virtue of his unique relationship with the sun as the son of Re, and, after the Osirianization of the royal solar ritual, with vegetation and the Nile as the living manifestation of Osiris.

It is out of this cycle of ideas we would suggest that the sacrificial ritual has emerged as a means of controlling the processes of vegetation. Any object especially charged with vitality, such as female figurines, new fruits, or water, may fulfil the same function as that exercised by blood in hunting magic and its subsequent developments. When this system of offerings is brought into relation with the death

[1] Foucart, E.R.E., vii, p. 713.
[2] Moret, Ann. de Musée Guimet, Biblio. de Vulg., 38, 1912, pp. 210 ff.
[3] E.R.E., xii, p. 780.

and resurrection drama, it assumes a mystery significance as part of the culture pattern centring in the divine kingship and its relations to the natural order, out of which the institution of sacrifice emerged, with its many strands in an ancient past.

Thus, it was around the practice of slaying the divine king that the Tammuz rites appear to have developed,[1] and it has been suggested that Osiris perished in the Nile flood.[2] While there is no definite evidence that the Egyptian Pharaoh was actually killed as a regular institution, Dr. Seligman has left no room for doubt concerning the existence of this custom among the Shilluk of the White Nile.[3] Moreover, we know that ancient Egyptian influence has spread to the upper reaches of the Nile.[4] It is, therefore, significant that the confirmation of Frazer's brilliant guess should come from this area.

Killing the King

As the divine reincarnation and representative of the culture hero, Nyakang, the Shilluk king is considered to be ultimately responsible for the well-being of his country and its people. Therefore, he " must not be allowed to become ill or senile, lest with his diminishing vigour the cattle should sicken and fail to bear their increase, the crops would rot in the fields, and man, stricken with disease, would die in increasing numbers." [5]   Something analogous to the rule of

---

[1] *Tammuz and Ishtar*, p. 26.

[2] Murray, *Zeits. für Ägypt. Sprache*, 1913, pp. 128 ff.

[3] *Cult of the Nyakang and the Divine Kings of the Shilluk* (Khartoum, 1911), pp. 216 ff.

[4] *J.R.A.I.*, 1913, p. 664.   [5] *Op. cit.*, p. 221.

succession to the priesthood of Diana at Nemi would seem to have prevailed at one time, since any member of the Royal family could attempt to kill the king, and, if successful, to reign in his stead. The tragedy, however, could only take place at night when the sovereign had dismissed his body-guard, and was alone with his wives in his enclosure. Under these circumstances, the sleep of crowned heads must often have " fled from them," and it is alleged that the night was passed in constant watchfulness, " the king prowling fully armed, peering into the shadows, or standing silent and watchful in some dark corner. Then, when at last his rival appeared, the fight would take place in grim silence, broken only by the clash of spear and shield, for it was said to be a point of honour for the *ret* (king) not to call the herdsmen to his assistance." [1] Although there is no contemporary evidence for anything of this sort, yet Dr. Seligman thinks that a survival of the custom may perhaps be detected in the common belief that the king keeps awake at night and sleeps only in the day—a report which seemed to be confirmed by the sleepy condition of the king whenever he saw him.[2]

In recent times the leading part in the act was performed by certain families called *ororo*, said to be descendants of the third ruler of the dynasty, but there is no reliable information regarding the method adopted. The old custom, in the opinion of Seligman, was to take the *ret* and wall him up in a hut till he died of starvation and suffocation ; a practice said to have been given up five generations ago at the dying request

[1] *Op. cit.*, p. 222.   [2] *Op. cit.*

74

of the last victim, whose protracted sufferings led him to endeavour to spare his successors his agonies. When decomposition was judged to be complete, the bones were removed, and buried with the skin of sacrificed oxen. A shrine was then erected over the grave, and enclosed by a fence in resemblance to the shrine of Nyakang. Groups of two or more huts of this description within a sacred area dedicated to the dead king occur in many villages. At them the harvest ceremony is performed, sacrifices are offered, and, after his installation, each new ruler is expected to send presents to the shrines.

The interregnum of some months which followed the death of the king was brought to an end by an effigy of Nyakang being carried to Fashoda from a shrine at Akurwa, near the northern border of the Shilluk country. This was placed on a four-legged stool, thought to have belonged to the culture hero, and immediately the effigy was removed the new king was seated thereon, a ceremony clearly indicating the transmission of the spirit of Nyakang to his earthly representative. This is a remarkable confirmation of Frazer's theory of the divine king since it reveals what was lacking in the ceremony at Nemi ; viz. the transference of the divine, or semi-divine, spirit to the new ruler.

As the controller of vegetation, the king was responsible for the great rain ceremony at Fashoda, and in the neighbouring Dinka tribes the rain-makers were also in the nature of divine kings. Thus, they were not allowed to die a natural death lest famine, disease and sterility resulted. When an aged rain-maker realized his end was approaching, and that he was growing old and infirm, he acquainted his children with the fact, who thereupon prepared a grave in which their father allowed himself to be placed. There he would remain for some twenty-four hours, reciting accounts of his deeds, and giving advice to his tribesmen. Then, when he had no more to say, he would tell his people to cover him with the soil, and soon all was over. Having passed out of the world in this orthodox manner, his spirit was transmitted to his successor, but if he were not killed ceremonially, his son could not succeed him, and the tribe would be without a rain-maker. Although not so serious as death from illness or old age, the accidental demise of a rain-maker brought sickness on the tribe.[1]

As Sir James Frazer has shown, in support of his brilliant conjecture, the practice is very widespread of the king reigning till he came to a violent end by his own hand, or at the hands of the community, or when a stronger than he arose and slew him.[2] Moreover, doubtless many of the legends in which aspirants to the throne fight and wrestle with one another for the kingship, or engage in tests of endurance and skill,[3] are reminiscences of the ritual killing of the sovereign when he showed signs of advancing age in order that his powers might be passed on unimpaired to his successor.

The custom, however, had its disadvantages, and as voluntary self-immolation lost its romance at court,

[1] Seligman, E.R.E., iv, p. 711.

[2] G.B., Pt. iii (Dying God), pp. 14 ff.

[3] Pindar, Isthm. 3(8), 70 ff.; Plat., Theæt., 169 B; Apollod., 2, 5, 11; Hyg., Fab., 31.

ways and means were devised by which effectual substitutes were provided for ageing divine kings to save
them from the painful necessity of coming to an un-
timely end. Instead of the actual monarch sacrificing
himself in the guise of the human god as a patriotic duty
to secure the continued prosperity of the land and the
vegetative processes, his son, or some member of his
family, paid the supreme penalty on his behalf.[1]   A
further modification of the rule is to be found probably
in the custom of a king reigning for a specified length
of time, and then either forfeiting his throne in favour
of another, or renewing his reign by some ceremonial
act such as a ritual marriage with the queen.[2]

There was, however, another way of approaching
the problem. It being firmly established that to
sacrifice life means to promote life, the throne, or the
creative power behind it, could be maintained as the
centre of vitality, by a continual outpouring of blood.
Therefore, instead of the gods being compelled virtually to immolate themselves in the persons of their
earthly reincarnations, in order that they might be
enabled to continue their beneficent vegetative functions towards mankind, sacrificial victims came to
figure more and more prominently in the ritual cycle
of ploughing, seedtime, and harvest, upon which the
agricultural community depends for its subsistence.
Thus in place of the one all-embracing divine sacrifice,
arose the practice of offering human hearts to augment
the powers of the gods, in particular the sun, and so
to ensure the maintenance of the agricultural year.

[1] G.B., *op. cit.*, pp. 160 ff.
[2] Homer, *Odyssey*, xix, 178 f. ; cf. G.B., *op. cit.*, pp. 70 ff.

CHAPTER III

HUMAN SACRIFICE

In developing a ritual cycle based on the agricultural year, the higher civilization of Central America introduced a calendrical system which was a ceremonial order providing the religious programme for each day in the year rather than a dating device. This " complete cycle of never-ending services " was a reflection of the cosmic order, so that by a perpetual round of human sacrifices the gods were kept alive, and as a result, the powers of Nature were enabled to fulfil their functions.[1]

Mexican Civilization

The origins of Mexican civilization are wrapped in mystery, but if it be assumed that the Maya culture was indigenous to the New World, a period of very considerable duration would seem to be required, corresponding to that of predynastic Egypt, for the development of the complex calendar and hieroglyphic systems to the point of graphic record. But of the existence of this we have no evidence. When it is first encountered, as Joyce says, it seems to spring " full-blown from the earth," [2] Mercer's investigations of the hill caves of Yucatan brought to light large quantities of good pottery but no remains of Pleisto-

[1] C. Wissler, *The American Indian* (New York, 1922), p. 192.
[2] *Mexican Archæology* (Lond., 1914), p. 368.

cene fauna,[1] while Mr. E. H. Thompson, who had previously explored the cave of Loltun in 1888-9, was convinced that " no people or race of so-called Cave People ever existed in Yucatan." [2]   The discovery of human teeth in one of these caves filed in the same manner as those of a skull found beneath one of the ruined buildings at Labna, and elsewhere in the Maya region,[3] supports Thompson's conclusion that the caves were occupied by " the same race and people who built the great stone structures now in ruins." [4]

Apart from the vexed question of origins, the civilization we know was fairly established by the second century of our era, the earliest phase apparently going back to a much more remote past.   At the close of the early period (i.e. about A.D. 300) the Maya seem to have penetrated into the Mexican valley by way of Oaxaca, and there to have come into contact with the primitive inhabitants of the Zapotec country, and subsequently with the Nahua-speaking Toltec invaders, who had made their way into the valley from the north.   In this case it was from a combination of these northern Nahua-hunting tribes, and the southern Maya immigrants, that the Toltec civilization arose in the Mexican valley.   After reaching its height about the middle of the eleventh century A.D., it fell before the successive incursions of tribes of kindred stock— the Chichimec hordes.   Other invading groups followed, and, finally, about the fourteenth century, the Aztec (the last of the invading Nahua tribes, who, on

[1] H. C. Mercer, *The Hill-Caves of Yucatan* (New York, 1903), pp. 34, 130, 160.

[2] *Memoirs Peabody Museum Amer. Anthrop. and Ethnol.*, iii, 1897, p. 22.

[3] Joyce, *op. cit.*, p. 228, 316.   [4] E. H. Thompson, *ibid.*

their arrival early in the thirteenth century were still a hunting people) rose to power, and extended their influence, and the culture they had imbibed, through Chiapas to Guatemala.

It was in the Aztec phase of the development that human sacrifice became the determining factor in the culture, and made the waging of extensive wars essential to provide the annual supply of victims required to enable the sun to continue his daily course across the sky, and ensure the fertility of the crops. While the early Maya worshipped a sun-god, there are no indications that he was associated with war or human sacrifice. In March they held a fire-ceremony in which they collected every species of animal available, and tore out their hearts, casting them into the flames. But the practice does not appear to have extended to human victims. Similarly during the May rites the heart of a dog was extracted in order that the land might be fertile, and the new crops abundant, but again without recourse to human sacrifice. Moreover, in the Mayan priesthood, the office of sacrificer was of little importance, whereas among the Mexicans it was the highest order, reserved for the king himself on certain occasions, such as the consecration of a new temple.

According to the *Popol Vuh*, the sun was not created, and mankind was without ritual, when the Quiche ancestors set out from Tulan, where each tribe had received its god under whose leadership it began its migration. The need of fire, however, after the general separation, led the other tribes to beg it from the Quiche thunder-god, Tohil, who was able to supply his votaries with it by simply striking it from his sandal. But the Quiche demanded in return that the recipients should consent to be united with their god " beneath the girdles and beneath their armpits."[1] In other words, they were requested darkly to give their hearts in sacrifice, and with the exception of the Kakchiquel, they all fell into the trap. Henceforth human sacrifice was practised secretly, till at length it became generally recognized that the sun and the powers of Nature needed continual regeneration which could only be secured by the offering of human victims in the prime of their vigour, whose reward in this life was a temporary enjoyment of living in the divine state, and hereafter a place with the warriors in the solar paradise.

Quetzalcoatl and Human Sacrifice

The break-up of the Toltec Empire seems to be directly connected with the institution of the rite, and it is possible that in the myths we have a reminiscence of the overthrow of Tulan, or Tollan, the capital, the murder of its last king, and the spread of Toltec influence into Yucatan. Human sacrifice necessitating aggressive wars doubtless played an important part in this series of events. The fact that the culture hero, Quetzalcoatl, the " father of the Toltecs," is represented as opposing the practice, suggests that it was introduced into Mexico by the pre-Aztec nomads, and this doubtless explains their successors (the Aztecs) regarding him as a foreign god, of alien character. Thus it was in the older towns, such as

[1] Brasseur de Bourbourg, *Le Popol Vuh* (Paris, 1861), pp. 215 ff.

Cholula, that his worship flourished, while in the capital, Mexico, he had but a limited following. Human sacrifice, moreover, was not an integral part of his ritual, and his priests were a separate caste ; the high priest of Quetzalcoatl, although next in rank to the Mixcoatl Teohuatzin (the Mexican Lord of Divine Matters, or head of the Aztec priesthood), having authority only over his own caste.

Quetzalcoatl may have been originally a divine king who instructed the Toltecs in the arts and sciences, and discovered the maize-plant. Later he was transformed into a Creator-god, and represented as the wind bringing the fertilizing rains to Mexico, and as the plumed-serpent, an emblem of fruitfulness. His name was derived from the early Maya Creator, Kukulcan, or Cucumatz, of the Quiche legends, " the feathered-snake that goes in the waters," the ripple born of wind and water, representing breath and life. In his snake and water aspects he was connected with the rain-gods, while the bird-like feathers associated him with the sky.[1] In all these forms he was connected with fertility, being the agent by which the earth brought forth in abundance.

As a divine king he sought ways and means of renewing his youth when his powers diminished through old age. To this end he travelled eastwards in search of the elixir of life, but his departure had serious consequences both on the vegetation and the bird-life. His aversion to shedding blood seems to have been the cause of his vacating the throne, brought about, according to the myth, by Tezcatlipoca descending

[1] Joyce, *op. cit.*, p. 225 ; Seler, 28*th Bull. B.A.E.* (1904), p. 40.

from the sky in the form of a spider ; and, disguising himself as a physician, giving the king a magical draught of *pulque*, which led him to lose his chastity. As a result, the priestly line was carried on without recourse to human sacrifice, and Quetzalcoatl betook himself to " Tlapallan " (i.e. Tabasco) in the hope of returning as king of a rejuvenated land. Instead, however, he elected to ascend to the sky on a funeral pyre, where he became either the planet Venus, or the Morning Star.[1] In his cult his representative was required to become intoxicated at certain festivals and while in this condition to have intercourse with a virgin,[2] so that by this literal reproduction of the incident recorded in the myth, the royal priestly line was carried on independent of human sacrifice.

Taking the evidence collectively, it seems that human sacrifice was introduced into Central America by the nomadic Nahua peoples after they had adopted a settled life, and borrowed from the indigenous Maya population their agricultural cults. At first the prosperity of the land rested, apparently, on the virility of the king. After the overthrow of the Toltec Empire, however, the Nahua invaders were less inclined to absorb the local Maya worship, preferring to adapt it to their original system. Thus in course of time the Aztec warrior-god Uitzilopochtli was transformed into a solar divinity demanding a state of constant warfare to furnish him with human hearts. It is this far-reaching change in the social and religious organization that is reflected probably in the legendary

---

[1] Joyce, p. 11.
[2] Sahagun, *Historia de la Nueva España*, vol. 3, Appendix, chap. ix.

account of the fall of the Toltec Federation, after Quetzalcoat[1] had been driven out of Tulan by his brother Tezcatlipoca, in which human sacrifice figures as an important factor.

In course of time sanguinary rites became associated with the worship of Quetzalcoatl when he was given a " place in the sun," and in Oaxaca the Zapotecs believed that it was he who first taught men to offer their own blood.[1] But, nevertheless, among the Aztecs he never lost his original character as an alien culture hero averse to the practice of human sacrifice, and his cult was always subordinate to that of the warrior-god. On the other hand, human sacrifice was prominent in the ritual of the mother goddesses, who were essentially associated with the sedentary agriculturists rather than with the pastoral Aztec.[2] Thus Centeotl, the goddess of maize and the earth, who in reality was the earth-mother, Teteoinnan, was the recipient of a female victim during the harvest festival, whose skin was taken to the temple of Centeotl the son, and worn there in the succeeding ritual by the officiating priest as the living image of the goddess.

It was, in fact, in conjunction with the culture of the soil, and the various phases of agricultural life, that elaborate ceremonial was performed on each of the eighteen sections of twenty days into which the ancient Mexican year was divided. In February children were sacrificed to the rain-gods to enable them to send the rain required for the crops of the new year.[3] Just

---

[1] Sahagun, *op. cit.*, chaps. 58, 64, 70 ; Seler, *28th Bull. B.A.E.*, pp. 276 ff.

[2] Joyce, *op. cit.*, p. 36.

[3] B. de Sahagun, *Histoire générale des choses de la Nouvelle Espagne* (Paris, 1880), pp. 57 f.

84

before the actual sowing, in the second twentieth, Totec, a form of the moon-god, required offerings to fertilize the earth in order that she might receive the germ and bring forth the crops. A virile and gallant prisoner of war was therefore selected, after which he was bound with extended arms and legs to a wooden frame, where he was shot with arrows, so that the blood might drop on the earth and fertilize it.[1]

In Mexico city, however, when the victim was exhausted, he was sacrificed in the normal manner by cutting open the breast and extracting the heart. Other prisoners were similarly treated, and their skins removed to be worn by men personating the god, to show that the earth-god had put on a new cloak. The feast concluded with a ceremonial dance in which priests disguised themselves as maize-ears, maize-stalks and similar crops, thereby indicating that the purpose of the rites was the promotion of the fertility of the cereals. The gladiatorial combat was symbolical of war, and doubtless had some connexion with the myths respecting the provision of blood and hearts of captives to feed the sun and the earth.

The ordinary form of sacrifice consisted in stripping the victim of his ornaments, stretching him over the convex sacrificial stones, and while five priests held his arms, legs and head, the high priest, or sacrificer, cut open his breast with a flint or obsidian knife, and tore out the heart. This was held up to the sun to provide it with nourishment, before it was cast into a basin of copal placed in a position to enable the blood and

[1] Sahagun, *op. cit.*, pp. 58 f.; cf. Joyce, *Mexican Archæology* (Lond., 1914), pp. 65 f., 40 f., Fig. 5 A.

incense to ascend to the gods. The body was hurled down the steps of the temple to the court where it was seized by the priests, or by the warrior who captured the victim. Sometimes a solemn feast was then held on the flesh, the skin having first been removed to be worn ceremonially by men who seem to have acquired thereby the fertilizing and health-giving qualities of the victim.[1] Some of the blood was carried to certain temples and smeared on the hips of the images of the gods.

In the third twentieth, Tocoztli (" awakening "), the month of the first-fruits, signified by the figure of a maize-goddess, children were sacrificed, and the first flowers were offered in the temple of Xipe, " the Flayed God," the patron of sowing, characterized in the MSS. by red and white paint. The men who had worn the skins of the victims slain in the previous festival as the living image of the god (Xipe), now discarded their gruesome and fetid garments, and solemnly buried them. The fourth month began on April 3rd with ceremonies and decorations appropriate to the condition of the maize, young girls being offered to the presiding deities, Centeotl and Chicome Coatl.[2]

Then came the great feast, Toxcatl, when the sun was at its zenith on April 23rd, symbolized by the figures of Tezcatlipoca, the Aztec Jupiter. This was the chief festival of the year, and it was on this occasion that the well-known sacrifice of the human god

---

[1] Frazer thinks that the skin was a representation of the resurrection of the deity ; cf. G.B., pt. ix., " The Scapegoat " (Lond., 1914), pp. 288, 296, 302 ff.

[2] Sahagun, op. cit., pp. 59 f., 94 f.

occurred. The event has been so often described that it is unnecessary to recapitulate the details. Briefly stated, it consisted in taking the most attractive prisoner of war, and disguising him as the divinity. For a year he lived in the temple, waited on by nobles, served as a prince, and treated as a god when he appeared in the streets. Twenty days before his death he consorted with four brides known as the goddess of Flowers, the goddess of the Young Maize, the goddess of " Our Mother among the Water," and the goddess of Salt. At length the destined day arrived, and the victim, still young and full of vigour, was led forth across the lake to a spot where a little hill arose from the edge of the water. Here he bade farewell to his wives, and repaired to a lonely pyramidal temple where he was seized by the priests awaiting his arrival, and made the great sacrifice in the usual manner.[1] This having been accomplished, his successor immediately was invested with the office for the next year, so that the substitute, like the divine king, never dies. " *Le Roi est mort, Vive le Roi.*"

The sixth twentieth was the rainy season, and therefore symbolized by the figure of Tlaloc. It was the occasion of a severe fast of the priests who gathered aquatic plants for the manufacture of mats on which small balls of a flour-paste made with maize in grain and beans, called *etzalli*, were placed to be offered and solemnly eaten. After a ceremonial bath in a lake, during which the motions and cries of aquatic birds were imitated, human victims were offered to the

---

[1] Sahagun, *op. cit.,* pp. 61 ff., 96 ff. ; Seler, *Altmexikenische Studien* (Berlin, 1899), ii, pp. 116–65.

Rain-gods, adorned with appropriate emblems. Then came the celebrations in honour of the sprouting maize in the seventh and eighth months (June 2 and 22), characterized in the first instance by the sacrifice of a woman as the representative of Uixtociuatl, the goddess of Salt, the sister of the Rain-gods. For ten days dances were held by women and girls holding garlands of flowers which on the last night continued till the fatal day (June 2nd) dawned when the victim and a number of slaves were sacrificed on the pyramid of the temple of Tlaloc.[1]

On June 22nd, when the maize was nearly ripe, a woman dressed as the goddess of the young maize, Xilonen, was sacrificed after the customary dances in which torches were carried, and complete decorum between the sexes was strictly enforced. The victim was arrayed in the robes and regalia of the goddess, the upper part of her face having been painted red, and the lower part yellow, in resemblance of the colouring of the ripe maize, while her legs and arms were covered with red feathers. In her left hand she carried a shield, and in her right a crimson baton. During the night she danced before the temple of Xilonen, and the next day she was led to the temple of Centeotl, the goddess of the maize, where she was seized by a priest, who carried her on his back while the sacrificer decapitated her, and tore out her heart. Then, but not till then, the green ears of maize might be eaten.[2]

The ninth twentieth (July 12th), symbolized by the

---

[1] Sahagun, *op. cit.*, pp. 64, 115 ff.; Bancroft, *Native Races of the Pacific Coast* (San Francisco, 1882), ii, pp. 325 ff.

[2] Sahagun, *op. cit.*, pp. 65, 118 ff.; Bancroft, *op. cit.*, pp. 326 ff.; Payne, *op. cit.*, i, pp. 421 f.

figure of Uitzilopochtli, or of a mummy, was happily free from human sacrifices, a more congenial flower feast sufficing at this stage in the growth of vegetation. The next month, Xocouetzi (Aug. 1st), however, witnessed the most horrible episode in the sacrificial ritual of the Aztec year. It was then that living victims were cast into a huge brazier and dragged by hooks to the place of sacrifice, where their hearts were torn out in the usual manner, as offering to Xiuhtecutli, the fire-deity, while prisoners were thrown into a fire to renew his energy. Similarly, young men full of vigour vied with one another in climbing to the top of a pole on which was the figure of a mummy, bird or butterfly symbolizing the god of Otomi, the " soul of the dead warrior." [1]

After this feast of the dead, the harvest festival and great expiation ceremony occurred in the eleventh month of the Mexican year (August 21st), during which a woman representing Teteoinnan, the " mother of the gods," was decapitated at midnight and flayed, the skin being worn by a young man as the living image of the goddess. One of the woman's thighs, however, was flayed separately, and the skin carried to another temple as a mask for the priest of Centeotl, the maize-goddess and daughter of the mother of the gods. The man personating the Mother Goddess was finally decorated in her apparel on the highest point of her temple, where at break of day he sacrificed four captives, while the priests completed the slaughter of all who remained. The purpose of this rite was the impregnation of the goddess by Uitzilopochtli, the

[1] Sahagun, *op. cit.*, pp. 66 f., 126 f.

ceremonies concluding with dances where Teteoinnan was replaced by the maize-goddess. Finally, the skin worn by the priest of Centeotl was deposited on a hostile frontier, and the goddess, in the person of the priest wearing the skin of the victim, was driven out of the town.[1]

The twelfth twentieth (September 10th), called Teotleco, was the feast of all the gods held in honour of the return to their land after a temporary absence during the rainy season. The deities were provided with universal rejoicings, and the proceedings concluded with a fire ceremony in which many slaves were thrown alive into the flames.[2] The harvest rites were continued in the next festival on September 30th, when victims, identified with the fertility gods, were sacrificed to Tlaloc, and offerings brought to the rain-gods (i.e. the gods of the mountains). In the fourteenth month (October 20th), a great feast called Quecholli, associated with Mixcoatl, the god of hunting, was observed, which necessitated the sacrifice of the representative of this deity, to Tezcatlipoca, together with a number of slaves, who were bound hand and foot like captive deer.[3]

The birth of Uitzilopochtli and his victory over his brethren, were re-enacted on November 9th, the slaves to be offered at the conclusion of the rites engaging in ceremonial combat. Then came the sixteenth festival on November 29th with more sacrifices to Tlaloc, followed in the next month (December 19th) by the offering of a woman at sundown in the temple of Uitzilopo-

---

[1] *Op. cit.*, pp. 18, 68 ff., 133; Bancroft, *op. cit.*, iii, pp. 353–9.
[2] Sahagun, pp. 69, 139 f.   [3] *Op. cit.*, pp. 141 ff.

chtli personating the goddess Uamatecutli. Her head was cut off and given to a priest wearing the costume and mask of the deity, who then led a dance round the platform, followed by priests similarly attired.[1]

The year terminated on January 8th with a feast called Izcalli, dedicated to Xiuhtecutli, the god of fire, who was honoured by offerings of animals captured by children and young men who passed them on to the priests to cast into a sacrificial fire. Human victims, consisting of men with their wives, were provided every fourth year when the festival assumed more elaborate proportions. These were dressed in the attire of the fire-god and thrown into the flames, but only to be raked out again to have their sufferings brought to an end by the removal of their hearts.[2] It would seem that the purpose of this inhuman procedure was to ensure the deity deriving the full benefit of the vital energy of his victims lest he should grow old and die. Therefore the victims were first dedicated to him in the flames before he renewed his energy from their palpitating hearts.[3]

The ritual of the Aztec solar calendar, as it has been recorded by Sahagun, has been set forth in some detail (wearisome as may be the description of rites having a consistent similarity on each occasion) inasmuch as it illustrates the cardinal belief of the Mexicans concerning the renewal by means of human sacrifice of the life-principle upon which vegetation depended. Since it was supposed that no less than

---

[1] *Op. cit.*, pp. 71 ff., 148 ff. ; Bancroft, ii, pp. 337 ff.

[2] Sahagun, *op. cit.*, pp. 164 f. ; Bancroft, ii, pp. 329 ff. ; J. de Torquemada, *Monarquia Indiana* (Madrid, 1723), lib. x, cap. 30 ; ii, pp. 285 ff.

[3] *G.B.*, pt. ix, " The Scapegoat," p. 301.

four previous suns had been destroyed at the end of succeeding world-epochs, causing incidentally universal destruction, the present luminary was hardly in a very secure position. Therefore the greatest possible care had to be taken to prevent a recurrence of the catastrophe, and be the cost what it may, he must be sustained by seasonal sacrifices. This entailed constant wars to keep up the supply of victims, and so the sun was the god of warriors, just as he was the lord of the vegetation deities who controlled the forces of Nature. Without the requisite number of captives the sacrifices would fail, and then natural processes would cease. Therefore the vegetation motive predominated in the calendrical rites which were ultimately solar in origin, and military in practice.

The association of the mother goddesses with these agricultural sacrifices doubtless explains the warlike qualities sometimes displayed elsewhere by the various manifestations of the Great Mother, as, for example, in the case of the Babylonian Innini who was identified with Antu, the goddess of war.[1] In Central America it was only when the pastoral Aztec civilization developed that the indigenous vegetation cults took over this military character, as the principle of fertility was made to depend on the extraction of human hearts.

Once it was established that the Sun—Ipalnemohuani, " He by whom men live "—could only be sustained in this way, human sacrifice assumed these alarming proportions, and since wars were carried on for the express purpose of obtaining victims to provide nourishment for Uitzilopochtli, this warrior-god was

[1] Langdon, *Tammuz and Ishtar* (Oxford, 1914), pp. 7, 45, 92, 95.

appropriately made to exclaim, " through me has the sun risen." [1] Notwithstanding the fact that the entire pantheon, male and female, tended to become incorporated in the calendrical ritual, and assume various *rôles* in the rites, it was a solar theory that dominated the ceremonial as a whole. Thus the sun was regarded as the *teotl*, the god *par excellence*, and if hearts were plucked out for the benefit of other deities, they were usually offered to him as well, inasmuch as he represented the ultimate source of life. Therefore, behind all the ghastly sequence of the solar calendar there lay the fundamental belief that the sun must be given nourishment if he was to continue his beneficent functions in supplying the kindly fruits of the earth through the good offices of the various departmental deities, and not least the mother of fertility. But since the king no longer sacrificed himself it became necessary to seek substitutes, and lest the nation should be deprived of her own sons, aggressive wars were continually waged to keep the altars adequately supplied from without.

The barbarous custom may be said to have reached its zenith in the Aztec civilization. Thus in the surrounding agricultural communities to the north, while there are traces of human sacrifice among the Skidi Pawnee,[2] the Natchez of Louisiana,[3] the Iroquois,[4] and sporadically in the Pueblo region, it is in the nature of a declining practice. Thus, for example, among the

---

[1] Sahagun, *op. cit.*, pp. 477–82.

[2] Wissler, *19th International Congress of Americanists* (Wash., 1917), p. 367.

[3] Du Pratz, *Histoire de la Louisane* (Paris, 1758), p. 314 ; cf. Swanton, *43rd Bull. B.A.E.* (Wash., 1911), pp. 138 ff.

[4] *Jesuit Relations*, xiii, pp. 37–79.

Huron the most characteristic sacrifice was that of the white dog at the New Year rites, but prisoners of war on occasions were also tortured to death apparently in honour of the war-god who seems to have been another form of the sun-god.[1] The ceremonies observed in connexion with the victim both before and after his death are almost identical with those of the Aztec at the feast of Toxcatl, and doubtless represent a northern survival of the same rite.

In the southern continent, again, the ritual recurs in a modified form under the Inca rule in Peru. Thus, sacrifices were offered to maintain the human representative of the sun-god in vigour. Whether the victims were actually human beings has been disputed, but while the Incas undoubtedly suppressed to a very considerable extent the human element in the rites, it is certain that before their rule, the practice was common among some of the tribes in the district. Our chief chroniclers—the Abbé de Molina, Fr. Coboa, Fr. Gavilan, and Cieza—bear witness to the continuance of the custom in the Inca culture, it being recorded that on the death of a ruler a considerable number of his attendants and wives accompanied him to the tomb. So great, in fact, was their ardour that many of those who clamoured to be buried alive with their sovereign had to be restrained.[2] Similarly, it is alleged that on the accession of a successor to the throne, women and children were collected from different villages to be strangled at the shrine, having first been treated as divinities on the way to the place of offer-

---

[1] Le Jeune, *Jesuit Relations*, xiii, pp. 37–79 ; xvii, p. 75 ; lxi, p. 65.
[2] J. Rankin, *The Conquest of Peru and Mexico* (Lond., 1827), pp. 229 f.

ing.[1]   The purpose of the sacrifices, we are told, was
to give the Inca " good health, and preserve his kingdom and dominion in peace, and that he might reach
a great age, and pass his time without illness." [2] Sometimes instead of being strangled the hearts were torn
out, and the blood sprinkled on the face of the image
of the deity of the shrine (usually that of the Sun,
Thunder or Moon god).   The bodies were then buried
together with appropriate offerings.[3]   This doubtless
explains the significance of the cemetery full of sump-
tuously dressed women in the precincts of the Sun-
temple at Pachacamac, where all the circumstances of
the interments point to the remains being those of
victims sacrificed to the sun.[4]

Taking the evidence collectively, it would seem
that however much human sacrifice may have been
mitigated in the Inca Empire, the welfare of the ruler
and of the community was believed to be dependent
in some measure on sanguinary rites having for their
purpose the renewal of the supernatural energy of the
representative of the sun and the natural processes he
controlled.   Moreover, not only were such sacrifices
required at the death and accession of the Inca, but
also in order to maintain the sun and the other gods in
health and strength.   Thus children were offered to
certain sacred stones " that the sun might not lose its
power," [5] and when the grains were removed from the
maize-cobs similar sacrifices were made to the maize-

---

[1] De Molina, *Relación de las fabulas y Ritos de los Ingas* (Lima, 1916), p. 89.

[2] *Op. cit.*, p. 90.

[3] *Op. cit.*, p. 91.

[4] Joyce, *South American Archæology* (Lond., 1912), p. 162.

[5] *Cobo, Historia. del nuevo mundo* (Sevilla, 1895), iv, pp. 31, 79.

images on a hill called Mantocalla, where the sun was supposed to descend to sleep.[1]   How deeply ingrained was this practice may be gathered from the statement that the native tribes in Ecuador were in the habit of sacrificing a hundred children annually at harvest,[2] and, therefore, however anxious the Incas may have been to suppress it, it still survived even after the Spanish occupation. Without such offerings the maize-crops would fail, the sun would be unable to continue its vitalizing functions, and mother earth would cease to bring forth abundantly.

Human Sacrifice for the Crops

Human sacrifice to secure good crops was common in West Africa in connexion with the sowing of the fields.   In March a man and a woman were killed with spades and hoes in order that their bodies might be buried in the middle of a newly-tilled field, while among the Bechuanas a short stout man was slain in the midst of the wheat to serve as " seed."   After his blood had coagulated in the sun, it was burned along with the frontal bone and the brain ; the ashes were then scattered over the ground to fertilize it.   The rest of the body was eaten.[3]   The most significant example, however, is the well-known case recorded among the Pawnees in 1837 or 1838 of a girl of fourteen or fifteen who, after being treated with great kind-

---

[1] *Op. cit.*, pp. 25 ff.

[2] Cieza de Leon, *Travels*, Eng. trans. by C. R. Markham (Lond., 1864), p. 203 ; Juan de Velasco, *Histoire du Royaume de Quito* (Paris, 1840), i, pp. 121 ff.

[3] *G.B.*, pt. vii, " Spirits of the Corn," etc., pt. i, pp. 239 ff., where numerous similar examples are given from many parts of the world.

ness and respect for six months, was put to death on April 22nd. Two days before the sacrifice she was led from wigwam to wigwam, accompanied by the whole council of chiefs and warriors. At each she received a present of wood and paint, and after her body had been painted half red and half black, she was slowly roasted over a fire, and then shot with arrows. The chief sacrificer thereupon tore out her heart, and devoured it, the rest of her body being cut up while it was yet warm, placed in little baskets, and taken to a neighbouring cornfield. There the head chief took a piece of the flesh from the basket and squeezed a drop of blood upon the newly-deposited grains of corn. The rest of the party did likewise till all the seeds had been " vitalized." They were then covered up with earth, and, according to one account, the body was made into a kind of paste which was rubbed on potatoes, beans and other seeds to fertilize them.[1]

A similar rite obtained in India among the Khonds, a Dravidian people in Bengal, who formerly offered to the Earth Goddess, Tari Pennu, a victim called Meriah to ensure good crops and immunity from disease. To be acceptable he had to be purchased, unless he was the son of a Meriah, or had been devoted to the altar by his father or guardian from childhood. However he was secured, he was treated with great reverence as a consecrated person, till at length, when the fatal day approached, after having his hair cut off, he was arrayed in a new garment, and led in solemn

[1] H. R. Schoolcraft, *Indian Tribes of the United States* (Philad., 1853-6), v, pp. 77 ff. ; J. De Smet in *Annales de la propagation de la foi*, xi, 1838, pp. 493 ff. ; xv, 1843, pp. 277 ff ; Frazer, *op. cit.*, pp. 238 f.

procession to the sacred grove amid music and dancing. There he was tied to a post, anointed with oil and tumeric, adorned with flowers, and reverenced with adoration. Having exonerated themselves from any guilt in making the sacrifice, and beseeching the earth to give good crops, fruitful seasons and robust health to the offerers, the sacrifice was consummated by strangling or squeezing the victim to death; though sometimes he was cut up alive, having first been fastened to a wooden elephant representing the Earth goddess. When death at length delivered the unfortunate Meriah from his sufferings, the flesh was divided into two portions, one of which was buried in the ground as an offering to the Earth goddess, and the other distributed in equal shares among the heads of houses, who rolled the sanguinary relic in leaves and buried it in the best fields, or hung it on a pole at the stream which watered them. The bones, head and intestines were then buried, together with a sheep, and the ashes scattered over the fields, houses and granaries, or mixed with the new corn.[1]

Westermarck describes this rite as a propitiatory sacrifice to appease the wrath of the Earth goddess,[2] but while there may have been a negative element latent in the ritual, the evidence does not suggest that it was the primary motive. As Frazer points out, the treatment of the victim implies that " to the body of the Meriah there was ascribed a direct or intrinsic power of making the crops to grow, quite independent

[1] J. Campbell, *Wild Tribes of Kurdistan* (Lond., 1864), pp. 52 ff.; S. C. Macpherson, *Memorials of Service in India* (Lond., 1865), pp. 113 ff.; Frazer, *op. cit.*, pp. 245 ff.
[2] *Origin and Development of Moral Ideas*, i, pp. 443 f.

of the indirect efficacy which it might have as an offering to secure the good-will of the deity."[1] The flesh and ashes were treated as magical manure endowed with fertilizing efficacy like the blood of the Pawnee girl which was employed to give life to the new corn. Similarly among the Aztecs and in Peru, the sanguinary rites were connected with the renewal of the sun's power, and the general promotion of the growth of the maize which constituted the staple diet of the community. Consequently they normally occurred at the time of the sowing of the fields, or at the ingathering of harvest, or at the beginning of the rainy or the dry season.

It would seem, then, that in so far as human sacrifice was a product of agricultural society, it was directed in the first instance to the growth of the crops and the maintenance of the sequence of vegetation. The efficacy of blood in general as a life-giving agent would naturally invest human blood with a unique significance as the vital essence of the highest organism in creation. Moreover, when it was supposed that the king was himself divine and endowed with supernatural powers upon which the welfare of the community and the natural order depended, the royal life stood at a premium. This involved the sacrifice of the king in order that his vitality might be transferred to a vigorous successor before it diminished. As solar ideas developed, and commoners came to take the place of the sovereign at the altar, human sacrifice occupied a conspicuous place in the calendrical ritual, which tended, as among the Aztecs, to promote a

[1] G.B., pt. iii, *op. cit.*, p. 250.

perpetual state of warfare to maintain the enormous demand for human hearts.

The practice, however, of people sacrificing themselves for the sake of others persisted in many parts of the world. Thus, in India, for instance, high-caste widows voluntarily took their place on the funeral pyres of their husbands to accompany them to the other world, until the rite of *Sati* was prohibited by law in British territory in 1827. From religious suicide it is not a very long step to loftier conceptions of self-sacrifice, while the idea of substitution for a royal victim easily leads to that of vicarious offering. To these aspects of the institution, however, we shall return in a later stage in the discussion.

CHAPTER IV

HEAD-HUNTING AND CANNIBALISM

In Indonesia, among the Dravidian tribes of India, and in the Pacific, head-hunting occupies a position equivalent to that of human sacrifice in relation to agriculture and the cult of the dead, the underlying motive in both rites being apparently identical. The head, as we have seen, has been considered to be especially rich in soul-substance,[1] and frequently, when the vital essence assumes a more personal guise, its permanent abode is placed in this section of the body. Thus, the Karens of Burma, for instance, suppose that the *tso*, or life-principle, resides in the upper part of the head, and therefore they wear an appropriate head-gear.[2] Similarly, the Nootka of British Columbia regard the soul as a tiny man who lives in the crown.[3] The vibrations of the membrane in the fontanel of infants is explained in the Ao Naga tribe as due to the movements of the soul,[4] and in Siam the greatest care has to be exercised in cutting the hair lest the indwelling *khuan* be disturbed.[5] The numerous tabus surrounding the cutting of the hair, and the elaborate protection of the head by various coverings and devices, take their rise in the

---

[1] Chap. i, p. 23.
[2] E. B. Cross, *Journal of American Oriental Society*, iv, 1834, pp. 311 ff.
[3] Boas, *Report Brit. Assoc.*, 1890, p. 396.
[4] J. P. Mills, *The Ao Naga* (Lond., 1926), p. 225, n. 2.
[5] A. Bastian, *Die Völker des Ostlichen Asien* (Leipzig, 1886), vol. ii, p. 256.

belief that the soul is therein located.[1]   Moreover, as
Mr. Hutton has pointed out, there can be little doubt
that the practice of head-hunting is based on this same
notion.[2]

Head-Hunting

In the Naga Hills the rite is mainly associated with
the well-being of the crops and of the cattle, so that
human heads appear to be extracted in order to increase the productivity of the soil, just as among the
Kayan of Borneo the custom is connected with rice-
growing.[3]   In Borneo the head is thought to contain
the ghost, or *Toh*, which, so long as it is not neglected,
produces fertility in the soil, promotes the growth of
the crops, and brings prosperity to the community in
general and to the person who captures the head in
particular.[4]   The soul is conceived as a sort of egg or
bladder filled with a vaporous substance which is
spread over the fields as a magical manure when the
balloon bursts.   Thereby the developing flowers of
the paddy and other plants are fertilized, since the
vapour contains the vitalizing principle.   When the
grain is eaten as food, its life-giving power is communicated to the blood, and thence imparted to the
seminal fluid, by means of which men and animals are
enabled to propagate life.[5]

It would seem, therefore, that there is an intimate

[1] Fox, *The Threshold of the Pacific* (Lond., 1924), pp. 230, 240 ; Norden-
skïold, *Indianerleben* (Leipzig, 1912), p. 106.

[2] *J.R.A.I.*, lviii, 1928, pp. 403 ff.

[3] C. Hose and W. McDougall, *The Pagan Tribes of Borneo* (Lond., 1912),
i, p. 114 ; ii, p. 23.

[4] *Op. cit.*, ii, pp. 20 ff.

[5] H. I. Marshall, *The Karen People of Burma* (Ohio, 1922), p. 222.

connexion in this district between the soul and fertili-
zation, and consequently it is reasonable to argue,
inasmuch as the head is the seat of the soul, that head-
hunting has been prompted by the idea of securing its
vitality to increase the productivity of the soil.[1] Soul-
substance being required to fertilize all vegetable and
animal life, and to add to the general supply of vital
essence in the village, it is essential that as many heads
as possible be acquired. Therefore, as the Aztecs
carried on wars on secure sacrificial victims, so in
Assam head-hunting expeditions become a normal
feature of native life.

The principal seasons for these escapades are
generally the times of planting and reaping the crops.
Thus in Upper Burma the Ida tribe set forth in March,
when the poppy fields are in full bloom, in search of
human heads, and woe betide any stranger who comes
within their reach. Having secured their trophies,
the head-hunters return to their village, where they
are received with uproarious delight, and universal
rejoicing because the fertilizing power of the newly-
acquired heads will make the rice grow green far
down in the depths of the valley, and the maize ripen
in the sun on the mountain-sides, and the hill-tops will
be white with the bloom of the poppy.[2] In the
Philippine Islands the Bontoc consider it essential that
every farm must have at least one new human head
added to the store at planting and sowing. The
raiders go out in twos and threes to lie in wait for a
victim, cut off his head, hands and feet, and bring

[1] Hutton, op. cit., pp. 403 ff.
[2] J. G. Scott and J. P. Hardiman, *Gazetteer of Upper Burma and the Shan
States* (Rangoon, 1900–1), i, pp. 430, 496 ff.

them back to the village in triumph, where they are exposed during the feast and dance that follow. Finally, when the flesh has decayed, the skull is taken home by the man who captured it, and preserved at his farm, his companions preserving the hands and feet.[1]

According to native tradition, head-hunting in Borneo is regarded as an ancient custom bequeathed by the tribal ancestors to give plentiful harvests, and keep off sickness and pains.[2] Therefore the presence of heads in a house brings prosperity and good crops ; and so essential to its welfare are these trophies, that if through fire they are lost, the occupants will beg a head, or a fragment of one, to supply the missing vitality.[3] Dr. Hose, it is true, thinks that the practice arose as a result of a desire to send slaves to accompany the dead in the hereafter,[4] but though this idea undoubtedly exists, it seems to be a later interpretation of a much more fundamental fertility concept.

The notion of the journey of the ghost to a mythical spirit-world, and theories concerning the provision of the dead with a guide and a retinue to do him service beyond the grave, constitute secondary developments of specialized eschatological beliefs, relative to the elaboration of funerary ritual originally designed for practical purposes.[5] Thus head-hunting is found among tribes unacquainted with these later speculations, and while McDougall and Hose may be correct in thinking that the Kayans (who kill slaves at the

---

[1] A. Schadenburg, *Zeits. für Ethnol.*, xx, 1888, p. 39.

[2] W. H. Furness, *Home-Life of Borneo Head-Hunters* (Philad., 1902), p. 59.

[3] Hose and McDougall, *op. cit.*, ii, pp. 20, 23.

[4] *Natural Man* (Lond., 1926), pp. 145 f.

[5] Cf. E. O. James, *Folk-lore*, xxxviii, 1927, p. 356.

death of a chief to accompany him on his journey) introduced head-hunting into Borneo,[1] it does not necessarily follow that their grave ritual represents the earliest and essential features of the custom. The fact that head-hunting was not confined to funerals, being a common feature at any great Kayan festival, particularly in conjunction with agricultural ceremonial, suggests that the eschatological interpretation belongs to a later stage in the development of the institution. The substitution of a slave for an enemy,[2] and of pigs or fowls in Kayan sacrifices,[3] and the holding of a sham fight on the return from the funeral, are doubtless reminiscent of a former head-hunting expedition.[4]

That the culture is in a state of flux is suggested by the fact that human hair is now substituted for a skull at the funeral feast,[5] and Kruijt considers that the killing of slaves and the provision of the dead man with a servant are probably more recent than head-hunting.[6] Hutton, again, is convinced that on the mainland the custom of taking heads to put on graves is merely the result of the influence of contact with head-hunters on a people practising human sacrifice in their funeral ceremonies.[7] In this connexion it may be recalled that Rivers maintained that the offering of the head of an enemy in Melanesia arose directly out of the practice of human sacrifice and the cult of the dead, but he recognized that head-hunting was the outcome of the idea of the head being the seat of magical powers

---

[1] *Pagan Tribes*, i, pp. 187 ff.
[2] Furness, p. 140 ; *Pagan Tribes*, i, p. 192 ; ii, p. 105.
[3] *Pagan Tribes*, ii, pp. 104 f.   [4] Furness, p. 141.
[5] A. W. Nieuwenhuis, *Quer durch Borneo* (Leiden, 1907), i, p. 92.
[6] *E.R.E.*, vii, p. 242.   [7] *Op. cit.*, p. 399.

of great potency in strengthening the foundations of a new building, or launching a new canoe.[1]

The association of the souls of the dead, and the practice of human sacrifice, with the fertility of the crops, has doubtless tended to make the fusion of the two rites easier since they both frequently have a common significance. Thus, if the head is the special abode of the vital essence, like blood, ochre, shells and similar life-giving agents, it serves the double purpose of revivifying either the corpse or the crops, according to the particular ritual with which it happens to be related. This explains the widespread custom of preserving the skull for a given time for use in connexion with spring and harvest rites, as, for example, in the case of the Ao who dry the corpse in the smoke of a fire in order to keep it till the first-fruits are eaten at the following harvest.[2] Similarly, in Indonesia the Cham of Annam bury the fragments of the frontal bone in a metal box at the foot of a tree for seven years, and then remove it to its final resting place " near the best of the family rice fields," where trees are planted round it, and a tombstone is erected."[3]

In Polynesia among the Maoris the dried heads of those slain and decapitated in war are taken from their graves to the fields where sweet potatoes are about to be sown in the belief that by so doing the growth of the crop will be promoted.[4] In New Caledonia in Southern Melanesia, heads of old women are set up on poles as charms for a good crop, and teeth are taken to the

---

[1] *History of Melanesian Society* (Camb., 1914), ii, p. 259.
[2] Mills, *op. cit.*, p. 279.
[3] H. Baudesson, *Indo-China and its Primitive People* (Lond., 1919), p. 314.
[4] E. Best, *Journal Polynesian Society*, xii, 1903, pp. 195 ff.

yam plantations to fertilize them.[1]   It is doubtless for a similar reason that a bride and bridegroom visit the skulls of their ancestors before their marriage.[2]   In New Guinea, as in Central America, the head is often mummified and treated as the portrait statue of the deceased because it contains the soul-substance,[3] just as in Melanesia it is believed to be full of mana which can be acquired for the benefit of the survivors.[4]   To participate in the soul of the deceased, the head is sometimes worn as a mask,[5] a custom which seems to be connected with masked dancing, to which reference has already been made.[6]

In Africa head-hunting, like human sacrifice, was frequently employed to aid the growth of the crops, the Ashanti, for instance, placing the head in the hole whence the new yams are taken.[7]   Again, in Nigeria, the dead are often thought to be more powerful even than Ale, the Earth goddess, in promoting the fruitfulness of the ground, and at her shrine, as recently as the outbreak of the Great War when the natives threw off restraints imposed by the government and returned to their old customs, two messengers of the native courts were seized and decapitated before the sacred drum.[8]   This was apparently an act of defiance to British rule, but the method of the crime followed

---

[1] Turner, *Samoa*, pp. 342 f.

[2] Ellis, *Polynesian Researches*, i, pp. 271 f.

[3] Frazer, *Belief in Immortality* (Lond., 1913), i, pp. 311, 321 ; James, *Amer. Anthrope.*, xxx, 1928, pp. 218 f.

[4] Codrington, *The Melanesians* (Oxford, 1891), pp. 264, 267.

[5] Ratzel, *History of Mankind* (Lond., 1897), p. 298.

[6] Chap. i, pp. 24 f.

[7] T. E. Bowdich, *Mission to Ashantee* (Lond., 1873), pp. 226 f.

[8] A. M. Talbot, *Some Nigerian Fertility Cults* (Oxford, 1927), pp. 1 f.

ancient custom. The drum was decorated with the unmistakable fertility emblems, suggesting that, as among the Kagoro and other tribes in this district, the removal of the head was associated with the fertility of the crops.[1]

Ritual Cannibalism

The practice of consuming the head or the body, either whole or in part, which is a common feature of head-hunting and sacrificial ritual, seems to have been prompted by the desire to imbibe the soul-substance in order to obtain the qualities of the deceased, whatever other motives, such as revenge or hunger, may have also led to anthropophagy. Moreover, when portions of the body are eaten as part of the ritual of vengeance, it is not improbable that the idea is that of cutting off or mutilating the life of the individual in the hereafter, since the preservation of the mortal remains is so intimately associated in the primitive mind with the "putting on of incorruption." Even when body and soul came to be divorced and assumed an independent existence, as the practice of cremation and the doctrine of metempsychosis developed, the fleshly integument still played some part in the process of immortality, either as the vehicle in which the soul ascended to the sky, or as the ultimate abode of the discarnate spirit in some future existence. Frazer, in fact, sees in the Australian practice of eating the dead a particular mode of ensuring the reincarnation of human souls.[2] This is not the place to

---

[1] Talbot, *op. cit.*, pp. 1-9; Tremearne, *Tailed Head-Hunters of Nigeria* (Lond., 1912), p. 178.

[2] *G.B.*, pt. i (" The Magic Art "), p. 106.

enter upon a discussion of this complex question, and here it need only be remarked that normally metempsychosis is possible only when the remains of the dead have been preserved. To destroy the body is to annihilate the soul-substance on which the life of man depends, and therefore to render impossible any further reincarnation. Hence the eating of slain enemies, and the destruction of their bones, in order to send forth the soul naked to wander endlessly in the forest, or to go down the holes of the earth that lead to the regions of the damned.[1] Thus, the most terrible act of revenge that can be indulged in is to cut off a man from the land of the living by rendering his soul incapable of attaining its proper and natural paradise.

Cannibalism as a ritual of vengeance, however, is probably a later phase in anthropophagous practice, when the original conceptions of the rite had become very considerably modified. The solemn eating of kinsmen, powerful warriors and persons set apart to represent and impersonate divinities, if not of the essence of sacrificial ritual, occupies a very prominent place in it. In the Aztec rites, as we have seen, after the offering had been consummated, the remains of the victims were usually given to the warriors who captured them, to hold thereupon a banquet with their friends. Moreover, twice a year, in May and December, a dough image of the god Uitzilopochtli was eaten sacramentally to secure health and strength.[2] At the winter festival the blood of children was kneaded into

[1] T. W. Whiffen, in *Folk-lore*, March 1913, pp. 53 f.
[2] Sahagun, *op. cit.*, pp. 203 ff.

the maize paste, and the heart of the image was cut out by a priest and consumed by the king, the rest being distributed in small portions among the men.[1] Similarly the body of the representative of Tezcatlipoca was cut up into tiny fragments and eaten as " blessed food " by the priests and nobles.[2]

Behind these rites there would appear to be the desire to imbibe the attributes and qualities adherent to and resident in the body of the victim by the simple process of eating his flesh. Thus among the native tribes of Australia the bodies of those who fall in battle, honoured chiefs, and new-born infants are frequently consumed to obtain their qualities,[3] just as in the Torres Straits the tongue and sweat of a slain enemy are imbibed in order to get his bravery.[4] The Sioux were in the habit of reducing to powder the heart of a valiant foe and swallowing it in the hope of appropriating his valour, and Chippewa women fed their children with the flesh and blood of English prisoners to make them warriors.[5] It was for this same reason that the Nahua ate the hearts of the Spaniards during the wars of the Conquest of Central America, while more recently the Ashanti chiefs devoured the heart of Sir Charles J. McCarthy to imbibe his courage.[6] If the powers of a warrior could be secured by eating particles of his mortal remains, or by smearing the body with his fat or blood, it is hardly

[1] *Op. cit.*, p. 203 ; cf. p. 33.
[2] Brasseur de Bourbourg, *op. cit.*, iii, pp. 510 ff.
[3] *J.A.I.*, xiii, pp. 135, 283 ; Howitt, *Native Tribes*, p. 753.
[4] Haddon, *J.A.I.*, xix, p. 312.
[5] W. H. Keating, *Narrative of an Expedition to the Source of the St. Peter River* (Philad., 1824), i, p. 412.
[6] J. L. Wilson, *Western Africa* (Lond., 1856), pp. 167 f.

surprising if the flesh of sacred sacrificial victims was regarded as the source of life and potency to those who were privileged to partake of it, since the food was charged with the supernatural virtues of the sacrosanct representative of the divinity.

In addition to the idea of gaining renewed strength and vigour from the sacred meal, the notion of entering into a blood-covenant with or through the deceased is also intimately connected with anthropophagous ritual. By sharing in the life, or soul-substance, a new kinship is established between the living and the dead, calculated to have beneficial effects upon the individuals concerned, and upon the general life of the community. Or, conversely, the custom of the slayer eating a portion of the man he has slain may arise from the desire to form a sacred bond with the victim as a means of escaping his revenge by making him his kinsman.[1] Thus he absorbs his vitality and at the same time prevents the ghost from doing him injury.

If there is any truth in the contention of Roheim that " there was a time in the prehistoric evolution of the Central Australian tribes when the women were supposed to conceive, not from eating the totem, but from eating human flesh," [2] the reason is not far to seek, whatever the psychological motive may be that lies behind the tradition. The flesh being charged with the vitality of the deceased, it was the equivalent of the churinga, or any similar agent, and therefore the life of the dead man passed into the body of the recipient to be born again in due course.

---

[1] Hartland, *Legend of Perseus* (Lond., 1895), ii, pp. 245 f.
[2] *Australian Totemism* (Lond., 1925), p. 391.

In the later developments of anthropophagy the original purpose and significance of the ritual became obscured by the introduction of secondary interpretations, generally those of revenge, gluttony, or fear of the dead. Hunger may have driven small communities to eat one another in times of great scarcity, but the practice is essentially ritualistic in origin, and prevails mainly in districts well supplied with food.[1] Thus the Bataks of Sumatra declared that they frequently ate their own relatives when aged and infirm," not so much to gratify their appetite, as to perform a pious ceremony."[2] Cannibalism on the whole is probably a less organized institution than human sacrifice, but where it is not the result of necessity for the satisfaction of hunger, the fundamental ritual motive is similar, inasmuch as both rites are so intimately connected with the giving and receiving of soul-substance.

[1] Westermarck, *Origin and Development of Moral Ideas*, ii, p. 556; vol. ii.
[2] *Op. cit.*, p. 568.

CHAPTER V

MYSTERY CULTS

IF life is the universal mystery in all states of culture, the social implications of this concept are not far to seek. Since eating to the primitive mind appears as life renewed, to kill to eat readily becomes a ritual whereby the soul-substance of the food—be it the flesh of a sacrificial victim, a totem or the head of an enemy—is imbibed to give strength and power to the recipient. But no man lives or dies to himself in primitive society, and, therefore, a social meal renews the life of the community, just as a crude cannibalistic feast on a corpse is animated by the notion that to eat of the dead is to eat with them; to share their soul-substance. So with the practice of blood-exchange, and the various rites whereby a person is initiated into what may be described as the sacramental covenant.

Initiation Ceremonies

The primary object of this ritual is to effect rebirth by the aid of a death and resurrection symbolism in order that the individual may take his proper place and part in society, both sacred and profane, fulfil his functions as a consecrated person in a holy estate, and finally attain to the hope of everlasting life when his mortal body shall put on immortality, or the soul be united with a mystery divinity in a bond that survives death. As in the case of the divine king, it is necessary to die to live, to pass through a mystic grave to a newness of life. Thus, the ritual consists virtually of a new birth of the novice as a complete and active member of society. Having been instructed in the tribal lore and customs, he is allowed to take part in the sacred mysteries and thereby is brought into relation with the culture heroes, totems, tutelary spirits, or other divinities who preside over the destinies of the community.

Frequently this incorporation into the social and religious organization is accomplished by severe tests of endurance which include the rite of circumcision and sub-incision, in addition to milder ceremonies such as lustrations and a symbolic rebirth. Thus, for example, every Akikuyu boy and girl is solemnly born again about the age of ten, the mother going through the act of childbirth in pantomime. On being brought to the birth the child cries like a babe, and after being washed it is fed on milk for several days. Formerly the ceremony was part of the circumcision rite, but now it is a separate function.[1] In New Guinea the principal initiatory rite among the Yabim consists of circumcision, which is performed on all youths before they are admitted to the privileges of manhood, and given their place in the male clubhouse. At the conclusion of the ceremony they are bathed in the sea, and then elaborately decorated with red paint. On returning to the village they walk with their eyes closed, presumably because they are in process of

[1] W. S. and K. Routledge, *With a Prehistoric People, the Akikuyu of British East Africa* (Lond., 1910), pp. 151 ff.

entering a new state, like newborn babes, having been reborn into the adult community.[1]

Death and Rebirth Symbolism

Before the process of initiation is complete, however, the neophyte usually is ceremonially installed into the fellowship of the ancestral spirits, totems or gods presiding over the destinies of the tribe or society. Thus among the Yuin in South-East Australia a figure of Daramulun is prepared and shown to the youths, and instruction concerning his office is given after they are raised to the dignity of manhood.[2] In some of the tribes, especially in Southern Queensland, a ceremonial combat forms part of the testing of the young men,[3] and on the Darling River the novices are placed alongside a grave from which an old man rises during a dance, accompanied by a dirge in honour of Daramulun.[4] A similar rite is performed in Fiji, but in a more realistic form.

On the fifth day of the ceremonies, the heads of the novices are shaven for the second time, and their bodies arrayed in the largest and best folds of cloth. Taking their choicest weapons in their hands, they enter the inner sanctuary of the sacred stone enclosure, or *Nanga*, where before their startled gaze they behold a row of dead men covered with blood, their bodies apparently cut open so as to reveal their entrails. Stepping over these ghastly relics, they form a line in front of the high priest who suddenly utters a great

---

[1] K. Vetter, *Nachrichten über Kaiser Wilhelms-Land und den Bismark-Archipel.* (Berlin, 1897), pp. 92 ff.

[2] Howitt, *Native Tribes of S.E. Austral.* (Lond., 1904), p. 540.

[3] *Op. cit.*, p. 639.   [4] *Ibid.*, p. 554.

yell, whereupon the dead men rise to their feet and rush down to the river to cleanse themselves of the blood and entrails of slaughtered pigs with which they have been smeared.[1]   In this way, through a crude death and resurrection symbolism, the initiates are incorporated into the mystical fellowship of the adult tribe and its ancestral spirits.

In the hill country of the main island, the Fijian cult of water-sprites has been described by Mr. Hocart, and interpreted by him as an initiation ceremony based upon a consecration ritual.[2]   He believes, in fact, that initiation, at least in Fiji, is a popular form of installation.[3]   " The rites of a king's consecration," it is contended, " mostly bear their own explanation writ large across them : death, fasting and quiescence, battle and victory, oath to preserve law and order, whether it be in the calendar, in the ritual, or in civil life, rebirth and lustration in the waters of ocean, crown, shoes and throne, circumambulation, marriage, are all episodes in the career of the sun who, overcome and slain by the powers of darkness, is mourned for, but again battles with his foes, defeats them, and can thus be reborn again to maintain order in the universe," and having ascended to the sky, " by his beams unites himself with earth to produce offspring and crops."[4]

The equation of the king with the sun-god is lacking in primitive communities, but the idea of death and rebirth, as we have seen, dominates the ritual, though often in a rationalized form as tests of endurance,

---

[1] Fison, *J.R.A.I.*, xiv, 1885, pp. 20 ff.
[2] *Kingship* (Oxford, 1927), pp. 58 ff., 134 f.
[3] *Op. cit.*, p. 135 ; *Folk-lore*, xxxv, December 4th, 1924, p. 321.
[4] *Kingship*, p. 155.

returning to the embryonic state, symbolic ceremonial, and proofs of adolescence. If, however, initiation is derived from installation in certain cultures, as Mr. Hocart believes, by royal and secret rituals gradually becoming secularized and popularized till they are regarded as the normal mode of entering upon the privileges and responsibilities of tribal life, a reason is forthcoming for circumcision, which is normally part of the puberty initiation ceremonies, being made a covenant sign in Israel.

Mr. Hocart further suggests that initiation persists mainly in those communities in which the divine king-ship has been discarded,[1] and if this cult existed in Palestine, as seems probable,[2] it was certainly in abeyance when the literature of the Old Testament took its present form. It is significant that as the ancient conception of kingship disappeared the institution of circumcision came into greater prominence, till after the Exile it was placed above the Mosaic ritual, and made second only to the Sabbath as the covenant sign, despite the fact that the oldest legal code ignores the custom altogether. If the fundamental conception was that of an installation into a god, or a sacramental alliance with him, as in the consecration ceremony, the rite would readily become a covenant sign once the divine kingship was abandoned in favour of a theocracy, as in Israel, since the sacred ruler was similarly united with his god and his people.

Secret Societies

Another development of this type of ritual occurs in

[1] *Op. cit.*, p. 158.　　　[2] Cf. Chap. VIII, p. 243.

the Secret Society in which the novice undergoes a process of rebirth by a ceremonial death and resurrection into the sacred community. While some of these societies were formed with social, political, or military aims, in the purely religious organization the cult centred in the securing of immortality for the initiates by a process of reanimation. Thus, in the North American confraternities, the candidates were slain by thrusting a medicine-bag at them, and restoring them by a similar operation.[1] The novice is clothed in new garments and presented to the society as a regular and completely initiated member. A ceremonial meal frequently constitutes part of the ritual, to which, as, for example, among the Winnebagoes, certain members of the confraternity are invited by the master of the feast. The neophytes are required to observe a fast of three days before admission, which seems to include a process of sweating. Having been secretly instructed in the mysteries of the society, on the appointed day they are duly killed by having a medicine-bag thrust at their breasts, and subsequently revived by placing these life-giving objects in their hands, and a small white sea-shell in their mouths. By this process of revivification they become full members of the fellowship.[2]

This pretence of death and resurrection appears to be the fundamental motive in all the initiation ceremonial in the American secret societies. Even in the

---

[1] H. R. Schoolcraft, *Indian Tribes of the U.S.* (Philad., 1853), iii, p. 287 v, p. 430 ; W. J. Hoffmann, *7th R.B.A.E.* (Wash., 1891), pp. 215 ff., 248, 265 ; *14th R.B.A.E.* (Wash., 1896), pp. 99 ff.

[2] J. E. Fletcher, in *Indian Tribes of the U.S., op. cit.*, iii, pp. 286 f. ; cf. Radin, in *Journal Amer. Folk-lore Society*, xxiv, 1911, pp. 149 ff.

elaborate ritual of the celebrated Grand Medicine Society, or Mide-wiwin, of the Ojibwa, the mythological background is the portrayal of the path from earth to heaven attainable through four degrees, or " lodges," which provide the necessary magic and occult powers of communion with the supernatural. Initiation involves the usual physical purifications and courses of instruction, the payment of fees and the provision of a feast by way of preparation for the actual killing of the candidate, and bringing him to life again by means of a magic shell (*migis*, or " life ").[1]

In the complex Pawnee ritual, which is no longer the possession of any particular secret society, the control of the crops and the securing of buffalo are dependent upon the performance of a death and resurrection ceremonial in spring, summer, or autumn to secure the birth of a Spirit of Life by a re-enactment of the process of creation. In the Hako ceremony, " the gift of life, of strength, of plenty, and of peace," is sought " when life is stirring everywhere." This is accomplished by songs and dances with mimetic action, embodied in some twenty rituals, and the rebirth of a child in which a ceremonial washing, anointing, and fumigation are part of the procedure.[2]

Although spoken of as a prayer, the Hako is more akin to a mystery since its purpose is the teaching of certain hidden truths unfolded during a series of ceremonies from an initial purification to a final act, consisting in part of a public festival, and in part of a secret mystery—a dramatic portrayal of the birth of

[1] Hoffmann, *7th R.B.A.E.* (1891), pp. 187 ff.
[2] A. C. Fletcher, *22nd R.B.A.E.* (Wash., 1904), ii, pp. 23 f.

a sacred child. That it is a ritual rather than a prayer appears again from the fact that the long series of observances and songs are so closely articulated that any variation of relationship, or any omission, would be disastrous alike to the structure and efficacy of the whole performance. Throughout the all-prevailing theme is a desire for children, long life and plenty—the abundance and prosperity represented by the Corn-mother; the symbol of fruitfulness and life.

The Mystery Cults

The aim and general setting of the Hako, therefore, presents a striking parallel to the Greek Mysteries which were based on the death and resurrection of a divine hero, such as Dionysos, Persephone, Attis or Osiris, represented in the form of a sacred drama by which the rebirth of the novice was secured. The experiences of these semi-divine heroes were recalled dramatically in order that those who took part in the rites might individually and as a society obtain a renewal of life which would endure beyond the grave. Their primary aim, in short, was to give assurance to their initiates of a blessed immortality in union with the divinity who presided over the cult, and who himself has passed through death to life. Greeks approached the divine order in two ways : the one was intellectual—the way of the philosophers ; the other was mystic—the way of the mysteries. The philosophical approach, however, was too sophisticated for the plain man who sought and found in the simulated death and resurrection of the mystery cults a more satisfying solution to his theological problems, and satisfaction for his inherent craving for life in ever-increasing abundance, both here and hereafter.

The Eleusinia

The mystical origin of the Eleusinia, the best known in its Athenian form of any of the cults, is contained in the so-called Homeric Hymn to Demeter, usually assigned to the seventh century B.C., or possibly later.[1] According to the legend, Persephone, the daughter of Demeter by Zeus, while gathering flowers in the meadow was carried off to the underworld with the connivance of Zeus. Only the Sun-god and *Hekate*, the Moon-goddess, saw her capture, but her mother heard her cries and instantly set out in search of her, going about the earth for nine days and nine nights, without food, and bearing in her hands blazing torches to light up the darkest recesses. On the tenth day Hekate led her to the Sun, who told her of the where-abouts of Persephone. Once more the sorrowing mother resumed her wanderings, and having changed herself into an old woman, she came at length to Eleusis, where she sat down by the public well, known as the Fountain of Maidenhood. Hither came the four daughters of Keleos, the king of Eleusis, to draw water, to whom she told a fictitious story of her escape from pirates. Having won their confidence, she asked to be allowed to act as nurse to their baby brother Demophoon. She continued, however, to sit day in and day out in silence, till the jests and raillery of Iambe, the maidservant, made her smile. She

---

[1] R. Foerster, *Der Raub und die Rückkehr der Persosphone* (Stuttgart, 1874), pp. 37 ff; A. Baumeister, *Hymni Homerici* (Leipsic, 1860), p. 280.

then consented to take a little gruel (χυχέων) of barley meal and water, but steadfastly refused wine. By day she anointed the child with ambrosia—a magical life-giving substance—and by night bathed him in fire, as did Thetis with Achilles. Had she not been disturbed in these operations, she would have made him im-mortal ; but one night Metanira, the wife of Keleos, saw her place her child in the fire, and cried in alarm. Thereupon the goddess declared herself and her in-tentions. " I am the exalted Demeter, the charm and comfort both of gods and men : I was preparing for thy son exemption from death and old age ; now it cannot be, but he must taste of both. Yet shall he be ever honoured, since he has sat upon my knee, and slept in my arms. Let the people of Eleusis erect for me a temple and altar on yonder hill above the fountain : I will myself prescribe for them orgies which they must religiously perform to propitiate my favour." [1]

Keleos did as she had commanded, whereupon the goddess took up her abode in her temple. But so great was her grief at the loss of her daughter that she withheld her blessings from the soil, so that nothing grew ; men were in danger of starvation, and the gods themselves were threatened with a similar fate since the altars lacked the life-giving sacrifices. In alarm Zeus agreed to send Persephone back to her, and Hades, unable to resist the command of his elder brother Hermes, yielded up his prize, but not before he had given her a pomegranate seed which bound her to him for one third of the year. With great rejoicing

[1] G. Grote, *History of Greece* (Lond., 1869), i, p. 37.

she returned to Eleusis in a golden chariot to dwell for the remaining two-thirds of the year with Demeter.

The goddess then consented to rejoin the gods in Olympus, but before her departure she revealed to the daughters of Keleos, and the rulers of the land, Triptolemus, Eumolpos, Diokles, and the king, the manner of performing her secret rites which would confer upon initiates a new birth to a blessed immortality. These mysteries became the prerogatives of the Athenians, according to another legend, as a result of a war by Erechtheus with the Eleusinians,[1] which gave them the political headship, but to the family of Eumolpus and the daughters of Keleos were assigned the high priesthood of the cult.

This constitutes the mythological background of the annual festival which took place just before the autumn sowing, on the 15th day of Boedromion (approximately September), and lasted for ten days or more. The entire festival may be divided into four distinct ceremonial acts—(1) the preparation and purification of the *mystæ* ; (2) the procession from Athens to Eleusis ; (3) the roaming about at the seashore ; and (4) the sacred drama in the Hall of Initiation.[2]

By way of preparation, feasting, seclusion, penance and asceticisms of various kinds were required. The initiate betook himself during the latter portion of the month before his installation to an instructor, or μυσταγωγός, who had himself successfully passed through all the degrees, and from him he received instruction concerning the rites of purification to be

[1] Pausanias, i, 38.

[2] C. A. Lobeck, *Aglaophamus sive de theologie mysticæ Græcorum causis* (Königsberg, 1829), pp. 206 ff.

performed, and the offerings to be made to gain the favour of Demeter. A fast of nine days followed— from the 13th to 21st of Boedromion in commemoration of Demeter's fast during her search for Persephone —when no food might be eaten between sunrise and sunset, and then domestic birds, fish, apples, beans and pomegranates were tabu. On the 16th wine was distributed to the people in the evening in honour of Chabia's victory at Naxon, and the next morning the festival began.

A proclamation was made driving forth all strangers and murderers before the *mystæ* were led to the sea-shore (ἄλαδε μύσται) to undergo a series of lustrations. Sacrifices were offered on the 17th in the Eleusinium at Athens for the safety of the State. On the following night (18th) some of the very devout may have slept in the temple of Demeter, or in the temple of Æsculapius, south-west of the Acropolis. Meanwhile sacred objects consisting of a bone (ἀστράγαλος), top (στρόβιλος), ball (σφαῖρα), tambourine (ρόμβος), apples (μῆλα), mirror (ἔσαπτρον), fan (λίκνον), and woolly fleece (πόκος) were brought from Eleusis. A procession formed in the morning of the 19th, from the Eleusinium and proceeded to the Iaccheum where the statue of the " fair young god " Iacchus, adorned with myrtle and holding a torch, was procured and carried amid ivy and myrtle crowned priests and people, and wealthy ladies in carriages. Along the Sacred Way to Eleusis stations were made, and appropriate ceremonies performed at the shrines and temples and baths which lined the route. On occasions buffoonery and gibing at one another, called γεφυρισμός, was resorted to on either the outward or return journey, as is common in initiation and coronation rituals. Sacrifices were then offered which seem to have included the offering of swine to Demeter.

On the evening of the 22nd, the votaries roamed about the seashore with lighted torches in imitation of the search for Persephone, to bring the *mystæ* into union with the passion of Demeter. Then came the climax of the sacred drama, when, after an all-night vigil, the neophytes, assembled in the great Hall of Initiation, veiled and in darkness sat upon stools covered with sheepskins. Some kind of dramatic performance took place which seems to have depicted episodes in the life and sufferings of the sorrowing mother.[1] But whether the rites included a sacred marriage, as might be expected under the circumstances, it is impossible to determine with any degree of certainty.

There are indications in the Christian writers that the union of the sky-god Zeus with the goddess Demeter was symbolised by the intercourse of the hierophant with the priestess of the goddess, a reaped ear of corn being the fruit of the divine marriage.[2] But the evidence is very hypothetical, and rests on the none too reliable testimony of late writers when the original rites had absorbed many extraneous local

[1] Clem. of Alex., *Protrept*, 12. 15 (ed. Potter) ; cf. F. Lenormant, " Eleusinia," in Daremberg and Saglio, *Dictionnaire des Antiquités Grecques et Romaines*, iii, p. 578 ; Lobeck, *Aglaoph.*, pp. 701 f.

[2] Tertullian, *Ad nationes* ; Asterius Amasensus, in Migne's *Patrologia Græca*, xl, col. 324 ; cf. P. Foucart, *Les Grands Mystères d'Eleusis* (Paris, 1900), p. 69 ; J. Harrison, *Prolegomena to Study of Greek Religion* (Camb., 1922), pp. 548 ff.

elements. Thus, the birth of the holy infant Iacchus, the son of Zeus and Persephone, is an addition to the Eleusinian deities, and the cry of the hierophant, " the lady-goddess Brimo has borne Brimos the holy child,"[1] recorded by Hippolytus, was derived from Gnostic sources. It is in this same context that the secret of Eleusis is revealed as a disclosing to the initiated of a " cut corn-stalk."

That a sacred marriage and the reaping of an ear of corn did occur at supreme moments in the cult seems very probable, at any rate in its later form, but how far they are parts of the original drama the evidence is insufficient to warrant a conclusion. The agricultural character of much of the ritual is obvious, but this does not justify the assumption that Demeter was a corn-totem whose divine substance was sacramentally eaten by the neophytes partaking of the cup of κυκέων, a gruel made of water and meal, mentioned by Clement of Alexandria.[2] Actually we have no definite evidence of the worship of the corn-stalk, still less of a corn-totem. Therefore, it is to go beyond any available data to say that " as the worshippers of animal totems at their annual sacrifice consumed the flesh of their god and thus partook of his divine life, so the worshippers of the Corn-Goddess annually partook of the body of their deity, i.e. of a cake or paste or posset made of the meal of wheat and water."[3]

Even supposing that Dr. Jevons were correct in

---

[1] *Refutatio omnium hæresium*, L. Duncker et F. G. Schneidewin (Göttingen, 1859), p. 162.

[2] *Protrept*, ii, 16, 18, 24.

[3] Jevons, *The History of Religion* (Lond., 1902), pp. 365 f.; cf. Kirsopp Lake, *The Earlier Epistles of St. Paul* (Lond., 1911), p. 214.

assuming Demeter to have been an Eleusinian corn-totem, and that the κυκεών really contained her substance, both of which assumptions have yet to be proved, it would not follow, for reasons already given, that the ceremonial meal was in the nature of a mystic sacramental communion with the divinity. All that could be deduced from such evidence would be a primitive attempt to imbibe the life and qualities of the sacred species, and to secure a closer ritual fusion of the totemite with the totem, which in the rites in question have been brought about by a coarser symbolism. Normally it is the quickening and strengthening power of the corn-spirit that is sought in agricultural cults of this nature, distinct from the loftier strivings after a mystical union with a divine being.

Now it would seem that at Eleusis the supreme " act of worship," to which all the preliminary ceremonies were directed, consisted in beholding a sacred action, and not in partaking of a sacred meal. Thus in the familiar phrase of Clement of Alexandria, " I have fasted, I have drunk of the κυκεών, I have taken out of the chest, having tasted thereof (or wrought therewith), I have put them into the basket, and from the basket into the chest," [1] the sacramental feast, if such is implied, was merely part of the preparatory rites, and not the culmination of the cult. Furthermore, there is no indication that the κυκεών was hallowed on an altar, or in any way connected with sacrificial ritual, while the theory that it contained the divine substance of the goddess is pure assumption. Therefore, until classi-

[1] *Protrept.*, ii, 21.

cal scholars can provide us with more evidence, the anthropologist and student of comparative religion must declare as unproven the theory that " the first great and solemn act of worship " at Eleusis consisted in a mystic sacramental communion with the goddess through the reception of her divine substance.

The same attitude must be maintained at present to the similar references to sacred meals in connexion with the other Mystery Religions, though in one or two cases the affirmative evidence is rather more convincing. It is possible that the admonition to the priest to " cut up and minister the cake, and distribute the liquid to the votaries," recorded in the fragmentary inscription of the Kabeiroi mysteries from Tomi in the Black Sea,[1] indicates a sacramental element in the Samothracian cult ; but the restoration is conjectural, and from the few fragments we possess it is impossible to determine what was done or implied at the meal. Taken as it stands, the inscription merely records the practice of communal meals in this society which may or may not have been sacramental in character.

The Dionysiac Ritual

In the orgiastic Thraco-Phrygian worship of Dionysos, which made its way into Greece in the Homeric period, and became definitely established as a public cult by the sixth century B.C., the devouring of the raw flesh of bulls and calves by frenzied votaries seems to have occurred.[2] It is not easy to determine, however, whether this earlier ritual survived when the new

---

[1] Dieterich, *Eine Mithrasliturgie* (Leipzig, 1903), p. 106 ; cf. Farnell, *E.R.E.*, vii, p. 631.

[2] Firmicus Maternus, *De err. prof. rel.*, vi, p. 16 (Ziegler).

wave of Dionysiac fervour passed through Greece in
the seventh and sixth centuries before our era, replac-
ing Bacchic frenzy by spiritual ecstasy. The orgiastic
cult is certainly unhellenic, and since the bull was a
luxury-animal in Crete, the ritual is hardly likely to
have had its origin in the Minoan culture, despite Miss
Jane Harrison's advocacy of a Cretan cradleland.[1] If
a local origin is sought, the cattle-raising areas of
Thrace are a more probable home of the worship,
where the tearing to pieces of a bull with the teeth
conceivably might have formed part of the wild
orgiastic rites of the rude and licentious tribes. But,
as Andrew Lang suggested, perhaps the legend is not
so savage as it looks.[2]

The similarity of the Greek Dionysos and the
Egyptian Osiris is so obvious that many scholars in
ancient and modern times have been led to regard the
two figures as aspects of the same person, and therefore to seek the original home of the legend and its
associated ritual in Egypt.[3] Thus, Herodotus found
the resemblance between the rites so great that he
thought it impossible that they could have been in-
vented independently, while Plutarch is equally insistent
upon their identity. As Frazer points out, " we cannot reject the evidence of such intelligent and trust-
worthy witnesses on plain matters of fact which fell
under their own cognizance. Their explanations of
the worships it is, indeed, possible to reject, for the

[1] *Prolegomena*, chap. viii.
[2] *Myth, Ritual and Religion* (Lond., 1887), ii, pp. 137 f.
[3] Herodotus, ii, 49, 144, 42 ; Plutarch, *Isis et Osiris*, p. 35 ; Foucart, *Le
Culte de Dionyse en Attique* (Paris, 1904), pp. 9 ff., 159 ff. ; Perry, *Hibbert
Journal*, xxv, January 1927, pp. 241 ff.

meaning of religious cults is often open to question ;
but resemblances of ritual are matters of observation." [1]

If Dionysos is associated with Osiris, his being torn
asunder and revived under the title of Zagreus
becomes the Thracian counterpart of the dismember-
ment of the Egyptian culture hero, just as his connexion with the vine and agriculture is explicable in
terms of the Osiris myth. On this interpretation, the
primary purpose of the Dionysiac would seem to have
been a death and resurrection ritual to obtain the rebirth of the initiate to a blessed immortality, and we
know that this was the object of the Orphic mysteries
in later times.

How far, however, if at all, this was achieved by or
through a sacred meal it is difficult to say. Something in the nature of a sacramental union with the
worshippers may have been established when the god
visited his votaries in early spring, a survival of which
may have occurred in the Orphic-Dionysos mystery
ritual. Thus, in Euripides the initiated votary in
Crete is said to have become one with his divinity
after he had fulfilled " the solemn rite of the banquet
of raw flesh," [2] a rite connected by the Christian
Fathers with Orphism. [3] But until we know with
more certainty how much of the literature attributed to
Orphism in antiquity really had any right to this title,
the passage must remain of doubtful interpretation.
Moreover, since the Orphics normally abstained from
a flesh diet, their partaking of a sacramental meal of

---

[1] *G.B.*, pt. vi (" Adonis," ii), p. 127. [2] Frag. 472, Nauck.
[3] Clem. Alex., *Protrept.*, ii, 12, 17; Fir. Mat., *De err. prof. rel.*, p. 84.

the character described can only be explained on the supposition that the tabu was removed on this occasion. This would be a perfectly reasonable and probable explanation of the rite if we could be sure that it was practised. The Orphic sacred books relate the story of the tearing in pieces of the divine huntsman (Zagreus), identified with Dionysos, but if it was connected with the rending of the bull in Crete, there is no evidence that this ritual was performed in the Orphic lodges.

Orphism, as it is actually known, was essentially a mystical movement resting on the belief that when Orpheus went to the underworld in search of his wife Eurydice, he discovered the secret of immortality which was imparted to the initiated in the private brotherhoods. Doubtless some of the old Thracian worship of Dionysos was continued in symbolic form in the cult-societies, though the brotherhoods, perhaps as early as the seventh century, raised the worship to a higher level, making it a means of the purification of the soul in this life and in the next full communion with God.

According to the theogonies, Zeus having slain with his thunderbolt the wicked Titans, after they had rent in pieces and eaten Dionysos, made man from their ashes, so that the human body partook of the evil nature of the Titans. The soul, however, was associated with Dionysos-Zagreus whom Zeus recreated, and therefore shared in his divine nature. But until the Titan element (i.e. the body) could be eliminated by a life of ritual and moral purity during the soul's incarnation in a series of bodies, the attainment of the divine state was impossible. Thus the aim of Orphism was the possibility of securing divine life, the immortal state being reached only by complete union with the gods, since " only to the gods in heaven comes no old age nor death of anything." [1] Salvation was wrought by Orpheus and mediated through the Bacchic mysteries, but how far, if at all, the representation of the passion of Dionysos and an *omophagia* in his divine life constituted part of the cult we do not know. It is possible that sacramental methods were employed in the *thiasoi*, or brotherhoods, but from Pindar and Plato it seems that their main preoccupation was the solution of the problem of immortality along the lines of Buddhist thought, and if the Indian philosophies can be taken as a guide, sacramentalism is scarcely likely to have been very prominent.

In any case, Orphism took the ancient ritual of Dionysos, and having stripped it of its Thracian orgies, gave it a new significance in an endeavour to free the soul from a " circle of births or becomings " by spiritual rebirth and regeneration to a higher life beyond the grave. It seems to have influenced the cult of Eleusis, and if it did not penetrate the inner secrets of these mysteries, the vegetation ritual of Demeter, like that of Dionysos, was interpreted in terms of destiny of the soul after death. [2] It was indeed this hope that gave the Eleusinia its widespread

---

[1] Soph., *Œd.*, col. 607.

[2] J. Harrison, *Prolegomena to the Study of Greek Religion* (Camb., 1922), pp. 539 ff.; *Psyche*, E. Rhode, Eng. trans. (Lond., 1925), p. 219; C. A. Lobeck, *Aglaophamus sive de theologie mysticæ Græcorum causis* (Königsberg, 1829), pp. 69 ff.

appeal, drawing worshippers from many lands to its annual festival not merely to behold a passion-drama, as in more recent times at Oberammergau, but, like the Ancient Egyptian practice of mummification, to secure a place among the glorified dead hereafter.

Nevertheless, if it became a generally accepted tradition that Orpheus was the founder of all mysteries,[1] the central feature of these cults as a whole was the primitive conception of the death and resurrection of the novice in association with the victorious survival and return of a divine hero, Dionysos, Persephone, Osiris, Attis, Adonis or Mithra. In all the various phases through which they passed in their complicated history, there was one predominant concept—the conservation and promotion of life, whether in the human organism or in nature. Occasionally this may have found expression in some crude form of sacramental communion, as perhaps in the Thracian worship of Dionysos, or in the Attis-Cybele mysteries of Phrygian origin where the fusion of the mortal with divinity in later times was brought about mainly by a blood ritual, together with a sacramental meal of food and some liquid.

The Attis-Cybele Mysteries

When we first encountered this cult in Athens in the fourth century, the initiation to a blessed immortality was secured by anointing the body of the novice with a mixture of mud and bran.[2] But, according to Firmicus Maternus and Clement of Alexandria, at

---

[1] Aristophanes, *Frogs*, 1032.
[2] Demosthenes, *De Corona*, xviii, 259.

some point in the rite the neophyte ate out of the timbrel and drank from the cymbal, and went down into the παστός (bridal-chamber).[1] Farnell thinks it was a sacrament of cereals or fruits that was received from the drum and the cymbal, bread being eaten by the Attis-votary " as the very substance or body of his divinity, for in the liturgy of Attis he was himself called the ' Cornstalk ' ; he was then the mystic Bread in a sense in which Demeter is never found to have been." [2] This is a possible deduction, yet Firmicus Maternus does not actually tell us anything more than that eating and drinking constituted an aspect of the initiation. Hepding maintains that in some cases there was an actual burial as part of the resurrection ritual, the initiate rising from the grave with the divinity to a new life.[3] The journey to the bridal-chamber commemorating the death of Attis would naturally suggest the rebirth of the *mystæ* from the cave-sanctuary of the Mother-goddess,[4] but, so far as the earlier cult is concerned, it has to be borne in mind that it is only the later writers who record this ritual.

The same applies to the *taurobolium* (and the parallel *criobolium*, or sacrifice of a ram) during which the initiate was drenched with the blood of the bull (or ram) slain on a perforated platform above a pit in which he stood.[5] For while this rite doubtless had a sacramental significance in the third and fourth

---

[1] Firm. Mat., *De err. prof. rel.*, xviii, 1 ; Clem. Alex. *Protrept.*, ii, 15.

[2] *Hibbert Journal*, xi, No. 2, 1904, p. 317.

[3] *Attis, Seine Mythen und sein Kult* (Giessen, 1903), p. 196.

[4] Cf. W. Scott, *Proceedings of Society of Historical Theology* (Oxford, 1917–18), p. 56.

[5] Hepding, *op. cit.*, pp. 185, 199.

centuries A.D., when it was supposed to cleanse from the past and bestow the life of immortality, the earliest references to it, which belong to the second century of our era, suggest that its object was the welfare of the Empire, Emperor, or community rather than the regeneration of an individual.

Moreover, there is no positive evidence that the taurobolium was originally connected with the Cybele cult in its Phrygian form. Cumont contends that it made its way into Italy in the second century A.D. from Cappadocia where it had been part of the worship of the eastern Artemis Tauropolos.[1] This view is upheld by Dill,[2] though it is controverted by Hepding, who maintains a Phrygian origin for the rite.[3] But even so it was only in post-Christian times that we encounter it in its mystic form as a bath of regeneration rendering the baptized *in æternum renatus*.[4] If it subsequently became part of the Mithraic cult, it was probably borrowed from the Cybele-Attis ritual in the last ages of paganism in the West.[5]

The Isis Ritual

It would appear from *The Golden Ass*, the curious work of the Egyptian Apuleius, that Isis initiates at

[1] F. Cumont, in *Revue d'Histoire et de Littérature religieuses*, VI, No. 2, 1901; *Les Religions Orientales*; Eng. trans. (Chicago, 1911), pp. 99 ff., 332 ff. According to Showerman, the difference between the *taurobolium* and the *criobolium* lies in the latter being a sacrament instituted subsequently to bring the Attis myth into greater prominence, whereas the *taurobolium* had a long sacrificial history—*The Great Mother of the Gods* (Madison, 1901), pp. 280 ff.

[2] *Roman Society from Nero to Marcus Aurelius* (Lond., 1904), p. 556.

[3] *Op. cit.*, p. 201.

[4] Dill, p. 547, n. 4, *Corpus Inscrip. Latin*, vi, 510; viii, 8203.

[5] Dill, *op. cit.*, p. 556; Cumont, *Mysteries of Mithra*, Eng. trans. (Chicago and Lond., 1910), pp. 180 f.

Corinth in the second century A.D. underwent a ceremonial bathing during the period of preparation, like the *mystæ* at Eleusis.[1] Having performed the necessary offices and asceticisms, the candidate was at length led into the inner chamber of the temple at night, where, by the aid of a sacred drama and occult methods, he was brought face to face with the gods to receive mystic revelations and witness sacred rites which Lucius, the hero of Apuleius, was unhappily not permitted to divulge. He admitted, however, that he had " penetrated to the boundaries of the earth ; he had trodden the threshold of Persephone, and returned to earth after being borne through all the elements. At midnight he saw the sun gleaming with bright light ; and came into the presence of the gods below and the gods above and adored."[2] The next morning he appeared before the people clad in the gorgeous array of an initiate, with twelve stoles, a coloured garment of linen, and a precious scarf on his back, all decorated with animal designs. In his right hand he carried a burning torch, and on his head he wore a crown of palm leaves. Thus adorned, he was revealed for the admiration of the crowd. At the end of the year he had to undergo further initiation into the mysteries of Osiris, and shortly afterwards he was initiated for the third time, when he became a member of the college of *Pastophoroi*.[3]

Making due allowances for the fanciful character of this record, there can be little doubt that it was based upon inner knowledge of the initiation rites of the Isis mysteries. It would seem, then, that the novice under-

---

[1] *Metam.* ix, 3.　　[2] *Op. cit.*, 23.　　[3] *Op. cit.*, 24, 26, 30.

went a ceremonial sanctification which was celebrated as a sacramental drama with an elaborate death and resurrection ritual, for the purpose of setting him in the way of salvation when he rose from a mystic grave. It was an initiation involving regeneration, and a voluntary dying, in order to enter into communion with the gods and rise to a newness of life through participation in a death and resurrection ritual. The Mystery Cult of a goddess, however, differs fundamentally from that of a god ; the one is the mystery of birth, of life coming forth from life ; the other is the mystery of death, of life issuing from death. It would seem that in Apuleius the votary embodies not the goddess but the sun since it was a vision of the luminary that was vouchsafed in a vision at midnight. Moreover, when the next morning he stood before the congregation he was arrayed in sacramental garments in the likeness of the solar deity with whom he was identified. That is to say, he passed through the experience of death in union with the Sun-god rather than with Isis before entering into the full service of the goddess.

In the original Egyptian form of the ritual (the cult of Osiris) immortality was secured through the death and resurrection of the divine hero who died to awake to life again.[1] It therefore required only slight modification in a syncretistic age to bring the worship of Osiris and Isis into line with the spirit of Græco-Oriental mysticism, in view of its strong resemblance to the cult of the Asiatic goddess and her consort. In the fourth century B.C. the Olympic religion began

---

[1] Chap. II, pp. 65 ff.

to decay as city states were merged into larger units, and new influences from Thrace, Phrygia and Egypt made their way in the Eastern Mediterranean. In this great welter of religions the Mysteries became firmly established, and finally, in the second century of our era, added the Persian Cult of Mithras to their number. Now while all these rituals with their varied histories were never entirely fused, so far as the scanty evidence available allows of any generalization, they all appear to have had this in common in their later guise that they were essentially sacramental dramas in the sense that they offered to all classes the promise of a blessed hereafter, and aimed at producing inner and mystical experiences calculated to quicken the religious life of the initiates through outward and visible portrayals of the passion and triumph of a divine hero.

Mithraism

In the case of Mithraism the ritual centred in the death of the sacred bull by Mithras rather than that of the hero himself, but the bull had been created by Ormazd, and when he was sacrificed by order of the Sun, the life of the world, animal and vegetable, sprang from his blood. Therefore, Mithras was the creator of life by virtue of this sacrificial act, and, like Osiris, he became the guide and protector of souls in quest of a blessed immortality. To his initiates he secured ascent through seven spheres to the supreme heaven, and full communion in the mystic beatific vision and celestial banquet, of which perhaps the sacramental communion of bread, water and possibly wine, administered to the votary on his admission to the higher degrees, and compared by the Christian Fathers to the Eucharist,[1] was the earthly counterpart.

In all the Mystery Cults the appeal was primarily mystic and emotional. As Angus points out, what Farnell says of Eleusis applies in a measure to all: " To understand the quality and intensity of the impression we should borrow something from the modern experiences of the Christian Communion Service, Mass and Passion Play, and bear in mind also the extraordinary susceptibility of the Greek mind to an artistically impressive pageant." [2] The triumph of life over death in nature and in the human soul was the predominant theme in the sacred drama, represented, intensified, spiritualized by all the emotional qualities of a carefully thought-out ritual elaboration calculated to " refine and exalt the pyschic life and give to it an almost supernatural intensity such as the ancient world had never before known." [3]

Thus, without respect of class or race, a sure and certain hope of immortality was offered freely to all who accepted this way of salvation. In the process of a quasi-spiritual, quasi-magical rebirth the initiate became regenerated, and received the gift of a new divine substance, so that having undergone a mysterious metamorphosis (i.e. become the recipient of the gift of a new divine substance), he was endowed with immortality. Lustrations and sacred meals played some part in most of the cults, apparently, but how far the ceremonial acts of eating and drinking were in

[1] Tertullian, De Præser. Hær., 40, Justin Martyr, Apol., i, 66.
[2] Angus, The Mystery Religions and Christianity (Lond., 1925), p. 59.
[3] Cumont, Textes et Monuments relatifs aux Mystères de Mithra (Brussels, 1896), i, p. 323.

the nature of mystic sacraments in the life of the deity it is impossible to determine with any degree of certainty. Speaking generally, the way of salvation revealed in the Mysteries, in striking contrast to the eternal hopes and aspirations of the philosophers, was the communication to the votary of the life-giving powers of the divine hero, through certain asceticisms, tests, rites and sacerdotal directions implicitly followed, in order to establish a vital union between the divinity and his devotees. The very popularity of the cults lay in the promise they gave to the ordinary man, incapable of philosophical reasoning, of an assured hereafter by the simple expedient of following the prescribed ritual.

The Mystery way of communion in many respects was thus more closely allied to the magical control of supernatural powers than to a religious mystic union with a divine personality, though in the death and resurrection drama a real fellowship of suffering seems to have been achieved. By dying in order to be reborn to a new life the votaries became identified with the mystery deity in an intimate and ecstatic communion. However crude some of the more orgiastic rites may have been, the scheme of redemption offered by the Cults was essentially of a sacramental character in the general sense applicable to a covenant relationship between a deity and his worshippers. But when we pass from the general to the particular the evidence fails us. How far, if at all, any real similarity existed, for example, between the mystery meals and lustrations and the Eucharist and baptismal rites of the Christian Church, it is very difficult to say since the only available comparative material comes from the second century of our era and onwards. To this intricate subject we shall return in the next chapter, but, so far as our present inquiry is concerned, without prejudicing the issue, the Mystery Religions may be described as sacramental dramas which were destined to play a significant part in preparing the way for the establishment of a Christian sacramentalism in Europe.

CHAPTER VI

THAT Christianity had the character of a Mystery Religion is suggested by the method and purpose of initiation as set forth in the Pauline literature. Thus, in Romans vi it is stated that the catechumen was baptized into the death of Christ and buried with Him in a regenerative bath from which the candidate emerged reborn, as from the grave, to newness of life like his risen Lord. Henceforth the Christian initiate lived under conditions different from those which constituted his former existence. Through a mystical sacramental union with Christ, the flesh had been freed from the law of sin and death and animated by a new life-principle so that he walked not after the flesh, but after the spirit (Rom. viii. 4) as " a new creature " (2 Cor. v. 17).

Now while the evidence of Baptism in the Mystery Cults is very slight, it might appear from what has been said above that the fundamental conceptions of the Pauline theology were identical with those which lay behind initiation in the Græco-Roman Mysteries. The early Fathers of the sub-apostolic period, in fact, saw a resemblance even in the outward rite, but, as we have seen, the precise significance of these lustrations has certainly not become easier to determine as our knowledge has increased. That writers at the beginning of our era, already familiar with Christian practice, should read a similar meaning into the apparently parallel pagan customs is understandable, but, as they were not themselves initiates, their testimony is of little value concerning what was actually said and done at these secret Cults, except as an expression of popular ideas on the subject at that particular time.

It would seem, however, that the bath of cleansing had an apotropaic efficacy, but when it was regarded as a symbolic and sacramental regeneration, as in the *taurobolium*, it belongs to a time when the Christian doctrine was well established. It is, in fact, conceivable, as Burckhardt suggests, that this interpretation of the rite arose as a pagan attempt to provide its devotees with the same hope of eternal life which was promised by the Church to the Christian initiates.[1] The evidence of a Mystery sacramentalism during the early centuries of our era, therefore, does not solve the problem of the *origin* of the Christian rites, however helpful it may be in determining their later developments. It is rather to the immediate antecedents of Christianity that we must turn for light on the ultimate question.

Jewish Proselyte Baptism

That the Church at a very early period came to be regarded as the New Israel, brought into being, as it was supposed, because the Messiah had come, and had inaugurated a new order based on the old dispensation, is now hardly open to doubt. Therefore Judaism is the most likely source of the ideas and practices which found expression in the Christian

---

[1] *Die Zeit Constantin's des Grossen* (Bale, 1857), p. 223, n. 1.

sacramental system, unless it be assumed that, like the Maya civilization, it sprang " full-blown from the ground." Thus, respecting baptism, in the Hebrew ritual lustrations to remove ceremonial defilement, and as a preliminary to consecration to the priesthood, or to a sacred ordinance (Ex. xix. 10, xxix. 4; xxx. 18; Lev. xiii–xiv., xvii. 16, xxii. 6; Num. xxxi. 21–24, cf. Heb. ix. 10), are sufficiently prominent to suggest a possible clue to the Christian mode of initiation, especially as they were given a spiritual significance by the prophets, and interpreted by them in terms of a change of heart (Ez. xxxvi. 25 f.; Zech. xiii. 1; Ps. li. 7). Moreover, these ceremonial washings, which in primitive thought were connected with the removal of non-moral pollution (cf. Lev. xiv. 5, 50), later were looked upon as efficacious as an initiation ceremony, in the form of proselyte baptism, when converts from the Gentile world were admitted into Judaism.

That this rite prevailed before the second century A.D. is clear from the Rabbinical literature of the Tannaitic period (*c*. A.D. 200),[1] and both Schürer and Edersheim have argued in favour of an earlier date.[2] As Büchler has pointed out,[3] this view is supported by the Maccabæan legislation concerning a purificatory bath, or *tebilah*, to which Gentile women who had had immoral relations with Jews had to submit on becom-

[1] *Mekhilta* on Ex. xii. 48 ; Mishna *Yoma* iii. 3. and viii. 9 ; Babylonian Talmud, *Yebhàmôth*, ff. 45–47 ; *Gerim* (extra-canonical treatise of Babylonian Talmud).

[2] E. Schürer, *History of the Jewish People* (Edin., 1890), II, ii, pp. 319 ff.; A. Edersheim, *Life and Times of Jesus the Messiah* (Lond., 1887), ii, pp. 745 ff.; i, p. 273.

[3] *Jewish Quarterly Review*, New Series, July 1926, p. 15.

ing proselytes to Judaism. This suggests that the custom prevailed at the beginning of the Christian era, though the decree may have lapsed after the victories of the Maccabees, especially as it was sometimes supposed that a Gentile was incapable of contracting " uncleanness." On the other hand, one Rabbinical tradition maintained that every Gentile " is in all respects like a man with an unclean issue," and, therefore, for those who held this view, a purificatory lustration would be an obvious outcome of the Levitical legislation. That this was actually the case in the second century of our era we are left in no doubt from the frequent references to proselyte baptism in the literature of the period,[1] while in Mishna Peśahim viii. 8 there are explicit references to the rite having been performed on non-Jewish soldiers, suggesting that the practice was of long standing.

It would appear, according to the Talmud, that " proselytes of righteousness " (i.e. those who became " perfect Israelites," or " children of the covenant," as distinct from " proselytes of the gate," who merely renounced heathenism and submitted to Jewish jurisdiction) were circumcised and baptized and then offered a sacrifice in the temple. This last prescription was modified, owing to the destruction of Jerusalem, by a promise that the burnt-offering would be made when the services of the sanctuary were restored, but the very fact that baptism was included among the two ancient rites of circumcision and sacrifice, suggests, as the Mishna presupposes, that it was a well-established custom.

[1] In its present form the Mishna is the work of Rabbi Judah ha-Nasi, " the Prince," who compiled it from earlier sources about A.D. 200.

Another question raised not later than the beginning of the second century A.D. was whether baptism alone without circumcision was sufficient to make a proselyte. The Rabbis decided in favour of the necessity of both rites,[1] though later reasons were found for the view that baptism alone sufficed, thereby showing the importance attached to this part of the initiation. This is also borne out by the injunction that it be performed, with appropriate exhortations and benedictions, in the presence of three witnesses, and in such a manner that the water touched every part of the body.[2] The *tebilah* must, if possible, be of " living water," and the question as to how far a certain quantity of " artificial " (i.e. drawn) water tended to invalidate the baptism is considered to be of sufficient importance to merit discussion.[3] In the case of the ceremonial washings of the Old Testament, sprinkling sufficed, but, despite Professor C. Rogers's criticism of the generally accepted view,[4] there seems no reason to doubt that at the close of the Tannaitic period total immersion was practised. The Mishnaic and Talmudic evidence can hardly be interpreted in any other sense without doing violence to the texts,[5] and it is implied by the Zadokite Fragment, a document, if it is genuine, which goes back to the second

---

[1] *Yebhāmôth*, 46a.
[2] Maimonides *Hilk. Milah*, iii, 4. Maimonides, a medieval Jewish teacher, died about A.D. 1204. On immersion, see Abrahams, *J.T.S.*, xii, July 1911, p. 609; W. Brandt, *Die jüdischen Baptismen* (Giessen, 1910), pp. 32 ff.
[3] Cf. *Mikwaoth of the Mishna* ; T. B. Sabbath 15a; T. B. Hagigah 11a.
[4] *J.T.S.*, New Series, xii, April 1911, pp. 437 ff.
[5] *Yebhāmôth*, 46–48 ; *Gerim*, chap. i ; cf. Abrahams, *J.T.S.*, xii, No. 48, July 1911, pp. 609 ff.

century B.C.[1] The dimensions of the bath given in the Talmud ($1 \times 1 \times 3$ cubits) is also suggestive of immersion.[2]

John the Baptist

Therefore, while the evidence is not conclusive, it seems probable that proselyte baptism was practised in Israel at the beginning of the Christian era and perhaps much earlier, since, when we encounter it in the second century A.D., it is as a definitely established rite of very considerable importance, and there are hints of baptismal lustrations in earlier times. Moreover, while there is no mention of the water-baptism of St. John the Baptist in the Rabbinical literature, there can be little doubt, whatever may be open to question in the traditional records of this strange figure, that the familiar episode in " the wilderness of Judæa in the days of Herod the king " is substantially historical.

In Josephus the Baptist is referred to as " a good man who exhorted the Jews to exercise virtue (ἀρετή), both as to justice (δικαιοσύνη) towards one another and piety (ἐυσέβεια) towards God, and to come to baptism (βαπτισμῷ συνιέναι). For baptism (τὴν βάπτισιν) would be acceptable to God thus, if they used it, not for the pardon of certain sins, but for the purification of the body, provided that the soul had been thoroughly purified beforehand by righteousness."[3] If, as some scholars are now inclined to admit, the passage is substantially authentic,[4] it gives a dif-

---

[1] S. Schechter, *Documents of Jewish Sectaries* (Camb., 1910), p. xlviii.
[2] *Erubin*, 46.   [3] *Antiq.*, xviii, v. 2.
[4] Cf. K. Kohler, *Jewish Encyclopædia*, vii, p. 218 ; H. St. J. Thackeray, *Dict. of Bible* (Hastings), extra vol., p. 471.

ferent account of the nature and purpose of the rite from that preserved in the Gospel traditions, since Josephus pictures it as a bodily purification rather than as a preparation for the coming of the Messianic kingdom.

In the Marcan narrative it is maintained that " John did baptise in the wilderness and preach the baptism of repentance unto the remission of sins " (Mark i. 4) ; a statement amplified in the parallel passage in the First Gospel by the addition of the phrase " the kingdom of heaven is at hand " (Mark iii. 2, cf. iv. 17; Mark i. 15), words apparently derived from Q,[1] the chief source employed by the writer for his account of the preaching of John. It would appear, therefore, that the earliest Christian authority (Q) represented the mission of the Baptist as apocalyptic and Messianic. This is confirmed by another Q passage in St. Luke (xvi. 16 ; cf. Mark xi. 12), and is in accord with the general setting and circumstances of the story.

Like his predecessors the Hebrew prophets, John bore witness to an approaching divine judgment which was actually at hand—a baptism with fire, as well as with water and the Holy Spirit—and calling upon his hearers to return in repentance to a right relationship with Yahweh. Thus the tradition which constituted the common source for Matthew and Luke sets forth the primary significance of the mission and baptism of John more fully than the Marcan narrative, though both traditions agree against Josephus as to the general character of the rite as a moral and spiritual cleansing symbolized and sealed by immersion in Jordan.

[1] Streeter, *J.T.S.*, July 1913, p. 550.

Naber, a recent editor of Josephus, explains the discrepancy as a deliberate and controversial attempt on the part of the Jewish historian to discredit Christian baptism, and as this was repulsive to Christian readers, the text was tampered with so that the baptism of Christ became altogether omitted.[1] Be this as it may, Josephus seems to have been trying to identify John with the Essenes who performed baptismal lustrations of a sacramental nature on the admission of candidates to their society, and with whom the Baptist betrays some very obvious points of contact.[2]

Essenism

That Oriental ideas of a " mystery " nature entered Palestine either in the train of Hellenism, or directly from the Orient, in pre-Christian times, is now fairly established. Thus from the Maccabæan age onwards the Essenes, whether they be regarded as a distinct sect or not, constituted an ascetic brotherhood of Palestinian Jews living a common life of prayer, study, manual work, and the practice of charity, ordered perhaps partly on Greek and partly on Persian models. Kohler, on the other hand, has shown that it is easy to exaggerate the non-Jewish character of Essenism, and, in his opinion, the cult was merely a " branch of the Pharisees who conformed to the most rigid rules of levitical purity while aspiring to the highest degrees of holiness." [3] This is probably an exaggeration, but,

---

[1] E. J. Kiehl, E. Mehler, S. A. Naber, "Mnemosyne," *Tijdschrift voor classieke litteratuur, onder redactic van* (Leyden, 1852–6), xiii. p. 281 ; cf. F. C. Burkitt, *Theologisch Tijdschrift*, 1913, xlvii, pp. 135 ff.

[2] Abrahams, *Studies in Pharisaism and the Gospels*, i, p. 34.

[3] *Jewish Encyclop.*, v, p. 224.

nevertheless, the essentially Jewish traits in this "great enigma of Hebrew history" cannot be over-looked.

The punctilious observance of the Mosaic law, for instance, and the rigid Sabbatarianism, ally the Essenes with the Pharisees rather than the Sadducees, while their asceticism and love of the simple life suggest the Rechabites more than Greek culture, except in so far as they practised agriculture and admitted outsiders into their ranks. Their insistence on the immutable nature of oaths, conversely, suggests a point of contact with Sadduceeism. In view of these divergent characteristics, the movement would appear in the light of a Palestinian syncreticism, Jewish perhaps in origin, but having incorporated various elements from extraneous sources, some of which may have come ultimately from Greece and the East.[1]

Since the Essenes were drawn from all classes, and were probably much less in the nature of a sect rigidly separated from the rest of the community than was formerly supposed, it is not unlikely that John the Baptist was influenced by the movement, even though he may not have been actually and officially a member of the brotherhood. Thus he was an ascetic, but his asceticism was not identical with that of the Essenes, nor did he strive to live a common life in his desert home. In place of a simple white garment he wore a girdle of skin about his loins; and instead of a secluded life emancipated from every object of sense, he took up the *rôle* of an eschatological prophet calling

---

[1] Cf. Moffatt, *E.R.E.*, v, pp. 400 f.; B. H. Branscomb, *Jesus and the Law of Moses* (Lond., 1930), pp. 58 ff.

upon his countrymen to prepare for the approaching Messianic judgment. To this end he urged them to a baptism of repentance, not as an act of ceremonial cleansing, but as a token of an inward and spiritual change of heart as representatives of a regenerative people.

Foreign Influences in Judaism

Whatever may have been the precise relationship between St. John the Baptist and the Essenes, both the allied movements testify to the existence of sacramental ideas in Palestine at the dawn of the Christian era. As early as the days of the Exile, ceremonial ablutions, as we have seen, were tending to be regarded in the light of spiritual purifications (cf. Ezek. xxxvi. 25), but it was not until the time of Alexandrian Judaism that Baptism in Palestine had a sacramental significance in the more mystical sense. Something akin to this may have been present in embryo in the earlier purifications,[1] but this definitely comes to the birth in the later ritual in which the notion emerges of a spiritual death to sin, and, in the case of the Johannine Baptism, entry into a new life in preparation for the coming kingdom of the Messiah. That this conception was in some measure influenced by the Mystery ideas of Hellenic and Oriental thought is highly probable, though, as has been demonstrated, the evidence on this point at present is insufficient to establish anything in the nature of a definite ritual analogy.

Sacramental ideas, either in a crude and primitive

[1] Oesterley and Box, *The Religion and Worship of the Synagogue* (Lond., 1911), pp. 287 ff.

form, or in a more mystical guise, were floating about the Græco-Roman Empire from the sixth century B.C., and if Jewish thought on the whole was little affected by foreign influences, Hellenic culture, especially on its deeper spiritual side, exercised no small sway over the general outlook of the educated classes in Palestine during the third and second century B.C., and doubtless penetrated to the rest of the population.[1] Schürer, in fact, believes that so strong was the Greek spirit among the Jews of Judæa at the beginning of the second century B.C., that had the process of hellenization been allowed to continue without the drastic intervention of Antiochus Epiphanes, the Judaism of Palestine would have been more syncretistic than that of Philo.[2] If this is an overstatement, the fact remains that Greek civilization had a powerful fascination for a considerable section of the population, and even in matters of religion, where it must be admitted a very marked reluctance to imbibe extraneous practices and ideas is manifest, post-Exilic Israel did not prove to be impervious to outside influences. Just as it borrowed the notion of Sheol, and a great deal of its cosmological mythology and demonology, from Babylonia, and probably some of its eschatological and apocalyptic speculations from Persian Zoroastrianism, so in the Wisdom literature, and Philo, we see unmistakable evidence of culture contact with Greece, where the Jews of the Dispersion were compelled to read their own Scriptures in the only language they understood, viz. Greek. It, therefore, seems highly probable that

[1] Hölscher, *Geschichte der israelitischen und Jüdischen Religion Volkes* (Leipzig, 1886), i, pp. 189 f.

[2] *Geschichte des Jüdischen Volkes* (Leipzig, 1883), i, pp. 189 f.

their brethren in Palestine, while remaining loyal to the traditions of Judaism, nevertheless tended to interpret their faith in Hellenic terms.

Thus in the matter of baptism, the ceremonial lustrations with which they were familiar may reasonably be suspected of having undergone a modification in a sacramental direction, especially as the Mystery ideas of death and resurrection were becoming current in Palestine at that time. The Covenant relationship inherent in Jewish theology readily assumed a sacramental significance once proselytes were admitted into the fellowship of Israel by initiatory rites which included the ancient puberty ceremony of circumcision, a ritual bath and a sacrificial offering. If we cannot be certain that this threefold form of entry into the ranks of the " Covenant People " prevailed before the fall of Jerusalem, it has every appearance of being an established institution in the first century A.D., with earlier antecedents. The custom may have been mainly ceremonial in character, but it was also connected with notions of rebirth and spiritual change, the newly baptized proselyte being like " a newborn child " by virtue of his incorporation into the congregation of Israel.[1] In the Essene and Johannine rites the sacramental and spiritual significance suggested by Ezekiel were more fully developed, and it is open to question whether Headlam is correct in believing that the " inspiration of the last of the prophets " was drawn wholly from the prophetical books of the Old Testament.[2]

[1] Yeb., 486.
[2] A. C. Headlam, The Life and Teaching of Jesus the Christ (Lond., 1923), p. 138.

In the post-Exilic period "baptism" (i.e. ceremonial lustration) unquestionably had a Messianic significance (Ez. xxxvi. 25 ; Zech. xiii. 1), and doubtless this conception played an important part in determining the Baptist's use and interpretation of the sign in his eschatological mission.   But living in an age saturated with mystical ideas, it is difficult to avoid the conclusion that he was affected by the thought current in apocalyptic circles where foreign influences were very strongly felt.   Furthermore, the Essenes were confined for the most part to the district round the Dead Sea, where Pliny maintains they persisted for " thousands of ages." [1]   Whether or not the Baptist was in any way connected, directly or indirectly, with this movement, his mission occurred in a district identified with the sect, and therefore doubtless not wholly oblivious of its general outlook.

Galilean Judaism

If the Christian doctrine of baptism derived inspiration from the teaching and practice of the " forerunner," John, it is also very significant that Jesus Himself was brought up in Galilee where a very distinct type of Judaism prevailed.   Surrounded by non-Jewish territory, the province was open to influences from the neighbouring Hellenistic city of Cæsarea Philippi, and it was within easy access of Antioch, the capital of Hellenistic Syria.   Moreover, it was cut off from Judæa by the antagonistic and despised Samaria, and held in contempt by the Rabbis as heretical.[2]   A

---

[1] Pliny, *Historia Naturalis*, v, 17.
[2] Cf. H. Loewe, *E.R.E.*, iv, pp. 6126 f.

saying ascribed to Jochanan ben Zaccai, a pupil of Hillel—" Galilee, Galilee, thou that hatest the law, therefore thou shalt yet find employment among robbers " [1]—has its parallels in the Gospels (John vii. 52 ; i. 42 ; Matt. iv. 13 f.), and doubtless expresses the general attitude of the exclusive mind of Judæa towards this cosmopolitan province, inhabited by a hybrid race devoid of the ethical and nationalistic spirit which characterized post-Exilic Israel. It was here that new movements of thought were most manifest in Palestine, as is shown by the fact that the Mandæan religion took its final form in Galilee in the Persian period, just as Christianity later was first proclaimed among its hills and on the shores of its lake. Therefore, as Dr. Headlam has remarked, " it is not without significance that within sight of the sea of Galilee, on the hills above the valley of Jordan, might be seen the signs of the religion and culture of the Greek world, and that Greek language and thought were permeating even Jewish life." [2]

Thus, at the beginning of the Christian era there is reason to think that Judaism outside Jerusalem was in some measure affected by Hellenism, though exactly to what extent cannot be determined. It is, however, important not to lose sight of the fact that Christianity was born in a changing environment in which new ideas were modifying the ancient Rabbinic Sadducæan traditions, especially in the north where Jesus passed his early years. There, probably, the great body of the people were devout Jews worshipping in the traditional way, but, nevertheless, subject to external influences, and

[1] *Jerus. Shabbath,* 15d.   [2] Headlam, *op. cit.,* pp. 74 f.

therefore suspect in the eyes of their more circum-
scribed compatriots in the south.   Farther afield, in
Alexandria and elsewhere, the Diaspora lived in an
atmosphere saturated with Hellenism, and it was from
these centres that pilgrims flocked to Jerusalem from
time to time, so that even in the Holy City itself
Judaism was not entirely untouched by external
influences.

Therefore, when it is claimed, and not without good
reason, that Christianity was originally the New Israel,
the modifications in Hebrew religion at the dawn of
our era should not be overlooked.   It was from the
peculiar province of Galilee that Jesus wended His way
to Judæa to begin His public ministry by undergoing
baptism at the hands of John.   In His northern home
He had been brought up as a devout and orthodox
Jew, though with certain important differences of outlook from His fellow-countrymen in the capital.   At
Nazareth He would have been instructed by the scribes
in the tenets of official Judaism, and it is recorded that
He disputed with the doctors of the law in the Temple
as a youth (Luke ii. 46 f.), according to current
custom.[1]   It is clear, however, that He did not have a
Rabbinical training, His education consisting in that
commonly given to a provincial artisan at the local
synagogue school, where He would learn the general
principles of the theory and practice of the religion of
Israel.   His own teaching in later years, as recorded
in the Gospels, reveals the general outlook of the
Hebrew scriptures current in His day, and it seems
probable, despite assertions to the contrary, that He

[1] Josephus, *Life*, 2. 9.

spoke in Aramaic rather than Greek. The Founder of Christianity, therefore, thought and spoke as a Jew, but, nevertheless, as a *Galilean* Jew, and consequently with the mental presuppositions moulded and modified through contact with certain phases of Hellenic and Oriental thought and culture. Thus equipped, He began His mission with a sacramental initiation.

The Baptism of Christ

In the earliest record of the event (Mark i. 9–11) John is represented as the forerunner of the Messiah who would " baptize with the Holy Spirit," whereas the First Gospel contrasts the Johannine lustration with an apocalyptic baptism with fire (Matt. iii. 11 f.), a conception more in line with Judaic thought than the Marcan expression which is suggestive of Christian interpretation. On the other hand, the idea of the " Anointed of the Spirit " is deeply rooted in the Old Testament (1 Sam. xvi. 13 ; Is. lxi. 1), and this aspect of the Messianic *rôle* would probably not be unfamiliar to John, if he regarded himself at all in the light of a forerunner. The subject is really one for the New Testament literary scholars to decide, but if the account of the baptism of Christ is in any sense historical, as the majority of critics are inclined to allow,[1] all the circumstances suggest that it had for Him a Messianic significance (Mark ix. 12, 13, and Saying from Q in Matt. xi. 7 ff. ; Luke vii. 24 ff., xvi. 16). Moreover, the alleged retirement to the desert immediately after the event (Mark i. 12 f. ; Matt. iv. 1–111 ;

[1] Streeter, *The Four Gospels* (Lond., 1926), pp. 187 ff.; B. W. Bacon, *Studies in Matthew* (Lond., 1930), pp. 214, 393 ; cf. K. E. Kirk, *The Vision of God* (Lond., 1931), pp. 98 ff.

Luke iv. 1–13) is indicative of His having undergone a profound religious experience which drove Him into solitude to reflect upon its meaning.

Henceforth He regarded Himself as the chosen servant of Yahweh in terms of the apocalyptic, Messianic and Isaianic figures, but while He permitted His disciples to baptize, He did not Himself administer the rite (John iii. 22, iv. 2, cf. Luke vii. 29 ff.). His message at first carried the same note as that of His predecessor (Matt. iv. 17, cf. Mark i. 15), and bore witness to His prophetic ministry, confirming the promise of a Spirit-baptism to which John had referred in his Messianic anticipations (Luke xxiv. 49 ; Acts i. 47, xi. 16 ; John xx. 22). If He did not actually Himself baptize, or institute the Christian sacrament,[1] He submitted to the rite at the hands of the Baptist, and sanctioned its continuance among His disciples so that the Apostolic Church used this method of initiation quite naturally from the beginning. It would seem, therefore, that the sacrament was a Johannine heritage which was adopted by Christ and the Church, and reinterpreted in terms of Christian thought.

The Pauline Doctrine

It was in this process of reinterpretation that the mystery ideas inherent in the institution developed in a highly spiritualized form, along the lines of the

---

[1] While the baptismal formula in Matt. xxviii. 19 occurs in all extant MSS., the Old Syriac and Old Latin versions are defective at this point, and there are reasons for believing that Eusebius quoted from a text which omitted the words. Cf. Conybeare, *Zeitschrift für die N.T. Wissen*, 1901, pp. 275 ff. If the lost ending of the Gospel contained the formula, it is surprising that Trinitarian baptism is not mentioned in 1 Cor. i. 14 ff., Acts ii. 38, viii. 12 ; xix. 5.

Pauline doctrine. In the complex personality of St. Paul, influences met, derived from his early Hellenic environment of Tarsus, his Rabbinical training at Jerusalem, and his later "twice-born" religious experience. The final product of this synthesis was an original theology welded together into a coherent scheme, based on Judaism but expressed largely in mystery and mystical language, though presenting certain fundamental divergences from the current belief of the Mediterranean and Oriental Cults. Thus, for example, there is no record of a baptism in the Mystery Religions into the name of any of the Mystery deities, nor is there any trace of a " gift of the Spirit," or divine πνεῦμα, in association with the ritual of lustration, although this concept was by no means absent in Mystery doctrine.[1] The prominence of these notions in the theology of St. Paul and the Early Church differentiates the Christian rite from the corresponding Mystery initiations, and the Jewish and Johannine counterparts. True, as we have pointed out, there are reasons for believing that the Trinitarian formula was not part of the original form of administration, but, nevertheless, the initiate was admitted to the fellowship of the baptized " in the name of Jesus " (Acts ii. 38 ff.), a phrase implying incorporation into the person of Christ (Acts i. 15 ; Rev. iii. 4 ; xi. 13). This was further developed by St. Paul into an explicit Covenant relationship ; a " putting on of Christ " (Gal. iii. 27) in a spiritual rebirth (Rom. vi. 3 f. ; 1 Cor. xii. 12 f.).

This Pauline interpretation of the initial sacrament

[1] Kennedy, *St. Paul and the Mystery Religions* (Lond., 1913), p. 230.

was by no means a typical Mystery initiation ceremony, as Dr. Kirksop Lake imagines,[1] since, according
to the apostle, " if any man hath not the Spirit of
Christ, he is none of his " (Rom. viii. 9). Clearly, to
the mind of St. Paul, Christianity was essentially a
personal, mystical experience achieved by an act of
self-renouncing trust involving death to the old life
and a " rising again " in newness of life and status in
Christ, in whom the initiate is " sealed with the Holy
Spirit of promise " (Ephes. 1–13).[2] Therefore, if
Baptism had its place in his scheme of redemption
and regeneration, it was not in the strictly Mystery
sense that he conceived the death and resurrection of
the catechumen, since what was implied was essentially
a putting away of the old life and its associations in
order that a new relationship of sonship with Christ
might be established (Rom. vi. 4 ; Gal. iii. 26 f. ;
1 Cor. vi. 17).

In all these utterances St. Paul was expanding his
own spiritual experiences as a " new creature " dead
to his old life, and in a new Covenant relationship
with his risen and ascended Lord, which he found
ethically superior to, and more soul-satisfying than, the
Judaic Law. The spiritual grafting of the faithful
into the New Israel was comparable, he thought, to

[1] Kirksop Lake, *The Earlier Epistles of St. Paul* (Lond., 1911), p. 233. To
the Hebrews, as to primitive people generally, the name was an integral part
of the human organism. Therefore Baptism in the name of Jesus would
appear to mean Baptism into His nature and fellowship, i.e. the Church.
There is no evidence for Lake's contention that " the name was the power
which gave the water its significance," p. 386.

[2] If the Pauline authorship of Ephesians is open to question, that this
view of Baptism is fairly representative of the teaching of the Apostle is
apparent from Gal. iii. 2 ; ii. 19 f. ; Rom. x. 17 ; 1 Cor. ii. 4, 5 ; iv. 15 ;
xii. 13.

the spiritual experiences his forefathers had undergone in the wilderness when they were " baptized " in the Red Sea ; an episode which was profitable only to those who were not disobedient to the ethical laws of Yahweh (1 Cor. x. 2). But what the Law failed to accomplish was carried into effect by the New Covenant. It was, however, to his own ancestral faith, not to the ideas and practices of contemporary religions, that he looked for the antecedents of his newly-discovered Christian ideals. Judaism was, he thought, a schoolmaster to bring the world to Christ (Gal. iii. 24) ; whereas Græco-Roman paganism, in his opinion, was a sink of iniquity (Rom. i. 21 ff.), from which many of his converts had been rescued, washed and sanctified (1 Cor. vi. 11). Therefore, having been at such pains to extricate perishing souls from the mire, he is scarcely likely knowingly and deliberately to introduce them afresh to pagan rites and beliefs. Nevertheless, it was in the atmosphere of a Hellenized Judaism that he was nurtured.

A Jew of Tarsus, St. Paul was a Roman citizen, and, therefore, by birth and early environment he belonged essentially to the Diaspora. Consequently his first acquaintance with his own nation and its creed was with the Judaism of the dispersion as it existed at Tarsus, rather than with that of Palestine. He was, therefore, familiar with a somewhat Hellenized type of the Hebrew religion, while during his most impressionable years he must have been in constant contact with Greek life and culture. On the other hand, his strict Jewish parentage must have isolated him from pagan society, and prevented his gaining an inside knowledge of the worship of the local religious cults. Moreover, he seems to have been educated at one of the Rabbinical schools in Jerusalem where he became a fanatical zealot for the Law.[1] His early environment, therefore, was very much modified by his subsequent training, which probably accounts for his essentially Rabbinical theological outlook, and almost complete ignorance, as it would appear, of Greek writers.

Thus, in his correspondence with the Gentiles it is always to the Old Testament Scriptures, and not to the classical or contemporary authors, that he makes his appeal, just as while he was proud of his Roman citizenship, and maintained an Imperial outlook, he proclaimed himself an Hebrew of the Hebrews, as touching the Law, a Pharisee. He was, in truth, narrower and more Pharisaical than his master, Gamaliel, recoiling with typical Jewish horror from anything that savoured of heterodoxy. In him Jew and Greek met, but it was the Jewish element that always prevailed. As he himself declared, as touching the Law he was blameless, having advanced in the Jew's religion beyond many of his own age among his countrymen, being more exceedingly zealous for the traditions of his fathers.

Furthermore, after his conversion to Christianity he did not abandon the religion of Israel, seeing in the New Covenant the fulfilment and expansion of the old dispensation. Thus, he brought over to Christianity current Jewish Rabbinical theology of the Pharisaic

[1] Cf. P. Wendland, " Die Hellenistisch-Romische Kultur " (Tübingen, 1912), p. 242, in Lietzmann's *Handbuch zum Neuen Testament*, i, Bd. 2.

school, modified in some measure, at any rate subconsciously, by his own early training and habits of thought at Tarsus. These preconceptions he reinterpreted in the light of his specifically " twiceborn " religious experience, in terms of the person, death, resurrection and early return of Christ. In welding together these component elements into a coherent scheme, he produced an original theology, the basic ideas of which belonged to Judaism, but the language and thought was a highly spiritualized Mystery conception of a mystical union with Jesus established through a spiritual *process* (as distinct from a ritual) of death and resurrection. In this way he created a Christian theology and apologetic, together with a philosophy of history, which proved to be readily adaptable to the needs and outlook of Jew and Gentile. Therefore, it was calculated to make a widespread appeal in an age of religious unrest and inquiry.

The amazingly rapid spread of Paulinized Christianity quickly created a Christian atmosphere in which Judaism tended to undergo further modification, and the Mystery Religions to assume a more mystical and sacramental character. The keenest and liveliest controversy being between Jews and Christians, the two theologies further reacted upon each other. Earlier likenesses in practice and belief not shared by the other tended to become obscured, while, conversely, the more attractive features were prone to be imitated or assimilated. Thus, as the liturgical expression of Baptism developed in the Early Church as a Mystery rite, a corresponding movement can be discerned in the contemporary religions, the one apparently reacting on the other.

In Church and Synagogue in the second and third centuries, baptismal ritual tended to approximate, so that in the early Roman rite in the so-called " Egyptian Church Order "—probably a recension of *The Apostolic Tradition* of Hippolytus written about A.D. 220 [1]—the order of procedure is similar and the rubrics governing the removal of ornaments on the body of the initiate identical with the corresponding parts of *Yeb.* 47 and the Tractate *Gerim.* i.[2] Similarly, the directions to the candidates, and the immersion, are of the same character in both rites.

In the Mystery Cults, despite their fundamental divergences from the Christian sacrament in its Pauline form, there was a tendency, as we have seen, for the initiation ceremonies and lustrations to assume a mystic sacramental significance. But, speaking generally, the antecedents of baptism in the Christian Church are to be found in the Synagogue rather than in the Græco-Roman temple. In its later developments, on the other hand, there was a closer approximation to the Mystery concepts so that Christianity exercised its controlling force in the declining Roman Empire mainly as a sacramental Mystery Religion.

The Eucharist

What applies to baptism is also true of the Eucharist. In the Mystery Cults, so far as it is known at present,

---

[1] Cf. G. Horner, *The Statutes of the Apostles* (Lond., 1904), pp. 245, 306 ff. ; R. H. Connolly, *The So-called Egyptian Church Order and Allied Documents, Texts and Studies* (Camb., 1916), vol. viii, No. 14.

[2] *Horner, op. cit.*, pp. 151 ff. ; Connolly, pp. 183 ff.

there are no real counterparts in the ritual, to a mystical sacramental meal of bread and wine partaken of as an act of spiritual communion with a particular divinity, or with the divine nature as a whole, and having at the same time a sacrificial significance. Such parallels as exist[1] have a very different history from the Christian rite, since the worship of Demeter, Dionysos, Attis and Osiris in its original form was essentially connected with the cult of the dead and the growth and decay of vegetation. Thus, if the ancient formula of the Attis ritual, " I have eaten out of the timbrel, I have drunk from the cymbal," referred to a sacramental rite, it was a ceremonial meal of cereals and fruits connected with Attis as a personification of the Cornstalk.[2] Moreover, if in their later and more spiritualized developments there was a Eucharistic element in the Mystery Cults, it was only incidental since the passage from sorrow to joy, from darkness to light, culminated in an ecstatic experience of a very different character from that implied in the Christian institution.

The Eucharistic Mystery was a weekly celebration of the Easter triumph over the forces of evil having an eschatological and a soteriological significance as the re-enactment of the drama of the *opus redemptionis* for those already initiate. The pagan parallels were in the nature of seasonal initiatory rites with a symbolism signifying the death and revival of vegetation, and if behind the Easter ceremonial there lies a long line of spring ritual, these observances represent a later development out of the Jewish Pascha.[3] The

---

[1] Cf. Chap. V, pp. 139 ff. ; Dieterich, *Eine Mithrasliturgie*, p. 174.
[2] Farnell, *Hibbert Journal*, ii, 1904, p. 317.
[3] E. Schwartz, *Zeitschrift für neutestamentliche Wissenchaft.*, vii, 1 ff.

Eucharist, on the other hand, became essentially a memorial of the death of Christ regarded as a sacrificial offering.

The Origins of the Eucharist

The earliest record of the ordinance (1 Cor. xi. 17–34) presupposes that by A.D. 55 the rite had been in existence sufficiently long for it to have become the scene of abuses. In attempting to set matters right, St. Paul appealed to the tradition he had received from the Church at Jerusalem concerning what took place on the eve of the crucifixion (1 Cor. xv. 3).[1] In the subsequent accounts of the event, the Synoptic narratives describe the disciples being assembled in the Upper Room " on the first day of unleavened bread, when they sacrificed the Passover " (Mark xiv. 21, Luke xxii. 13 ; Matt. xxvi. 18) ; i.e. on the 15th of Nisan. The Fourth Gospel, on the other hand, without making any attempt to narrate the proceedings, maintains that the gathering occurred " before the feast of the Passover " (John xiii. 1), and alleges that the bodies were taken down from the crosses on the Preparation to prevent their remaining at the scene of execution over the feast, " for the day of that Sabbath was a high day " (xix. 31*f.*, *cf.* 14 ; xviii. 28).

Notwithstanding the ingenious arguments of such theologians as Dalman[2] and Chwolson[3] to establish the Synoptic date, it is very difficult to reconcile the

---

[1] The phrase " received from the Lord " seems to indicate receiving a tradition rather than a special revelation, since the word παρέλαβον (1 Cor. xv. 3) is employed elsewhere for instruction from a Christian teacher (παραλαμβάνειν) : 1 Thess. iv. 1 ; 2 Thess. iii. 6 ; Gal. i. 12.

[2] *Jesus-Jeshua* (Leipzig, 1922), pp. 86 ff.

[3] *Das Letzte Passamahl Christi* (Leipzig, 1918), p. 11.

events described in connexion with the trials and crucifixion with the Jewish observance of the Feast day.
It may be true that a rebellious teacher could be executed on a festival,[1] but the priests and people presumably would have been too much occupied at this season
with their Paschal duties to conduct a public trial amid
popular demonstrations. Furthermore, although the
Synoptic tradition places the Supper on the night of the
Passover, it records the warning of the Sanhedrin
against taking action during the festival—" not on
the Feast-day, lest there be a riot " (Mark xiv. 2 ;
Matt. xxvi. 5)—and it is possible to read into Luke xxii.
15, 16 an unfulfilled desire on the part of Jesus to partake of the Passover.[2] It is also remarkable that no
mention is made of the Paschal victim in either the
Marcan or the Matthæan accounts of the meal.

Taking all the facts into consideration, the Johannine
date (Nisan 14) is the more probable, and if this is
correct, it follows that the Last Supper occurred in the
night before the Paschal Feast began. The Synoptic
record, therefore, seems to be deficient and contradictory
at this point, and it is possible that it is not an account
of the institution of the Eucharist as described by
St. Paul. The Fourth Gospel preserves a complete
silence regarding the Christian rite, and, as Bate has
suggested,[3] it may be that St. Luke merely recorded
the Paschal meal without any mention of the institution, ending his narrative with the words, " I will not
drink henceforth of the fruit of the vine, until the

[1] *San.*, xi. 3.
[2] Oesterley, *The Jewish Background of the Christian Liturgy* (Oxford, 1925),
p. 181.
[3] *J.T.S.*, July 1927, p. 362.

kingdom of God shall come " (xxii. 8). This would explain the omission of the words " this do in remembrance of me " in important manuscripts such as the Græco-Latin Codex Bezæ (D), the Old Latin MSS., the Curetonian Syriac version, and certain cursive MSS.[1] The placing of the cup of blessing before the reference to the bread in the current version becomes intelligible on this hypothesis as an insertion of the longer text at a very early date to incorporate the Pauline tradition (1 Cor. xi. 34 ff.), where the breaking of bread seems to have come first, though 1 Cor. x. 16, 21 reverses this order, as does the *Didache*.

In view of this textual and documentary confusion, we cannot be certain of the precise significance of the Synoptic record, and how far it represents the institution of the Pauline sacrificial-sacramental rite, but the narratives give a general idea of the character of the meal eaten by Christ and the disciples on the eve of the Passover. The circumstances point to the gathering having been of a quasi-religious nature as groups of friends (Ḥaburôth) were accustomed to meet in private houses on Friday evenings in preparation for the Sabbath, and before the great festivals.[2] Before the ceremonial meal, in later times the head of the family chanted the praises of a virtuous wife (Prov. xxxi. 10–31) and the family joined in singing songs on some theme. Singing after the meal is probably very

---

[1] Westcott and Hort, *The New Testament in the Original Greek* (Camb., 1881), appendix, pp. 63 f.; introduction, p. 175.

[2] Elbogen has shown that it was the custom in the early Tannaitic period to hold Sabbath meals early on Friday afternoons before the Sabbath had begun; the *Kiddûch* cup of wine being blessed and drunk at sunset. Cf. M. Braun and J. Elbogen, *Festschrift zu Israel Lewys Siebzigstem Geburtstag* (Breslau, 1911), pp. 173 ff.

much earlier than the preliminary chant. The *Kiddûsh*, or sanctification, consisted of two blessings : (*a*) the benediction over the wine, and (*b*) the sanctification of the day. After drinking it himself, he passed it to the rest of the company. The solemn washing of hands followed or preceded the wine, according to the particular rites observed. The two loaves were reminiscent of the double portion of manna, one of which was cut in pieces and distributed to the guests, and the other was reserved to the next day. These blessings were in the nature of a " grace " or thanksgiving, " Blessed art thou, O Lord our God, King of the universe, who createst the fruit of the vine " ; " Blessed art thou, O Lord our God, King of the universe, who bringest forth bread from the earth." [1]

In ordinary circumstances there would have been no *Kiddûsh* save on the Sabbath or a festival, the " feria," or weekday, rite consisting simply of a blessing appropriate to the nature of the meal. This would vary according to the viands.[2] In the case of the Last Supper, the evidence is against the meal having been actually the Passover, but if it was the *Kiddûsh* it must have been put forward a day by Jesus in view of His approaching death. Realizing that the blow might fall at any moment, and having a particular desire to eat, or rather to anticipate, this Passover with His disciples before He suffered (Luke xxii. 15), He seems to have gathered them together on the Thursday evening,[3] as doubtless He was wont to assemble them from time

---

[1] *Tosephta, Berākhôth* vi, 1, 24 ; cf. *Daily Prayer Book* (S. Singer), p. 124.
[2] *Ber.* vi, vii.
[3] Cf. Kennett, *The Last Supper* (Camb., 1921), pp. 35 ff. Cf. W. C. Allen, *St. Matthew* (I.C.C., Edin., 1907). pp. 273 f.

to time to discuss at a meal the Messianic mission.[1]

The stories of a miraculous feeding of a great multitude appear to be connected with ritual gatherings of this nature. That the Early Church attached considerable importance to these traditions is clear since they are the only miracles recorded in all four Gospels. Indeed, there is no other *incident* before the Passion, except the work of John the Baptist, which is related by all the Evangelists. St. Paul, at an earlier date than the Synoptics, had connected the Eucharist with the " spiritual food " which sustained Israel in the desert (where the feedings are alleged to have occurred), and a reference to the manna forms the transition from the Feeding story to the Eucharistic discourse in John vi. If, in historical fact, the " feedings " were regarded as anticipatory of the coming Messianic banquet, as Schweitzer suggests,[2] the sacramental interpretation is near at hand ; and the whole setting of the miracles is indicative of a mystical significance. Thus emphasis is laid on Jesus (who is here called ὁ κυρίος)[3] first giving thanks (John vi. 23), and the five loaves are called ἄρτος in the singular, as in 1 Cor. x. 16 f., xi. 27. The disciples are rebuked for their hardness of heart because " they understood not concerning the loaves " (Mark vi. 52). Similarly, judgment is passed on the crowd for following Jesus not because they saw σημεῖα, but because they " ate of the loaves and were filled." As St. Paul condemned the sordid excesses

[1] Schweitzer, *Quest of the Historical Jesus*, p. 374.

[2] *Op. cit.*

[3] Nowhere else in the Fourth Gospel is this term used of Jesus until the Resurrection.

at the Corinthian Supper (1 Cor. xi. 20 ff.), so the
Fourth Evangelist contrasts the barley loaves with the
" true bread," Jesus ; " Labour not for the meat which
perisheth, but for the meat which abideth unto
eternal life " (John vi. 26 ff.). It is the deeper sacramental significance of the ritual-meal that matters, for
" the flesh profiteth nothing ; the ῥήματα of the Logos,
made flesh, are spirit and life.

It would seem, then, that the origin of the Eucharist
must be sought in whatever lies behind the feeding
stories, reaching its climax in the Upper Room on the
eve of the Passion. The Synoptics agree that it was
during the supper that the rite was instituted, but the
narratives suggest certain departures from the normal
order of the Jewish observance. Either the meal did
not begin with bread and wine, and Jesus blessed these
elements when they came ; or, if the meal began with
the blessing of the bread and wine, the duplication of
the blessings points to an innovation implying that
the previous blessings, *Kiddûsh* or otherwise, were
invalid, and they were repeated because henceforward
they were to have a new significance.

The reason for the *Kiddûsh* of every festival and
Sabbath is its historical significance. On the Sabbath
the remembrance of the creation and the Exodus both
occur because of the differing reasons in the two
recensions of the Fourth Commandment (Ex. xx. 10 ;
Deut. v. 15).[1] Jewish chronology is thus divided into
two parts : from the creation to the Exodus, and the
Exodus onwards. By identifying the cup with the
blood of the covenant, Jesus made the Eucharist a new

---

[1] I am indebted to Mr. Loewe for this information.

Kiddûsh introducing a new division of time. As Lietzmann says, in offering Himself like the Paschal lamb at the last of the solemn banquets with His disciples Christ in effect said, " Ich bin das Opfertier, dessen Blut für euch, d. h. für das gläubige Volk, vergossen wird, um einen neuen Bund mit Gott zu besiegeln, und dessen Leib für euch geschlachtet wird." [1]

Therefore, if it is not strictly true to affirm that Christ " instituted and in His holy Gospel commanded us to continue a perpetual memory of His death and passion " in a Eucharistic sacrificial-sacramental ritual, there is very good reason to believe that, consciously or unconsciously, He provided the inspiration for the Christian rite by His words and actions in the Upper Room on the night of his betrayal, as they are recorded in the Synoptic narratives. The meal was already an established institution in Jewish social life, and endowed with a quasi-liturgical character.[2] The disciples consequently continued their regular *Ḥaburôth* when their Master had passed from their midst, and at these gatherings, it may be conjectured, they recalled with increasing vividness the unique occasion when they assembled with Him for the last time on the eve of His passion.

If, as seems probable, the crucifixion took place on the day on which the Passover lambs were sacrificed, His death would inevitably tend to become associated in their minds with the significance that festival had for them both as Jews and Christians. Therefore, under the circumstances, the most natural thing for

---

[1] *Messe und Herrenmahl*, p. 221.
[2] S. Krauss, *Talmudische Archäologie* (Leipzig, 1910), Bd. iii, p. 51.

them would be to equate the Last Supper *Kiddûsh* with the Paschal meal, and to interpret their weekly *Habúrôth* in terms of a sacrificial-sacramental action, such as that described by St. Paul, irrespective of whether anything was actually said on the original occasion about the repetition of the rite. Henceforth, as St. Paul affirmed (1 Cor. xi. 26), the "breaking of the bread" became a sacrificial communion proclaiming (καταγγέλλετε) the death of the Lord till He come.

In course of time as converts were added to the Church, the *Habúrah* fellowship meal inevitably underwent changes to bring into greater prominence the mystic sacramental and sacrificial elements. None but the eleven disciples were present in the Upper Room, and for the wider group of initiates, especially those who had come under the influence of St. Paul, it was the death and resurrection of Christ which were of supreme importance. In the mystery atmosphere of the syncretistic age, which characterised the formative period of Christianity, the Eucharist, without undergoing any essential change in constitution or significance, developed along the lines of a sacramental drama setting forth the re-enactment of the Covenant offering which it was believed Jesus had made in the mystery of the *opus redemptionis*.

The Eucharistic Sacrifice

Very early He was identified with the Paschal lamb on whom, it was supposed, the faithful feed as the true Passover (1 Cor. v. 7; John xix. 36). From this conception it was but a step in the thought of the age to the identification of the broken bread and poured-

out cup with the flesh and blood of the victim offered
on Calvary. Thus the way was opened for the
interpretation of the Eucharist as an *anamnesis* of the
atoning death of Jesus comparable with the Paschal
memorial before Yahweh of the deliverance from
Egypt. As the former covenant had been sealed with
blood, so the Eucharistic wine was none other than
the blood of Christ in which He sealed the new
covenant (1 Cor. x. 1–5).

The Agape

What the doctrinal implications of this analysis
of the historical situation may be, it is not our purpose
to inquire. Here we are merely concerned with the
rite as a development within the institution of sacrifice
as a whole, using the term " Sacrifice " in its broad
anthropological sense employed throughout this investigation. That the Eucharist arose out of a
ceremonial meal is now very fairly established, and if
there is some doubt concerning the original intentions
of Jesus at the actual institution, that it was continued
by the disciples and the Apostolic Church cannot be
denied. The separation of the *Agape* and the Eucharist
(1 Cor. xi. 34) doubtless had the effect of eliminating to
some extent the social character of the *Ḥabûrah*, and
emphasizing its religious aspect.[1] Lietzmann thinks
that the Agape-Eucharist was a proper meal derived
from the fellowship meal of the Jewish Christians at
Jerusalem, whereas the Pauline rite was a later and
independent development.[2] Völker, on the other

---

[1] Cf. Abrahams, in *Jewish Daily Prayer Book*, ed. by S. Singer, pp. cxxxix f.
[2] *Op. cit.*, p. 255.

hand, regards the Agape as an independent institution which arose in the second century in the Christian struggle with Gnosticism.[1] It is true that common meals without a Eucharistic significance at the end are of very uncertain occurrence in the Apostolic Church, and Batiffol has argued skilfully, though one may suspect not without theological motives, against the existence of such *agapai*.[2] But in view of the foregoing evidence it is difficult to deny that originally the Eucharist was incorporated in the common meal of the feeding-story type, in which the breaking of the bread perhaps came first in the Pauline rite, then the meal proper, and finally the blessing of the cup; the Eucharist being originally "after supper." Out of this composite observance the later liturgical sacrificial rite emerged.

At Troas, as at Corinth, the common meal (δεῖπνον) was partaken in the evening. Then followed a lengthy discourse by St. Paul, who subsequently celebrated the Eucharist (Acts xx. 7–12 ; 1 Cor. xi. 20). In the manual of Church order of Jewish origin and uncertain date and provenance called the *Didache*,[3] the Christian rite is still associated with a common meal, although the Last Supper is not expressly mentioned. By the middle of the second century, however, the separation was complete, and as the fellowship meal tended to drop out, the Eucharistic oblation remained as

---

[1] *Mysterium und Agape die gemeinsamen Mahlzeiten in der alten Kirche* (Gotha, 1927), pp. 1–11.

[2] *Études d'histoire et de théologie* (Paris, 1905), pp. 228, 283 ff.

[3] This document is usually assigned to the beginning of the sub-apostolic period ; cf. A. S. Maclean, *The Doctrine of the Twelve Apostles* (Lond., 1922); A. Robinson, *J.T.S.*, xiii, 1912, p. 329 ; Streeter, *The Primitive Church* (Lond., 1929), pp. 279 ff.

an act of sacrificial communion, the Christian equivalent of the Jewish meal-offering, and the drink-offering (Ex. xxix. 40; Lev. ii; xxiii. 13; Num. vi. 15, 17; xv. 5, 7, 10; xxviii. 14). The words, "Do this as my memorial," recorded in 1 Cor. xi. 24, 25, and in the *textus receptus* of St. Luke, were capable of a sacrificial interpretation, since ποιεῖτε is the equivalent of the Hebrew עשה, used to describe the daily offering of the morning and evening sacrifice (Ex. xxix. 39; c.f. Lev. ix. 7; Ps. lxvi. 15), while " memorial " (ἀνάμνησις) is the Greek translation in the Septuagint of the Hebrew לְאַזְכָּרָה in Lev. xxiv. 7, and of לְזִכָּרוֹן in Num. x. 10.[1]

As the New Covenant began to take the place of the Old in the allegiance of the first generations of Christians, so the central act of worship assumed more and more the position occupied by the sacrificial offerings in Judaism and the Græco-Roman world. The term " sacrifice " occurs at the end of the first century,[2] and speedily passed into more general use.[3] The Eucharistic offering was then regarded as an act of thanksgiving for the good and perfect gifts bestowed by a beneficent Creator,[4] material gifts being part of the oblation.[5] According to Irenæus, the sacrifice is an offering of first-fruits which should be offered to

[1] As Dr. Lock has pointed out, ποιεῖν is commonly used in the LXX to indicate the celebration of a festival, and it is similarly employed in Heb. xi. 28; cf. *Theology*, Nov. 1923, vii, pp. 284 ff.

[2] Clement, *Ad Cor.*, 40–44.

[3] *Didache*, xiv. 1; Ignatius, *Smyrn.*, 6; Justin Martyr, *Dial. cum Tryphone*, 117. 7–10, 41–70; Cyprian, *Ep.* lxiii, 17; Irenæus, *Adv. Hær.*, IV. xviii, 1–3, 6; cf. Volker, *op. cit.*, pp. 46 ff.

[4] Ignat., *Ephes.* xiii, 1; Justin Martyr, *Dial.*, 29, 41, 116, 117, cf. 70. *Didache*, xiv, 1.

[5] *I Clem.*, xliv, 4.

God, "not as though he is in need," but as a token of thankfulness for creation.[1] This conception may have been suggested by the *Kiddûsh* being the weekly commemoration of the Sabbath, and, therefore, in the Jewish mind a memorial of creation, and the Exodus an aspect of the observance retained in its Paschal form. The blessing of the wine is, again, reminiscent of vegetation ritual, and its Christian symbolism is a highly spiritualized development of the sacrifice of the first-fruits and of the first-born, with the accompanying life-giving sacramental attributes.

If, as seems probable, the discourse in John vi. has a Eucharistic significance, this primitive and fundamental aspect of the institution is emphasised in metaphysical language, since the spiritual eating of Christ's flesh, and drinking of His blood, are represented as bestowing upon the recipient the boon of immortality (John vi. 53 ff.). Whether the words in their present form were spoken by Jesus or not, they at least reveal the theology of the school from which the Gospel proceeded at the end of the first century A.D. The blood is the life, and to partake of it sacramentally is to assimilate the life-principle. On this hypothesis, the eating of the flesh of the victim and the presentation of the blood become integral in the sacrificial action.

In Pauline theology the Eucharist is regarded as the means by which the life-giving blood of the New Covenant, offered in complete surrender and obedience to the will of God, is partaken of by the worshippers in union with the sacrifice of the Cross. But

[1] *Adv. Hær.*, iv, 17 ; and of redemption, cf. Justin *Tryph.*, 41.

it was the blood (i.e. the life-principle) shed on Calvary and offered and received in the Eucharist, that constituted the act of redemption rather than the act of dying.[1]   Therefore Christ is represented in the Fourth Gospel as describing His sacrifice in terms of a surrendered life to be shared with His followers, thereby revealing a profound insight into the fundamental character of the ritual in its manifold forms.

Always and everywhere the primary purpose of sacrifice has been the bestowal of life, and if Christ to His followers was the " true wine," Whose life's blood was poured out for the life of the world, to partake sacramentally of " the flesh of the Son of Man, and to drink his blood " was to imbibe His life.   This seems to be the thought behind the Johannine theology, and it is strictly in line with the evidence brought under review in the foregoing pages.   But it did not find a ready acceptance apparently among the Jews (John vi. 60, 68), either in Palestine, if the words were spoken by Jesus, or in Antioch, if they represent a dialogue between the Church and the Synagogue.   This may be partly explained by their highly metaphysical and mystical character, but also because sacrificial theology had developed along other lines in post-Exilic Israel, the drinking of blood having become strictly tabu.

The Liturgical Eucharistic Drama

The Church, on the other hand, saw in the Eucharist a sacramental drama of the passion and death of Christ, so that, as Professor Chambers has said, " from the fourth century, the central and most solemn rite of

---

[1] For a further discussion of this question, cf. Chap. VII, pp. 218 ff.

that worship was the Mass, an essentially dramatic commemoration of one of the most critical moments in the life of the Founder. It is His very acts and words that day by day throughout the year the officiating priest resumes in the face of the people. And when the conception of the Mass developed until instead of a mere symbolical commemoration it was looked upon as an actual repetition of the initial sacrifice, the dramatic character was only intensified." [1]

As the daily repetition [2] of the original offering once made on Calvary, the Liturgy reproduces the salient features of the institution of sacrifice. The drama opens with the *asperges* as a kind of initiation ceremony, or new birth, by which the worshipper is initiated as it were into the Mystery. As a ceremonial cleansing the rite precedes every other ceremony, such as the blessing of palms or candles, and being no part of the Mass proper the celebrant wears a cope, not a chasuble (the sacrificial garment), nor a maniple. The altar, choir, ministers, and congregation having been sprinkled, the *preparation* follows, which includes the " confiteor," as the conclusion of the " expulsion ritual." The sacred ministers then ascend the steps of the altar to the " footpace," symbolizing the entrance to the heavenly sphere wherein the Eucharistic action is preformed. [3] At this point the liturgical drama actually begins with the incensing of the altar and the celebrant, who then says the *Introit* and *Kyrie eleison.*

---

[1] *The Mediaeval Stage* (Oxford, 1913), ii, pp. 3 f.

[2] The word " repetition " is used in a purely ritual sense, since in Catholic theology the sacrifice once offered on the Cross is " represented " rather than repeated at the altar.

[3] Cf. Chrysost., *Ep. ad Heb.*, hom. xiv, 1, 2.

At the Reformation the reading of the Decalogue was added to the *Kyrie* in the Anglican rite, thereby reviving the primitive practice of giving instruction in the moral law during initiation ceremonies, while the lections after the collects have a similar significance. The true note of the heavenly worship, however, is struck by the singing of the *Gloria in Excelsis* at the beginning of Mass, according to ancient custom, followed by the solemn rendering of the *Gospel* in a setting of incense and torches.

By gradual stages the drama proceeds through the *Credo* to the *Offertory*, wherein the " victim," in the form of the elements, is prepared, and the *secret*, or silent oblation is made, all of which in the Eastern rites are connected with the *Great Entrance ;* a ceremonial procession of the sacred gifts to the altar, corresponding to the triumphal procession in which the king played the part of the god at the head of the train of lesser deities. Then comes the *Anaphora*, the most ancient part of the service, consisting of the *Sursum Corda*, the *Sanctus*, the acclamation of Christ as King (*Benedictus*) and the *Canon*, with its commemoration of the hierarchy on earth, the communion of saints, the Incarnation, Passion, Resurrection and Ascension, together with the recitation of the words of institution.

The sacrifice is thus made by the whole Christian community, living and dead, which in the Eastern rites reaches its climax in an invocation of the Holy Spirit to consecrate the elements. In the Latin canon this *epiklesis* survives in its traditional place *after* the words of institution in the prayer that the oblation may be received at the " heavenly altar "—" supplices te rogamus, omnipotens Deus, jube hæc perferri per manus sancti Angeli tui in sublime altare tuum, in conspectu divinæ Majestatis tuæ, ut quotquot ex hac altaris participatione, sacrosanctum Filii tui Corpus et Sanguinem sumpserimus, omni benedictione cœlesti et gratia repleamur." The *Fractio* follows, symbolizing the death of the victim, with which is associated the *Agnus Dei*. Neither this ceremony nor the *Agnus* occurs in the documents of the fourth century, though in the Liturgy of St. Chrysostom the priest was directed to divide the Holy Bread into four parts, " with care and reverence," saying, " The Lamb is broken and distributed ; He that is broken and not divided in sunder ; ever eaten and never consumed, but sanctifying the communicants." [1]

As greater emphasis came to be laid upon the death of the victim, and the theory of immolation developed in conjunction with the " conversion theology " of Ambrose [2] and Paschasius Radbertus—a doctrine which subsequently found expression in the scholastic definition of transubstantiation—the Fraction assumed increased importance and significance. The particles of the Host were arranged upon the paten in such a manner as to represent the human form, until the practice was denounced by the Council of Tours in 567. It was then decreed that the portions should be placed in the shape of a cross. In the Mozarabic Liturgy the Host is still broken into nine parts, each having its special designation corresponding to a mystery in the life of Christ : (1) Incarnation ; (2)

---

[1] J. M. Neale, *History of the Holy Eastern Church* (Lond., 1850), p. 650.
[2] Cyril, *Cat. Myst.*, v.

Nativity ; (3) Circumcision ; (4) Apparition ; (5) Passion ; (6) Death ; (7) Resurrection ; (8) Glorification ; (9) Kingdom. In Ireland the Host was divided into seven particles arranged in circles on the paten in the form of a cross, the remaining two being placed on the right of the cross outside the circles.[1]

This elaboration of the original " breaking of the bread " tends to overshadow the *Commixtio*, or mingling of the Eucharistic species, which follows as a symbolical representation of the resurrection in which the body and blood were again reunited and reanimated. But, nevertheless, it is the life-giving aspect of the rite that is the most ancient and fundamental feature. Thus the rehearsal of the drama of the Passion culminates in the *Communion*, i.e. the bestowal of the life of Christ on the duly initiated and fasting communicants in order to impart a renewal of spiritual vitality, and to effect a mystical union of the soul with God. This accomplished, the Liturgy concludes with the ablutions, and the descent of the sacred ministers from the heavenly sphere. *Ite missa est.*

From this rapid analysis of the Liturgy it is apparent that in the Mass the main features of the ancient sacramental drama are re-enacted in terms of the birth, death and resurrection of Christ in a highly metaphysical form in which the sacrificial action is transferred to the celestial realms. First a severance from the world is represented, then a communion with the divine, and, lastly, a return to the world, though to a new and higher plane of it. The worship of heaven is thus brought into relation with that of earth by

[1] Duschesne, *Christian Worship*, 5th edn. (Lond., 1919), p. 219.

means of a ritual repeating symbolically the series of historical events upon which the initiates depend for their spiritual sustenance here, and the hope of immortality beyond the grave. From the standpoint of comparative religion, therefore, the Christian liturgical drama is true to type, but, as Dr. Marett has recently remarked, it is all too easy to slip into " the fallacy of deeming all religion more or less fraudulent because it employs a symbolism which, if taken literally, would be contrary to common sense. But this is to confuse the imaginative with the imaginary, the ideal with the merely unreal. Prefiguration is the only possible language of hope and faith ; so that every true visionary, civilized or savage, takes liberties with the actual in order to provide the soul of his dream with some sort of picturable body." [1] In the institution of sacrifice this is a complex ritual pattern representing certain situations connected with the promotion and conservation of life.

[1] *Faith, Hope and Charity* (Oxford, 1932), p. 145.

CHAPTER VII

PROPITIATION AND ATONEMENT

So far comparatively little has been said about the more negative aspects of sacrificial ritual which, as we saw in an earlier stage of the discussion, are fundamental to the institution. If life, health and prosperity are to be promoted in this world or the next, evil, however the term may be construed, has to be removed and driven forth. The old formula, " Out with famine, in with Health and Wealth," has its counterparts in every state of culture.[1] To the primitive mind good and evil, life and death, are in the nature of materialistic entities capable of transference or expulsion by quasi-mechanical operations. Any unusual misfortune or disaster is regarded as a manifestation of divine displeasure demanding some definite and concrete act of propitiation by way of atonement in order that the evil may be removed, and a right relationship restored between man and the supernatural order. By the anger of the gods is meant little more, therefore, than the failure of the crops, or outbreaks of plagues and diseases, and similar calamities, attributed to some ritual defilement, independent of ethical values, and which is removable by life-giving substances, such as blood or water.

It follows, then, that as sacrifices in this state of culture are the normal means of transferring life and

[1] Chap. II, p. 61.

184

power to mortal deities to keep them vigorous and render them beneficent, so they readily become vehicles for carrying away dangerous traits and harmful influences. For this reason human victims have figured prominently in rites of this character, a practice which had led Dr. Westermarck to base human sacrifice mainly on the idea of substitution. " In various cases," he maintains, " the offended god is thought to be appeased only by the death of a man. But it is not always necessary that the victim should be the actual offender. The death of a substitute may expiate his guilt." The expiatory sacrifice, therefore, may be vicarious for " by sacrificing a man they hope to gratify that being's craving for human life, and thereby to avert the danger from themselves." [1]

This is doubtless substantially correct so far as it goes, but it does not supply a reason for the action. Why should human victims be offered for the purpose of saving the lives of the sacrificers before the beginning of a battle, or during a siege, previously to a dangerous sea-expedition, during epidemics, famines, or on other similar occasions, when murderous designs are attributed to some supernatural being in whose will the lives of men are supposed to depend ? Dr. Westermarck concludes that " it is impossible to discover in every special case in what respect the worshippers believe the offering of a fellow-creature to be gratifying to the deity." [2] This, again, is no doubt true, but while it is most unlikely that they had always definite views on the precise significance of their

[1] *Origin and Development of Moral Ideas* (Lond., 1906), i, pp. 65, 440.
[2] *Op. cit.*, p. 440.

sacrificial ritual, yet it seems that their primary general aim was to save their lives and avert danger from supernatural sources by a renewal of vital energy. The gods have become inert through lack of nourishment, and therefore morose. Consequently human sacrifice, as we have tried to show, is essentially a transference of life to enable the gods to continue their beneficent functions on earth.[1] So men offer the lives of their fellow-men to their gods to save themselves from the disastrous results which must inevitably follow when the supernatural control of the processes of nature fail, and life is in danger.

In this practice of offering life to preserve life may be discerned the beginnings of the idea of substitution and propitiation, which, in many of the higher religions, have taken over a lofty ethical significance. In its primitive modes of expression, however, expiation was nothing more than the " wiping away," or ritual removal, by quasi-mechanical means, of a substantive pollution, contracted generally involuntarily and unwittingly. When it was the nature of the god, and therefore the processes dependent upon him, that were primarily involved, suitable offerings had to be made to secure the continuance of divine benevolence, and set up a supernatural barrier against the forces of evil. Conversely, when the condition of the worshipper was at fault, the ritual impurity, or contagious evil, contracted must be purged and removed by mechanical means, such as washings, confession, offerings of propitiatory value, or transference of the " sin " to some animal or human victim.

[1] Cf. Chap. IV, pp. 98 ff.

Behind these materialistic conceptions there is the desire to restore and maintain right relations between man and man, or man and the supernatural order, which may have been temporarily destroyed by the infringement of a tabu, or other ritual non-observance. Since misfortunes inevitably follow when the bond is broken uniting those in whose veins the same soul-substance circulates, something has to be done to " atone " for, or " cover," or " wipe out " the offence, and so to re-establish the vital union upon which the welfare of the individual and the group depends. When man is " desacralised " he ceases to be under the protection of the supernatural powers, very much as the first-fruits become common property after a *sacrifice de désacralisation*.[1] Therefore he is liable to be a ready prey to the malevolent forces surrounding him, just as the new crops are freely consumed as soon as they cease to be under divine ownership.

Thus, the early Semites, for example, developed an elaborate demonology consisting of invisible jinn, afrit and ghul capable of assuming animal forms.[2] These spiritual beings were associated chiefly with deserted and unhealthy localities, but they were also liable to be disturbed and become malicious when fresh ground was broken, a new house erected, the first-fruits of the harvest were gathered, or new trees cut down. Consequently, it was thought to be prudent to perform sacrificial rites on these occasions in order that those most intimately concerned might be pro-

[1] Cf. Chap. II, pp. 61 f.
[2] R. Smith, *Religion of the Semites*, pp. 119 ff. ; Langdon, *Mythology of all Races*, vol. v, Semitic (Lond., 1931), pp. 352 ff.

tected by the out-pouring of vital energy from the seat of life.

So persistent, in fact, has been this belief in Arabia that the custom of sprinkling blood on new land, new houses and new wells has survived into modern times. Thus, Curtiss records having witnessed the application of the blood of a goat to the cords of an Arab tent at Rubeibeh, and, on the authority of Mr. H. C. Harding, he gives an account of the pouring of sacrificial blood on the ground in the harvest-fields, on the lintel of the house of a newly married couple, at the laying of the foundations of a new government school at Kerak, and when the rail from Beirut to Damascus was commenced. Arab butter (semn), coloured with henna, was also daubed on the lintel and doorposts as a substitute for blood, leaving the imprint of hands.[1] Thus, despite the opposition of the Moslem authorities, the ancient blood rites survived among modern Semites down to modern times.[2]

The Paschal Ritual

These customs throw an interesting sidelight on the Hebrew Paschal blood ritual associated with the great spring festival celebrated by the Jews in later times in commemoration of that terrible night when it was supposed that the angel of Yahweh set forth on his bloody campaign to destroy all the first-born of the Egyptians (Ex. xii; Deut. xvi. 1–8). That this

[1] S. I. Curtiss, *Primitive Semitic Religion To-day* (Chicago, 1902), pp. 182 ff. It is possible that we have here a sidelight on the hand designs in Palæolithic caves, such as Gargas.

[2] Cf. C. M. Doughty, *Travels in Arabia Deserta* (Lond., 1921), new ed., i, pp. 136, 499; Spoer, *Folk-lore*, xviii, 1907, pp. 66 ff.

strange observance has its origin in a very primitive ritual is now generally agreed by scholars, and signs are not wanting in the narratives pointing to this conclusion, since the Israelites are represented as making request to go into the wilderness to sacrifice ; the Passover being actually referred to as an established institution before the Exodus (Ex. iii. 18 ; v. 1 ; vii. 16 ; xii. 21).

In its earliest form it seems to have been connected with the offering of first-born children, and in that case the destroying angel may represent the mythological version of the earlier sacrifice, the offering of the firstlings of sheep or goats being a survival of the subsequent modification of the original practice. As Frazer says, " the one thing that looms clear through the haze of this weird tradition is the memory of a great massacre of firstborn."[1] What is less certain is the precise reason for and occasion of the offering.

There is reason to think that in former times demonology prevailed among the Hebrews, as among other Semites, although most of the traces of the practice in the post-Exilic literature have undergone considerable modification in the process of bringing all spiritual beings under the control of Yahweh (1 Sam. xvi. 14 ff., 1 Kings xxii. 19–23 ; Amos iii. 6). Thus, for example, the seraphim, or " burning ones," apparently began their career as the dreaded flying serpent of early Semitic cult (Num. xxi. 6 ; Deut. viii. 15 ; Isa. xiv. 29 ; xxx. 6), before they were exalted in pre-Exilic Israel to the rank of attendants of Yahweh (Isa. vi. 1–7). Similarly, the " satyrs " (Isa. xiii. 21 f.), the " golden calf "

---

[1] Frazer, *G.B.*, pt. iv (" Dying God "), p. 176.

(xxxii. 4 ff., Lev. xvii. 7; Deut. ix. 21); and the " scape-goat," or *Azazel* (Lev. xvi. 8–10), probably represent the hairy jinn in the form of a calf, or *seirim*, who haunted waste places, and were worshipped among the Assyrians and Phœnicians. The *Lilith* of Isa. xxxiv. 11–15 (cf. Ps. xci. 5) was, of course, a well-known Assyrian night-demon, and the strange creatures mentioned in the desolation of Babylon (Isa. xiii. 21, 22) apparently refer to demons such as *Iyyim* (wolves), *tannim* (jackals), and *ochim* (doleful creatures).

In the Passover ritual blood is directed to be sprinkled on the lintel and two doorposts in order to prevent the forces of evil from entering the house (Ex. xii. 23). As Buchanan Gray says : " What the ancient Hebrews endeavoured to repel from their houses were spirits, demons of plague, or sickness and the like, much as the modern Bedawy or Syrian peasant." [1]   Death must be met by life, and to this end an efficacious barrier against " the destroyer " has to be set up on the threshold. The door is strengthened by the vital essence just as the houses of the newly wed, or the natural orifices of the human body, which are particularly exposed to evil spirits, have to be re-inforced in primitive society by substances rich in soul-substance and magical virtues calculated to give renewed strength in time of grave peril.

Now according to Deut. xvi. 1, it was at the spring equinox, on the night of the full moon, that the ritual was performed. Since there is nothing in the Old Testament to suggest an alternative date for the observance, it may be assumed that the Deuteronomic

[1] *Sacrifice in the Old Testament* (Oxford, 1925), p. 364.

legislature followed the traditional use, and therefore the Passover may very likely have had a lunar significance in its original form. If this was so, its connexion with fertility is readily explained inasmuch as the Mother-goddess and the life-giving powers of women frequently were identified with the moon in ancient practice, as, for example, in the case of Diana, who, under this guise, gave abundance to the harvest and bestowed offspring on childless women.[1] But deities concerned with the processes of fertility invariably require revivification. Thus, in the Aztec calendrical rites the heart of a human victim was offered to the moon in February at midnight for this purpose, and on the following day a feast was held on his flesh.[2]

The Paschal victim, therefore, may have been originally an offering to the moon during a spring festival, comparable with that in the Aztec calendar, to enable the deity to continue its fertilizing functions. At first it may have been a human offering, and there is abundant archæological evidence that this form of sacrifice was very common in ancient Palestine.[3] With the substitution of an animal victim (Deut. xii. 31, xviii. 10, cf. Gen. xxii. 1–19) came other modifications in the ritual which included a prohibition against eating the flesh raw (Ex. xii. 9). This tabu would be meaningless unless it were directed against a custom that was at one time in vogue,[4] and if the rite was origin-

---

[1] Catallus, xxxiv, 9–20 ; Cicero, *De natura deorum.*, ii, 26, 68 ff.

[2] J. de Acosta, *The Natural and Moral History of the Indies* (Hakluyt Society, Lond., 1880), ii, 384 ff.

[3] Macalister, *The Excavation of Gezer* (Lond., 1912), ii, pp. 426 ff.

[4] *Religion of the Semites*, p. 345.

ally in the nature of a fertility sacrifice, it would be very likely to include a sacramental meal to absorb the vitality inherent in the sacred victim. Moreover, if it were a moon festival there is a reason for the feast being concluded before the divinity disappeared with the break of day (Deut. xvi. 4).

The spring equinox, however, doubtless had a negative as well as a positive aspect, for it was at this season that malign influences were generally considered to be rampant, and consequently had to be kept at bay. Therefore, the blood ritual probably was directed against the attacks of " destroyers " roaming about in search of blood on Passover night (i.e. during the full moon festival), very much as death was expelled by similar rites in Christmas and New Year observances.[1] Moreover, the fact that the moon was the lesser light that ruled the night, and mythologically sometimes connected with the underworld, may have given lunar cults a sinister aspect, so that, like the Cailleach, the luminary was on occasions regarded as a malignant being. It is possible, therefore, that underlying the Passover ritual there is a demonology connected directly or indirectly with a moon cult.

Be this as it may, running through the general pattern of sacrificial myth and ritual there is the dual conception of getting rid of evil to secure good, of expelling death to gain life. Therefore, propitiation is an essential attribute of the institution of sacrifice since to conserve and promote life, decay and death must be removed. If by appropriate ritual man may share in the beneficence of the world, in addition to

---

[1] *Religion of the Semites,* (chap. ii, pp. 7 f.).

a bountiful " Providence " there are also adverse powers, a whole hierarchy of demons ever on the alert to compass his downfall.

Thus, in Babylonia, where the sin-offering occupies an unusually prominent place in the ritual texts, all sickness and ill luck were attributed to some offence or ritual error unwittingly committed,[1] so that the daily cry of the Sumerian penitent was the pathetic protest, " I know not the sin which I have done ; I know not the error which I have committed."[2] Somehow he had " missed the mark," and brought down upon him the wrath of tyrannical deities ever on the alert for the slightest infringement of the ritual order. In course of time in this circle of ideas there developed concepts of an ethical character so that the Babylonian penitent was led to exclaim, " My heart is distressed, and my soul faileth. I cry unto thee, O Lord, in the pure heavens. Faithfully look upon me, hear my supplication."[3]

It was, however, always within the sphere of ritual holiness that Babylonian thought moved, even the lofty prayer to Ishtar, in which the goddess is besought by the penitent to " dissolve my sin, my iniquity, my transgression, and my offence ; forgive my transgression, accept my supplication," concluding with a rubric concerning ceremonial lustrations with pure water, and cleansings by means of aromatic woods,

---

[1] Farnell, *Greece and Babylon* (Lond., 1911), p. 154.

[2] Langdon, *Babylonian Penitential Psalms* (Oxford Edition of Cuneiform Texts, Paris, 1927), pp. 40, 19–21, 41, 42–7 ; Zimmern, *Babylonische Busspsalmen* (Leipzig, 1885), iv, pp. 19–21, 42–5.

[3] Zimmern, *Beiträge zür Kenntnis der Babylonischen Religion* (Leipzig, 1899), pp. 23, 58 ff.

and sacrificial offerings.[1]   Nothing could sound more sublime than the prayer :

" Turn thou into good the sin which I have done ;
  May the wind carry away the error which I have committed !
  Strip off my many evil deeds as a garment !
  My god, my sins are seven times seven ; forgive my sins !
  My goddess, my sins are seven times seven ; forgive my sins ! "[2]

yet the sins bewailed were for the most part ritual errors, and the general outlook was that of the primitive conception of propitiation.

Believing themselves to be surrounded by a hierarchy of evil spirits of various kinds and shapes, the Babylonians developed an elaborate propitiatory ritual and system of ceremonial atonement in which the three life-giving elements, light, fire and water, figured prominently.   The revivifying powers of water have been considered in some detail,[3] and fire and light had a similar significance in view of their solar associations. Therefore it is not difficult to understand why their aid was sought in dispelling the forces of darkness, decay and death, in conjunction with the corresponding deities.   Thus, Ea, the water-god, was lord of the *apsū* (i.e. the deep) whence all rivers and springs were thought to take their origin, and out of which arose the sun-gods bringing release from the evils wrought by the demons of *tiāmat*, the waters of death.   It was with the restorative " waters of life " that Ishtar was sprinkled on her return from the underworld, and it

[1] L. W. King, *The Seven Tablets of Creation* (Lond., 1902), i, pp. 233, 237.
[2] Zimmern, *Bab. Busspsalmen*, iv, pp. 100–106 ; Langdon, *Bab. Pen. Psalms*, pp. 43, 41–5.
[3] Cf. Chap. II, pp. 62 ff.

was Ea who gave his son Marduk his own power over demons :

" Go, my son Marduk, this man the son of his god pacify.
Bread at his head place, rain-water at his foot place.
Smite the headache.
The words of the curse of Eridu utter.
Of his limbs the ache allay.
May the headache ascend to heaven like smoke.
Into the beneficent hand of his god restore the man." [1]

Eridu, the home of the Ea-cult, was a sacred and undefiled place at the mouth of the Tigris and Euphrates whence Marduk was directed by Ea to sprinkle the sick man with the sacred water from the mouth of the two springs to drive out the evil spirits within him.[2] The " curse of Eridu," or *šiptu* (the technical term for the curse of expiation), therefore, seems to have derived its efficacy from the potency of the water employed in the ritual, and only in later times is there evidence of the incantation alone sufficing to banish the powers of evil.[3] Ultimately the spoken *šiptu* became the all-important spell, and the water dropped into comparative insignificance, the rite then consisting essentially in a series of exorcisms. Originally, however, the water would appear to have been the absorbing or neutralizing agent, driving forth the malevolent influences, and so freeing a man from evil contagions. So permeated with impurity

---

[1] *Babyloniaca* (Paris, 1910), iii, p. 16.
[2] W. H. Rawlinson, *The Cuneiform Inscriptions of Western Asia* (Lond., 1880-1884), iv, 22, No. 1 ; *Cuneiform Tablets in the British Museum*, xvii, pp. 25-6 ; R. C. Thompson, *Devils and Evil Spirits*, ii, pp. 86-97.
[3] *Cuneiform Texts from Bab. Tablets, etc., in Brit. Mus.* (Lond., 1903), xvii, pp. 34-6.

did the water become that it was able to exercise a ban upon anyone who touched it, or even looked upon it. Therefore, it had to be put away at once lest it should become a snare to the unwary.

The act of expelling evil was called *kuppuru*, a word which has been the subject of considerable discussion in recent years.[1] Upon the technical philological question involved in the determination of the signifi-cance of the term the present writer has no qualifica-tions to pass an opinion, but if Zimmern is correct in regarding the original meaning to be that of " to wash away," [2] it is not difficult to understand why it was widely employed to signify a mechanical act of atone-ment in connexion with the removal of the sacred elements into which evil had passed. The holy water, grain, bread, or sacrificial victim by absorbing the un-cleanness of the defiled person or object, or by carrying it away, purified the sinner and so made atonement.

The Ritual of the Scapegoat

Closely associated with this notion of purging or removing evil is the kindred ritual of expiation by means of a scapegoat. As impurity was carried away by running waters, so animals were employed as sacrificial substitutes.[3] True, there is no definite evidence of the communication of evil to living animals in Babylonia comparable with that in the Hebrew ceremonial (Lev. xvi), but instances are not lacking of a victim slain for the purpose of removing malign

---

[1] Cf. B. Gray, *Sacrifice in the Old Testament*, pp. 69 ff.

[2] Zimmern, *Beiträge zur Kenntnis*, etc., p. 92; *Zeitschrift für Assyriologie*, xxviii, p. 76.

[3] S. Langdon, *Expository Times*, xxiv, 1912, pp. 9 ff.

influences from human beings, as, for example, in the case of the white kid of Tammuz whose heart was extracted in order that it might be placed by the priest upon the hand of the patient to make " atonement for the man." [1]

In a Sumerian ritual-test describing an " incantation by means of the horned wild goat " reference is made to Ea commanding his son Marduk to take a scapegoat to the king bound by a curse, and place its head against his head as an act of atonement so that " his poisonous tabu into his mouth may be cast."

> " May the king be pure, may he be clean.
> He who knows not the curse by which he is cured,
> From his body may he chase it away.
> May the demon of his device stand aside." [2]

Moreover, on the reverse, according to Professor Langdon's translation, the scapegoat is said to have been " unto the plain let loose," like the Hebrew Azazel. The atonement seems to have been made for the king rather than for the nation as a whole, as in Lev. xvi, but since in early society the life and prosperity of the people were bound up with the health of the divine king,[3] the Hebrew rite may only represent a later interpretation of the original conception. In the text in question the king is referred to as the " son of his god," and the demons which had attacked him had also " seized upon " the cattle and kids " which thrive in the field. The wild goats, the antelope, and the rams after (?) they caused to go."

---

[1] *Cuneiform Texts*, xvii, 10 f.; cf. R. C. Thompson, *Semitic Magic* (Lond., 1908), p. 203.
[2] Langdon, *op. cit.*, p. 11.   [3] *Ibid.*, chap. ii, pp. 73 ff.

It seems, therefore, to be more than just the curse upon the king as an individual that was removed by the scapegoat, and Dr. Langdon is probably correct in concluding that " the king communicates the sins of his people, the curse and ban of the devils, to the scapegoat by shooting it with an arrow." [1]

Gradually as a more ethical element developed in the Babylonian ritual of expiation, the higher conceptions of penitence began to appear. But in most of the Penitential Psalms sin is spoken of only in general terms, and until the stage is reached when the tablet of sins was broken in token of forgiveness,[2] atonement was little more than a mechanical process.

The same fundamental attitude to sin and propitiation lies behind the Hebrew ritual. Thus even after the Exile the infringement of tabus was punished by the Priestly Law with the same severity as moral offences (Ex. xxx. 33, 38; xxxi. 1, 5; xxxv. 2; Lev. v. 2, 6; xiv. 40, 52; xvii. 4, 9, 14; Num. xxxv. 31; xix. 12, 13, 19, 20), and the Hebrew priest was purged by ritual absolution like his Babylonian counterpart (1 Sam. iii. 14; Isa. vi. 7; Ps. xvi. 14; Lev. v. 18). The term *kipper* (כפר) is commonly translated "to cover," but, as Dr. Langdon has contended, in the light of the Babylonian evidence, the original significance of the expression is to be found in the technical term *kuppuru* used in the Babylonian ritual of atonement in the sense of " to remove," or possibly " to wipe away." [3] In his opinion, however, while in Sumerian *kuppuru* means " to turn away," " remove,"

---

[1] Langdon, *op. cit.*, p. 12.
[2] King, *Babylonian Magic and Sorcerers* (Lond., 1896), pp. 31 ff.
[3] *Expository Times*, xxii, March 1911, pp. 320 ff., 380 ff.

and was employed by the Babylonians to indicate absorbing the curse and the uncleanness, the idea of covering is not thereby necessarily excluded since the root meaning involves both the ideas of *covering* and *removing*. Thus, he thinks "the Babylonian ritual gives us the clue for fixing upon this Semitic conception of atonement from which both Babylonian and Hebrew started. We take the root *kaparu* to mean fundamentally 'wash away with a liquid'; *apply* and *wipe away* are two concepts inherent in this root, and although Babylonian appears to have lost almost completely the idea of applying or covering, yet Hebrew has apparently retained traces of it, certainly in Gen. xxxii. 21."[1]

Leaving the solution of the philological problem to those competent to deal with it, so far as the sacrificial ritual is concerned, there can be little doubt that the original idea was that of removing the taint of material and ceremonial evil by means of purifying and life-giving agents. Thus in the Hebrew ritual, it was the blood that made atonement "by reason of the *nephesh*," or soul-substance, therein contained (Lev. xvii. 11; Deut. xii. 23), which removed evil in the manner of the Babylonian "waters of life," while on the Day of Atonement the goat assigned to *Azazel* (Lev. xvi. 8–10) carried away the sin of the nation.

The identification of Azazel is not without its difficulties,[2] but whether it be regarded as one of the

---

[1] E.R.E. vol. v, 1912, p. 640, n. 3.

[2] Confusion has been caused by associating Azazel with the scapegoat instead of with the supernatural being to which the term obviously refers (Lev. xvi. 8 ff.). Clearly the Hebrew spelling has been changed deliberately to avoid mentioning this being, the word being unintelligible as it stands.

dreaded *se'irim* who, in the form of goat-demons, were thought to haunt waste places, to whom sacrifices were offered in post-Exilic times (Lev. xvii. 7); or, as Cheyne conjectured, an evil genius not unfriendly to man who supplied the scapegoat to remove the danger of the *se'irim*,[1] in either case he is a personal being directly associated with the *Elohim*. Now it was these *Elohim* who were thought to be responsible for introducing evil into the world (Gen. vi, Enoch vi. 7, viii. 1, ix. 6, x. 4) and, therefore, whether the Azazel was a satyr or a leader of the " fallen angels," he was intimately concerned with the absorption of evil through the scapegoat who bore away the sins of the people to a " solitary land " (Lev. xvi. 21, 22) wherein the demons made their habitation.

In an attempt to explain the ritual in terms of Zechariah's allegory (Zech. v. 5–11), the late Dr. R. H. Kennett suggested that Azazel was looked upon as a cause of trouble to Israel very much as Babylonia was thought to be guilty for its treatment of the Jews. On this hypothesis, Azazel becomes the receptacle or recipient of the sins of the nation in the sense that the land of Shinar was regarded as the depository of Judah's guilt in the allegory, the supposition being that " a pagan or semi-pagan man named Azazel gave his name to a place within easy reach of Jerusalem but in a district not actually inhabited by the Jews, and that he there instituted heathen rites." The place

---

[1] *Zeitschrift für die Alttestamentliche Wissenschaft*, xv, 1895, pp. 153 ff. Azazel, according to Cheyne, originally meant " God strengthens " rather than " complete removal," the present designation being of literary and religious origin rather than a description of popular belief.

being thus desecrated, it became "the dumping-ground for Jewish sin." [1]

The Day of Atonement

That the Day of Atonement was essentially a post-Exilic observance seems certain. It was apparently unknown either to Ezekiel or Zechariah, who regulated the offerings and fasts in commemoration of national disasters without reference to the Levitical ordinance governing the annual day of expiation (Ezek. xlv. 18 ff., Zech. viii. 19). This breach is hardly likely to have been committed if "the great fast" on the tenth day of the first month had been in existence at the time. Similarly, Nehemiah mentions a joyous feast on the first day of the seventh month, and the subsequent celebration of the Feast of Tabernacles (Neh. vii. 73–viii.), but he makes no reference to the Day of Atonement, though he records a general fast on the twenty-fourth day. Dr. Kennett thinks that actually it arose from a rite of expiation for the sins of the people held on the tenth day of the seventh month, which became "the annual commemoration of the solemn act of penitence with which the Jewish community under Nehemiah inaugurated a new phase of religion at Jerusalem." [2]

This is not improbable since it was the growth of a deeper realization of ethical values which characterized the development of the sacrificial system in post-Exilic Israel, and this concept reached the zenith of its expression in the institution of the Day of Atonement

[1] R. H. Kennett, *Old Testament Essays* (Camb., 1928), pp. 110 ff.
[2] *Op. cit.*, p. 109.

(Lev. xvi.). According to the Levitical legislation, on the first day of the seventh month (*Tishri*) the priest shall " make atonement for the holy sanctuary, and he shall make atonement for the priests and for all the people of the assembly " (Lev. xvi. 33). But although this event became the most important observance in the Jewish calendar, it is only once definitely mentioned in the Old Testament (i.e. in Lev. xvi.), and it has every appearance of constituting a unique development, inasmuch as, on the one hand, it holds a peculiar position in the Pentateuch, and on the other, it represents the climax of the post-Exilic notion of sin and atonement.

'*Āshām* (guilt-offering) and *Ḥaṭṭāth* (sin-offering), though pre-Exilic terms (2 Kings xii. 16), were not applied to sacrificial expiation through the agency of an animal victim till after the Exile. Hitherto they had reference to money payments made to the priests in compensation for injury, though it would seem from Ezek. xl. 39, xliii. 18, 20, 26, that the idea of a sacrificial cleansing was associated with these offerings while the people were still in Babylonia. In the subsequent Levitical legislation the '*āshām* was essentially an atonement for trespass (Lev. v. 14 ff., vi. 6, Num. v. 6–10), as distinct from the *Ḥaṭṭāth* which constituted a ceremonial removal of ritual offences committed " unwittingly " (Lev. v. 1, 4 ; xxiii. 19).[1]

Out of this post-Exilic sacrificial development the annual purification of the whole nation emerged, and later in the Talmud assumed predominant importance.

---

[1] Lev. xxiii. 19 was probably the work of the Priestly redactor, and not part of the earlier Law of Holiness.

Despite the silence of the Old Testament apart from the isolated reference in Lev. xvi., the observance has every appearance of representing the climax of the new religious movement instituted by Ezekiel in Babylonia and his priestly successors after the return from the Captivity. It is therefore not improbable that its origins are to be sought in Nehemiah's governorship, and that it constituted in its earliest form an inaugural act of penitence with which the exiles commenced the new phase of their theocracy at Jerusalem.[1] But if this conjecture is substantially correct, the ritual seems to belong to a more primitive state of culture with Babylonian affinities.

The fundamental conception of sin and atonement is that of a ritual uncleanness which can be removed by substances charged with magico-religious potency, or driven forth by means of a scapegoat. That the Azazel episode owed its origin to a " pagan or semi-pagan man " of that name seems to us less probable on the whole than that it was the designation of a pastoral deity, like the Babylonian Ninamašazagga, " the shepherd of the sacred goats of Enlil,"[2] and so the patron of herdsmen to whom offerings were made to protect and conserve the life of the group and its flocks. His character, however, may have undergone considerable modification in his abode in " solitary lands," since waste places were regarded by the Semites as haunted by demons. In such an environ-

---

[1] It is not improbable that Nehemiah took advantage of the New Moon Festival in the seventh month to re-dedicate the altar and the priesthood, the rite of expiation being the concluding ceremony on the eighth day.

[2] Langdon, *The Expository Times*, 1912, xxiv, p. 12 ; *Mythology of All Races*, vol. v (Lond., 1931), pp. 356 f.

ment a beneficent deity would readily become associated with the *se'irim*, and in this rôle, if his memory and individuality were sufficiently sustained by ritual, he would be well on his way to becoming the leader and author of the forces of evil (cf. Enoch vi. 7 ; ix. 6; x. 4–6).

But whatever may have been the original nature of Azazel, when he is first encountered in the Old Testament, and the later Jewish writings, he is represented as a sin-receiver not altogether unfriendly to man inasmuch as he is the recipient of the sins of Israel carried away by the animal dedicated to him. What was the fate of the goat in the " solitary land " we are not told in the Levitical narrative, but the Mishna Tract *Yoma* says it was thrown over a precipice.[1] This suggests that by the second century A.D. the victim was definitely regarded as a " substitute " whose death was part of the act of atonement. In the Biblical account, however, the dismissal of the living animal, like the living bird in the purification of the leper in Lev. xiv. 7, was apparently sufficient for the removal of the uncleanness, Azazel and not the goat being the ultimate depository of the guilt of the nation. The actual atonement was made by the application of the blood of the sin-offerings, and the smoke of the life-giving incense, so that the scapegoat was merely the vehicle by which the sin was carried away to Azazel in the wilderness.

So far, then, as our knowledge of the ritual of the Day of Atonement recorded in Leviticus is concerned, it would appear that at the close of the fifth century

[1] *Yoma*, 6.

B.C. the general principles of the ceremonial belonged to a conception of sin and its removal far nearer to the primitive ideas than to those of either Moses or Ezra.[1] The expiation was mainly a mechanical process dealing with material uncleanness, though doubtless it had also an ethical significance. The book of Leviticus is a *rituale* rather than a manual of private devotion like the Psalms (cf. Ps. xl., l., li.), and consequently the more spiritual aspects of the sacrificial worship are no more apparent than in the rubrics of the Latin Missal. Since the goat was loaded with *all* the sins of Israel (Lev. xvi. 34) it may be conjectured that, despite the primitive setting of the ritual, something more than expiation for the impaired ceremonial holiness of the community was involved. At the same time, it is misleading to assume with Delitzsch that the Day of Atonement was the Good Friday of the Law inasmuch as the ideas which found expression in the Christian doctrine of propitiation belong to a later and different stage in the development of the institution of sacrifice.

Mishnaic Atonement

In later Judaism the Rabbinic penitential theory advanced religiously to a much higher level, the earlier crude notions of atoning sacrifices undergoing a profound change in an ethical direction. As Dr. Büchler says, " acts of repentance, restitution, conciliation and confession preceding the sin-offering, and their religious and moral values give insight into the Rabbinic concepts of sin and sacrificial atone-

[1] Cf. Frazer, *G.B.*, pt. ix. (" The Scapegoat "), p. 210; G. B. Gray, *Sacrifice in the Old Testament* (Oxford, 1925), p. 315.

ment." [1]   The Mishnaic atonement, in fact, consists in a complete act of repentance, and if " good works " include almsgiving, fasting, and other asceticisms, together with the appropriate sin-offerings, the ultimate aim is the ethical righteousness insisted on by the Hebrew prophets. [2]

The blood of the sacrifices no longer had a magico-religious purgative action in wiping away non-moral uncleanness, and having acquired a spiritual and symbolic significance, repentance alone sufficed for venial sins. More " grievous " (in Christian terminology, " mortal ") offences required ceremonial expiation through the Day of Atonement ritual, but the rites must be performed with sincerity of heart and true repentance to be efficacious. [3]   Moreover, the sinner must make peace with an offended brother before he could claim the forgiveness of heaven, so that the prophetic and ethical conception of repentance was brought into relation with the priestly and sacrificial by the Rabbinical doctrine in a manner which gave the prophetic element the predominance.   Thus, even before the cessation of sacrifice after the destruction of the temple, the supreme importance of prayer and penitence as a means of atonement, emphasized by the prophets, was maintained in the Rabbinic penitential theory, and survived the catastrophe of A.D. 70. [4]

Mediation

The idea of mediation, however, which became a

---

[1] *Studies in Sin and Atonement* (Oxford, 1928), p. xiv.
[2] Cf. C. G. Montefiore, *Jewish Quarterly Review*, Old Series xvi, 1904, pp. 215 ff.
[3] *Yoma*, viii. 9.
[4] Cf. Chap. ix, pp. 263 ff. for further discussion of the Rabbinic theory.

cardinal doctrine of Christianity, was never developed on the same lines in Judaism. The notion of vicarious atonement can be discerned perhaps in the suffering of the nation for the individual (Josh. vii. 10–15), and the individual for the family (2 Sam. xxi. 1–9 ; Deut. v. 9–10), or the nation [1] (Ezek. xxxi. 3, 4 ; Isa. liii.), while intercessory prayer was also a familiar feature in Hebrew religion (Jer. xxvii. 18 ; xlvi. 25 ; Isa. liii. 12 ; cf. Gen. xx. 7, 17 ; Deut. ix. 26 ; Job xlii. 8). But such mediators as Moses, Jeroboam, Job or David are not represented as priests, and their intervention and intercession on behalf of others was not of a sacrificial character. It may be possible, as Dillmann maintains, to read into some of those passages the sinner's need of a mediator who " absorbs into himself the wrath of God, and procures divine grace for him who has made himself unworthy of it." [2] But, nevertheless, the conception of an individual redeemer making an act of atonement as priest and victim to reconcile God and man, in terms of the theology of the Epistle to the Hebrews, was alien to Judaism. To a Jew the idea of anyone being at once a perfect sin-offering and at the same time an ideal high priest of the human race entering the heavenly sphere through his own blood to obtain eternal redemption for mankind, could be but the rankest blasphemy.

The scapegoat ritual, as we have seen, tended to take over a substitutionary character, but not in the sense

[1] Nevertheless, as the individual, apart from the community to which he belonged, had no standing, so conversely he infected all the rest with his own guilt. The doctrine of race solidarity rather than vicarious atonement, therefore, may lie behind these instances.

[2] A. Dillmann, *Handbuch der Altestamentlichen Theologie* (Leipzig, 1895), p. 473.

in which it has been interpreted in Christian theology. The nearest approach to the Christian conception of atonement is in the Servant Saga incorporated in the composite book, Isaiah (Isa. lii. 13–liii.) [1] where suffering and death appear to be regarded as having an atoning value—" he was wounded for our transgressions, he was bruised for our iniquities; the chastisement of our peace was upon him, and with his stripes we are healed " (Isa. liii. 5, cf. 8). It has yet to be proved, however, that the " Servant " was originally identified with the Messiah. Undoubtedly, there is a Messianic tone about such phrases as " I have put my spirit upon him," and " he shall bring forth judgment to the Gentiles " (Isa. xlii. 1), but the rest of the picture, however applicable it may be to the Christ of history and religious experience, scarcely depicts the prevailing Jewish expectations of the greater David, who was destined, it was thought, to restore the former prosperity of Israel.

Such a leader might well be " a man of pains, and known unto sickness," but it would have been fatal to his campaign if he were despised and rejected of men, and if the people hid as it were their faces from him, and esteemed him not. Some of the later Jewish interpreters in the Talmud and the Targums identified the Servant with the Messiah, it is true, but even so they explained away the references to his death in Isa. liii. in terms of the " sickness " fallen upon Israel.[2]

---

[1] While the style and general thought of the Servant Songs (xlii. 1–4; xlix. 1–6, l. 4–9, lii. 13–liii.) are reminiscent of the Deutero-Isaiah, many critics believe them to be the work of a separate author.

[2] R. S. Driver and A. Neubauer, *The 53rd Chapter of Isaiah according to the Jewish Interpreters* (Oxford, 1877), pp. lxvi. ff.

The problem of the sufferings of the righteous became one of increasing perplexity in a monotheistic community as the appreciation of ethical values developed, and the conviction of sin as a moral concept deepened. The strange enigma sent the Psalmist into the temple in despair (Ps. lxxiii. 16 f.), and it inspired the author of the Book of Job to write a magnificent vindication of the moral perfection of Yahweh, but in neither case was any light thrown upon the ultimate question. Some advance was made in the Servant Songs since, whoever the righteous sufferer may have been, his (or their) " sickness " was regarded as having a redemptive significance, since the agony of his soul was likened to the sin-offering (*'āshām*) of a sacrificial victim (Isa. liii. 7, 10). If the " Servant of Yahweh " bore the sins of the people, and worked out their salvation in the travail of his own soul, vicarious suffering is given an expiatory value.

That this interpretation of sin and suffering was unusual is suggested by the reference to the astonishment of all who beheld the strange spectacle (lii. 4), and unquestionably it represents the fullest expression of the doctrine of substitution in Old Testament theology. A mechanical conception of sin, however, underlies the notion of the justified being merely passive partakers in the process of redemption in which they had no active share. Moreover, it failed to vindicate the ethical righteousness of Yahweh inasmuch as it made him satisfied with something less than the moral integrity of the offender. The old notion of the propitiation of angry gods by ritual observances seems to lurk somewhere in the background of this solution of the problem, despite the sublime literary form of the immortal saga.

Nevertheless, it was this exalted picture of the Suffering Servant giving his life a ransom for many which became the inspiration of the Christian doctrine of reconciliation. Originally it may have had little connexion with the Messianic hope, and the notion of a suffering Messiah may have been as vague as in the later Midrashic teaching on the subject,[1] but if, as can hardly be denied, the testimony of the Synoptic Gospels has any veracity at all, it clearly shows that Jesus equated the Messiahship with the Isaianic Servant, and on one occasion He is alleged to have declared that even the apocalyptic Son of Man must suffer (Mark viii. 31). Whatever His attitude towards the notion of the Davidic priest-king may have been, it was the ideal of the Servant, according to the Gospel narratives, which became increasingly the dominant theme of His teaching from the assembly at Cæsarea Philippi onwards (Mark viii. 27–33 ; Matt. xvi. 13–23 ; Luke ix. 18–22). Thus, it is recorded that " he began to teach them that the Son of Man must suffer many things, and be rejected by the elders, and the chief priests, and the scribes, and be killed, and after three days rise again."

The title " Son of Man " is derived from Dan. vii. 27, where the figure is employed to symbolize the " people of the saints of the Most High " (vii. 13 ff.). The imagery is brought into line with the prophetic conception of the Messianic kingdom in the later

---

[1] F. J. Foakes-Jackson and K. Lake, *The Beginnings of Christianity* (Lond., 1920), i, p. 356.

Jewish apocalypses, the Son of Man being interpreted as a celestial quasi-angelic being appointed as the agent of God to judge the world and usher in the New Age when He " comes in the clouds of heaven." [1] Twice He is called " the Anointed " (Enoch xlviii. 10 ; lii. 4), but it is only in the Gospels that the conception is brought into relation with the idea of the Suffering Servant who " came not to be ministered unto but to minister, and to give his life a ransom for many " (Mark x. 44 f. ; Matt. xx. 28).

If the genuineness of these far-reaching words as an original saying of Jesus has been questioned by not a few New Testament critics and theologians, [2] there can be no doubt as to their appropriateness as an interpretation of early Christian thought when the death of Christ came to be regarded as the Son of Man entering into His glory through suffering. Moreover, it must be admitted that the attempt to discredit the authenticity of the words has not been very successful. It is not part of our present purpose to enter into theological and metaphysical questions concerning the Messianic consciousness of Jesus, but in the light of the recent work of Schweitzer and the eschatological school of interpreters, [3] which incidentally is not now as moribund as is sometimes imagined by *English* theologians, the attitude of Christ to the Servant Songs, and His own approaching death to set up the kingdom,

[1] R. H. Charles, *Apocrypha and Pseudigrapha of the Old Testament* (Oxford, 1913), ii, p. 214 ; cf. *Ethiopic Enoch*, xlvi ; xlviii, 2 ff. ; lii. 4 ; lxix. 26 ff. ; 2 *Esdras*, xiii.

[2] H. Rashdall, *The Idea of Atonement in Christian Theology* (Lond., 1920), pp. 49 ff.

[3] Schweitzer, *The Quest of the Historical Jesus* (Lond., 1910), Eng. trans., pp. 388, cf. 353 ; cf. J. Weiss, *Die Predigt Jesu vom Reiche Gottes* (Göttingen, 1892), pp. 58 ff., 158 ff.

take over a new significance. If, after the Cæsarea Philippi gathering, He realized that the Messianic hopes could be fulfilled only through some great act of self-sacrifice, the Isaianic notion of the Servant bearing the sins of the "many," and working out their salvation in the travail of His own soul, could hardly fail to be an inspiration for what lay ahead. In other words, it is reasonable to suppose that He accepted the *rôle* of the Servant just as apparently He had seen already in the current eschatological ideas concerning the Son of Man a reference to Himself and His mission.

Taken together, these two figures constitute the background of the Messianic thought in the Gospel narrative, and whatever may have been the precise evaluation put upon them by Jesus Himself, that He first realized the Messianic import of the prophecies is suggested by the reluctance of His followers to look upon His death as anything but a catastrophe and the death-blow to all their hopes and aspirations (Matt. xvi. 22, xxvi. 22; Luke xxiv. 21). It was not until the crisis was over that it dawned upon them that it behoved the Messiah thus to suffer and die (Acts xvii. 1–3); still less did they realize that the tragedy was capable of a sacrificial interpretation.

The Christian Doctrine of the Atonement

By about the year A.D. 55 we find St. Paul as part of the tradition which he had received proclaiming that "Christ died for our sins according to the scriptures" (1 Cor. xv. 3), and if we are correct in thinking that he derived his initial information from the Church of Jerusalem,[1] the origin of the Christian

[1] Cf. Chap. VI, p. 166.

conception of atonement must be sought in the interval between the crucifixion and St. Paul's conversion.[1]
In the formulation of his theory of mediation the apostle was undoubtedly influenced by the sacrificial ideas in which he had been trained, and by his own spiritual experience. He was conscious of having been " bought with a price " (1 Cor. vi. 20, vii. 23), and for him Jesus was the victorious Messiah who had established a new covenant through His sacrificial death, whereby He satisfied the justice of God and secured the " acquittal " or " justification " of a guilty race (Gal. ii. 17; iii. 15ff., iv. 5–7; Rom. iii. 24; viii. 1, 17, 33; 1 Cor. i. 8; 2 Cor. v. 21). Sin he regarded as a moral disorder, and since God is essentially righteous and just, atonement entailed the vicarious suffering of one who knew no sin " set forth by God to be a propitiation through faith in his blood, to show his righteousness " (Rom. iii. 19–26).

In its later guise this forensic interpretation of the death of Christ developed into the grotesque theology which represented the offering on Calvary as a ransom paid by God to Satan to rescue a ruined race from his clutches. The theory is differently expressed by different writers, but from the third century to the eleventh a transactional doctrine prevailed. In the skilful hands of Anselm and the scholastics the more extreme presentations were modified by the introduction of the term " satisfaction " in place of " ransom," the emphasis then being laid on the vindication of God's honour rather than the pseudo-legal transaction with the devil.[2] The death voluntarily borne

[1] Cf. Rashdall, *op. cit.*, pp. 75 f.　[2] *Cur Deus Homo* (Lond., 1889), pp. 8 ff., 100 ff.

when it was not due was the infinite satisfaction which secured the salvation of man. But it still remained a vicarious offering of a substitute differing from the former theory in making the rights of God instead of those of Satan the object of the act of satisfaction.

Against these legalistic interpretations the moral aspect of the atonement was brought into prominence by men like Gregory of Nazianzum.[1] This movement found its fullest expression in Abelard, who in his *Commentary on the Romans* described the death of Christ as the supreme exhibition of the love of God rather than either a ransom to Satan or a satisfaction of divine wrath. The justification of man, on this hypothesis, is " that loftiest love inspired in us by the passion of Christ." [2] This view was never adopted by the Church, and it was completely repudiated by the reformers who redeveloped the penal theory in its crudest form, denying the Anselmic distinction between satisfaction and the infliction of penalty.[3] This attitude has remained characteristic of Protestant theology though various attempts have been made to restate in modern terms the notion that the death of Christ owed its saving power to its penal quality.[4]

In popular theology of a Catholic type, and in the more learned works, some modification of the objective or Anselmic Satisfaction Theory has usually held the field. All forensic interpretations have tended to

[1] *Poemata Dogmatica*, i, viii, 65, 69 (Migne, xxxvii, 470).

[2] iii. 22–6.

[3] Calvin, *Institutes*, II, xii, 1 ; cf. J. Köstlin, *The Theology of Luther*, Eng. trans. by Hay (Philad., 1883), ii, pp. 388 ff.

[4] Cf. J. McLeod Campbell, *Nature of the Atonement* (Lond., 1886) ; R. W. Dale, *The Atonement* (Lond., 1875) ; J. Scott Lidgett, *The Spiritual Principle of the Atonement* (Lond., 1901).

be rejected with every conception of a substitutionary imputation of righteousness.[1] R. C. Moberly in *Atonement and Personality*[2] retains McLeod Campbell's theory of vicarious penitence in place of vicarious suffering, and against Dale he holds that punishment is not primarily retributive in character ; though both Dale and Moberly regard the Cross as the central fact of Christianity. Like the early Fathers, Moberly interprets the Atonement in terms of the incarnation,[3] the perfect penitence and obedience of a sinless representative of ideal humanity being regarded as an adequate atonement for human transgression.[4]   Thus he retains a vicarious transaction, and preserves the independent value of Christ's sacrificial action, while by insisting on His universal humanity and the mediatorial work of the Holy Spirit, he passes from the objective to the subjective aspect of the problem. Nevertheless, as Dr. Mozley points out, " he pushes the Irenæan *recapitulatio* to a point where a crude realism seems the inevitable result."[5]

Rashdall, on the other hand, breaks away entirely from all objective sacrificial notions, and falls back on the subjective Abelardian view which involves no idea of substitution or expiation at all, and makes " the atoning efficacy of Christ's work depend upon the subjective and ethical effects produced by the contemplation of that work upon the mind of the

---

[1] H. N. Oxenham, *The Catholic Doctrine of the Atonement* (Lond., 1869), pp. 172 ff., 248 f. ; Grensted, *A Short History of the Doctrine of the Atonement* (Manchester, 1920), pp. 184 f.

[2] J. F. di Bruno, *Catholic Belief* (Lond., 1884), p. 49.

[3] Irenæus, *Adv. Haer.*, v.

[4] Moberly, pp. 110, 130, 259, 405.

[5] Mozley, *The Doctrine of the Atonement* (Lond., 1915), p. 213.

believer." [1] The mission of Christ, it is contended, was to proclaim that God is willing to forgive sin. "Forgiveness is dependent upon no condition whatever but repentance, and the amendment which is the necessary consequence of sincere repentance." [2]

That the Bampton Lectures for 1915 represent one of the landmarks in the interpretation of the Christian doctrine of the Atonement is a mere truism, and Dr. Rashdall had no difficulty in showing that, from the point of view of scholarship, most of the standard treatises on the subject are obsolete. Dale's book he dismisses as "absolutely pre-critical and unconvincing," while Moberly's volume is merely "an attempt to combine modern or liberal with traditional theories which, in spite of all his subtlety, still stand apart in his pages like oil and water." [3] All this, and similar strictures on other modern writers, is true enough, but Rashdall's own treatment of the historical evidence is open to serious criticism. As to what the death of Christ signified in ultimate reality, it is not our purpose to inquire, but as an historical phenomenon it belongs essentially to the institution of sacrifice. It may be true that to-day sacrificial ideas do not play a prominent part in the modern mind, but it was otherwise at the beginning of our era. Then, as Dr. Glover has said, " sacrifice was a language used by all men," [4] and the New Testament is certainly no exception to the rule. It is impossible to eliminate the notion of propitiation and atonement in these documents without doing violence to the canons of scienti-

[1] *The Idea of the Atonement*, p. 437.
[2] *Op. cit.*, p. 25.   [3] *Op. cit.*, pp. 46, 496.
[4] *Jesus in the Experience of Men* (Lond., 1921), p. 63.

fic criticism. From the earliest times of which we have knowledge the mystery of Calvary was interpreted in the light of the Old Testament theology and the Isaianic Servant prophecies. This is borne out, as we have seen, by a critical analysis of the Synoptic Gospels, the Pauline writings and the literature of the Early Church,[1] while the Epistle to the Hebrews is an elaborate discourse on the high priesthood of Christ.

The authorship of this last-mentioned book has been a matter of conjecture, of course, from the days of the ancient Fathers, when Tertullian regarded it as the work of St. Barnabas, and Origen, after defending the Pauline theory, became more cautious, concluding finally that " who wrote it God only knows certainly." But if the writer is lost in obscurity, he must have lived before A.D. 96, since the epistle is quoted by St. Clement, who worked out an analogy between the Jewish and Christian ministries along the lines of the similarity of function of Christ and the High Priest.[2] The general circumstances point to the second generation of the Church as the most likely date of composition (cf. xiii. 2), perhaps before the destruction of Jerusalem (cf. x. 25 ; viii. 13 ; xiii. 13), between A.D. 64 and 70, though the reference to Timothy in xiii. 23 may suggest a later period. In any case, the document reveals the theological outlook of the Church in Rome (cf. xiii. 24) at the end of the first century.

The central theme is the conception of Christ sealing the new dispensation with His blood as that of the

[1] A. E. J. Rawlinson, *The New Testament Doctrine of the Christ* (Lond., 1926), pp. 45 f.
[2] Clem. xl, 5 ; cf. xxxvi.

true Paschal Lamb in fulfilment of the sacrificial system of the Old Testament. That the offering on Calvary made a real expiation for sin is clearly established in contrasting the perfect sacrifice of His own blood with the ineffectual and impotent offerings of the blood of bulls and goats, which, except as shadows of the true, could have no real atoning significance (Heb. ix. 11–28). As the High Priest of the new Covenant, Christ is represented as entering " the holy place " through the outpouring of His blood in sacrifice, and there ever living to make intercession as " a ministering priest in the true tabernacle, the immediate presence of God." [1]

A significant feature in this argument is the emphasis laid on the victory rather than the sufferings of the mediator, the act of atonement being completed in the heavenly sphere of its eternal operations. The Cross is set forth as the path to the " new and living way " by which the triumphant Saviour passed into the heavens. It is still by virtue of His passion that He is qualified to make propitiation for the sins of His people, but the notion of the Suffering Servant is carried to what the author regards as its ultimate conclusion, viz. to " bring many sons to glory " (ii. 10) by the removal of the barrier set up by human transgression (ii. 14). The propitiatory value of the death of Christ, on this hypothesis, therefore, lies in the gift of life secured by His atoning sacrifice.

In developing this line of thought the author is nearer to the general theme running through the institution of sacrifice in its various manifestations

G. B. Stevens, *The Christian Doctrine of Salvation* (Edin., 1905), p. 87.

than is the case when the death of the victim is made the central feature of the offering. In all its manifold modes of expression the fundamental idea in sacrifice is the promotion and conservation of life, and while this often entails the death, or destruction, of the person or thing offered, this is merely incidental in the process of liberating *life*. It may be a far cry from crude notions of the reanimation of mortal gods to a voluntary act of self-giving on the part of one whose whole being was animated by entire dedication to a sacred purpose, yet there is a unity of principle in the desire for " newness of life " which finds expression in a complex death and resurrection ritual pattern.

As Mr. Hocart has said, " the sacrificial lamb is no longer the young of an ewe slaughtered at the Paschal Feast as the embodiment of some god in order to promote the life of the crops, but a symbol expressing, by what psychologists call condensation, a sum of innocence, purity, gentleness, self-sacrifice, redemption and divinity which no words could express with such forceful appeal." [1] The old drama of creation and redemption is repeated through a divine kingship, the new Spiritual King, " incarnated once for all in order ever after to rule over the souls of men," invested in a scarlet robe, a crown of thorns, and a reed for a sceptre,[2] dying to live on a cross which has become symbolized as the tree of life.

The Adam-story ends in ruin, but it is ruin which has the promise of redemption (Gen. iii. 15). The sacrificial drama of Good Friday has been interpreted,

[1] *Kingship*, p. 243.   [2] *Op. cit.*, p. 16.

therefore, in terms of the original catastrophe embodied in (or read into) the creation legend, so that Christian mysticism has found in the Cross the way of the tree of life which ultimately leads to the celestial paradise in which " in the midst of the street of it, and on either side of the river was there the tree of life, which bare twelve manner of fruits, and yielded her fruit every month ; and the leaves of the tree were for healing of the nations " (Rev. xxii. 2). Thus, true to type, the tree of life has the promise of immortality, the divine kingship finding its consummation in the celestial realms when the " kingdoms of this world become the kingdoms of our Lord and of his Christ ; and he shall reign for ever and ever " (Rev. xi. 15). In this repetition of the creation story in a ritual of redemption a fundamental aspect of the culture pattern is preserved in the institution of sacrifice.

CHAPTER VIII

PRIESTHOOD AND THE ALTAR

BEFORE bringing to a close this analysis of the principal elements in the institution of sacrifice, the question of sacerdotal intervention requires some consideration, inasmuch as an organized mediatorial priesthood reserving to itself the service of the altar is an integral part of the later developments of the ritual. Moreover, in the capacity of magician, the " consecrated man " occupies a prominent position in the lower cultures, though it does not thereby follow, as Frazer suggests, that the priest is the linear successor of the medicine man who was led to renounce his attempts to control directly the processes of nature, and sought to attain the same end indirectly by appealing to the gods to do for him what he no longer fancied he could do for himself.[1]

This theory is more simply stated than proved since it rests on the assumption that a pre-theistic age of magic preceded an age of religion in which the magician alone held sway, essaying to " bend nature to his wishes by the sheer force of spells and enchantments, before he strove to mollify a coy, capricious or irascible deity by the soft insinuation of prayer and sacrifice." [2] But no tribe or group exists in which a period of pure " godless " magic prevails, and while it is not possible to speak with the same degree of

[1] *Early History of Kingship* (Lond., 1905), p. 127.   [2] *Op. cit.*, p. 90.

assurance concerning the prehistoric cultures, there is no actual evidence of a Palæolithic age of magic.

Magic and Religion

If Frazer's distinction between magic and religion be accepted, it follows that it is the psychological approach to the category of the sacred which characterizes the nature of a rite as one of compulsion or supplication.[1] It may be more probable, on this hypothesis, that the emotions of a worshipper kneeling before an altar will be more strictly religious than those of a Palæolithic hunter engaged in a pantomimic dance in the inner recesses of a Pyrenæan cavern sanctuary, but until it has been ascertained whether the desire is to placate or compel the superior power, the precise nature of the action, on this estimation, cannot be determined. It is, therefore, exceedingly difficult to draw a hard-and-fast line between a magical and a religious traffick with the supernatural where any external source of strength is involved.

In almost every community certain persons have been accredited with powers to control at will the normal course of natural laws and forces independent of any external agency, and this may go back to the time when the chase was controlled by depicting the figures of animals in certain sacred spots presumably by certain sacred persons. But in addition to this organized ritual, probably every man had his own magical devices whereby he secured for himself health and good luck by the aid of teeth, claws, shells and similar objects charged with soul-substance and super-

[1] Cf. *G.B.*, pt. 1 ("Magic Art"), p. 222.

natural properties. That is to say, at all times man has believed that by the aid of certain objects and substances, usually connected with the notion of vitality, he could turn the course of nature to his own advantage, with or without the help of a professional practitioner. In this sense it is true to speak of a primitive " age of magic," but it does not represent a stratum in an evolutionary process.

In any complex religious rite a great deal of the ritual, separated from its context, would appear to belong to the category of magic. Thus, in the case of the institution of sacrifice with which we are here concerned, the disposition of the blood at the altar, and of special parts of the victim, the wearing of the skin by the officiant, and similar aspects of the ceremonial, are efficacious by virtue of an inherent potency. Yet, on Frazer's definition, the whole observance is charged with a religious sanctity inasmuch as the supernatural power which gives the ceremonies their significance is derived from supernatural beings superior and external to man. Magic, as Malinowski says, is " an essentially human possession, enshrined in man and can be handed on only from man to man, according to very strict rules of magical filiation, initiation and instruction. It is thus never conceived as a force of nature, residing in things, acting independently of man, to be found out and learned by him, by any of those proceedings by which he gains his ordinary knowledge of nature." [1] The real virtue of magic is embodied in spell and in specific rites performed for a definitely magical purpose in conjunction

[1] Malinowski, in *Science, Religion, and Reality* (Lond., 1926), p. 71.

with certain mystic formulæ which constitute the vehicle of the spell.

If a time ever existed when the magician alone held sway, at least we have no knowledge of it. The earliest traffick with the supernatural order known to archæology is connected with the cult of the dead and the food supply. In both there is undoubtedly a magical element inasmuch as the power is exercised in some measure by human agencies through natural objects, or formulæ. But permeating the whole *cultus* are influences outside a purely magical control. Thus in the case of the funerary ritual, death is regarded as the gate to a new life which must inevitably belong to another world, and if we know little of what this "otherness" signified to Neanderthal man, the hope of immortality is a religious concept, however much human enterprise may seek quasi-magical ways and means of meeting the final crisis. Similarly, in the effort to maintain the food supply, if man resorts to his own devices to secure the desired end, he also endeavours to conciliate and establish right relations with animal species whom he regards as in many respects his superiors.[1] In the Palæolithic cults in question, therefore, we are on the border-land between magic and religion which seems to be best described by the cumbrous and question-begging phrase, "magico-religious."[2]

Again, in the higher systems, the mutual dependence of the gods on man, and man on the gods, a notion which, as we have seen, is fundamental in the early

[1] Cf. Chap. I, pp. 25 ff.
[2] *Notes and Queries on Anthropology* (Lond., 1912), p. 251.

developments of sacrifice, comes into this same category inasmuch as the superior powers are not entirely
outside the sphere of human control, though at the
same time they are recognized as supreme so long
as they are able to perform their functions. Their
agents on earth, in like manner, are not magicians
uttering spells, but mediators with the supernatural
order to secure the welfare of the community by their
administrations. The ritual they perform may contain a constraining element because agent and act are
not clearly differentiated, but the action is directed
mainly outwards.

Thus, in the matter of rain-making, while the
officiant in his private practice may exercise magical
rites, in his public capacity he acts as a mediator with
the gods, ancestral spirits or totems. The *bain*, or
Dinka rain-makers, for example, attain very considerable power in the tribe as consecrated persons, but it
is really Dengdit, Great Rain, the high god, who
sends the rain from the rain-place, which is his special
home. The ancestral rain-making ceremony takes
place at his shrine in each tribe, where the god has his
abode as well as " in the above," and whither the Agar
people resort to install their new rain-maker.

Moreover, in the case of a powerful and highly
successful practitioner, it is thought that the spirit of
a renowned ancestor has come down to him through
a succession of rain-makers, and thus given him insight and wisdom superior to that of other *bain*. The
Shish maintained that a spirit named Mabor, one of the
four sons of Dengdit, was immanent in their rain-
maker, and, according to Dr. Seligman, " the per-

sonality of the rain-maker was submerged in that of the spirit immanent in him, so that when they spoke of Mahor, the dominant idea in their mind was that of the ancestral spirit of this name working in the body of the man in whom it was immanent." [1]

Again, in the much-discussed conception of *mana* as a kind of impersonal mystic influence attached to sacred objects, it would seem, as Codrington maintained, that " this power, though itself impersonal, is always connected with some person. If a stone is found to have a supernatural power, it is because a spirit has associated itself with it." [2] Similarly, the Iroquoian *orenda* is analogous to will and intelligence rather than to purely mechanical force,[3] while *wakonda*, " the power that moves," is ascribed anthropomorphic attributes by the Omaha who address prayers to it.[4] The term *manitu* is only applied by the Eastern Algonquian to sacred objects, such as an arrow, into which a spirit, or *genius loci*, has transformed itself,[5] while among the Dakota *wakan*, or the divine power, is only assigned to objects or functions which come from wakan beings.[6]

Behind all these more or less impersonal notions, therefore, there is the shadowy form of a personal being. Thus in Melanesia the *mana* which gives sacredness to stones also equips chiefs for their office, so that in the Eastern Solomons hereditary chieftain-

[1] Seligman, " Dinka," in *E.R.E.*, iv, p. 711.
[2] *Melanesians* (Oxford, 1891), p. 119; cf. Hocart, *Man*, 1914, p. 46.
[3] Hewitt, *Handbook of American Indians* (Wash., 1907-10); ii, p. 147.
[4] *27th R.B.A.E.* (Wash., 1911), pp. 134, 597.
[5] *Journal of American Folk-lore*, xvii, 1914, pp. 349 ff.
[6] W. Jones, *Journal of American Folk-lore*, xviii, 1905, pp. 183 ff.

ship seems to rest on the belief that a particular person has inherited from the *tindalo*, or ghosts, sufficient *mana* to qualify him for the post.[1] Similarly, in Morocco the sultan, who is regarded as the vicegerent of God, owes his position to the *baraka* which he inherits or appropriates from his predecessor.

This *baraka* is in the nature of an indwelling animating principle, or soul-substance, upon which both the life and office of the chief and the welfare of the whole country depend. " When it is strong and unpolluted the crops are abundant, the women give birth to children, and the country is prosperous in every respect; in the summer of 1908 the natives of Tangier attributed the exceptionally good sardine fishery to Mûläil-Ḥâfiḍ's accession to the throne. On the other hand, in the reign of his predecessor the deterioration or loss of the Sultan's *baraka* showed itself in disturbances and troubles, in drought and famine, and in the fruit falling down from the trees before it was ripe. Nay even in those parts of Morocco which are not subject to the Sultan's worldly rule the people believe that their welfare, and especially the crops, are dependent upon his *baraka*." [2]

But *baraka* is not the peculiar possession of the Sultan, though he has it in an exceptional degree as " the vicegerent of God on earth," and also the head of the 'Alawîyin, or family of shereefs (i.e. descendants in the male line of the daughter of Muhammed), whose ancestors came from Yanbo in Arabia and settled down in Tafilelt. Since Muhammed was of all men filled

[1] Rivers, *History of Melanesian Society* (Camb., 1914), ii, pp. 101 ff.
[2] Westermarck, *Ritual and Belief in Morocco* (Lond., 1926), i, p. 39.

with " blessed virtue " (*baraka*), his descendants, the shereefs, inherited a portion of it, though not to a sufficient degree to enable them to be regarded as saints, except in a few very special cases. The term saint in Morocco is applied to a person with an unusual endowment of *baraka*, and this being a transmissible quality, the descendants (*mrâbṭin*) of a saintly ancestor become a religious nobility, independent of the shereefs.

Moreover, though *baraka* is a personal quality it is also capable of communication as a sacred contagion to a place which is in some way connected with a saint, rendering it tabu because charged with mystic power. Similarly, objects personified as saints, or directly associated with them, such as wells, springs, trees, rocks and caves, derive their sanctity and life-giving powers from this contagion, and in consequence they are ascribed fertility and medicinal properties.[1] *Baraka* is also attributed to animals or birds connected with a saint, or which have acquired sacredness in some other connexion. Anything, in fact, which gives evidence of being in possession of inherent vitality, or which has in some particular way come into contact with *baraka*, is regarded as permeated with it. Thus wheat and barley are especially sacred and the last portion of the crop on the field is left untouched for a while, so as to transmit its *baraka* to the next year's crop, as " the bride of the field " from which the corn is to be reborn when the field comes to life again.[2] For a similar reason the threshing-floor must remain unswept in order that the *baraka* in the grain may be transmitted to the next season's crops.

[1] *Op. cit.*, pp. 66 ff. [2] *Op. cit.*, p. 106.

The Priesthood

Baraka, therefore, like *mana*, has a dual character. On the one hand it is in the nature of an inherent, impersonal, vital essence, as in the case of the seed corn, and, on the other hand, it is the underlying relation to a personal being, either the Sultan, a saint, or the shereefs. But the fundamental conception seems to be the personal quality capable of transmission from one generation to another. Now we would suggest it is this notion of handing down divine soul-substance, and the associated supernatural powers, resident in chiefs and kings, that lies at the root of priesthood, and gives religious efficacy to sacerdotal ministrations. The priest *par excellence* is, of course, the divine king himself who in his royal capacity is the natural mediator between the gods and mankind. Thus in Egypt he built the temples and is depicted in the reliefs as worshipping the gods and making offerings to them.[1] But while he had to perform daily ceremonies in connexion with the sun-god,[2] it was only on rare occasions that he was able to fulfil his high-priestly functions. In the performance of his sacerdotal office he was assisted, therefore, by members of his own family, his wife and son,[3] and the more prominent representatives of the local priesthoods.[4]

In Egypt from the fifth dynasty, when the king was regarded as the physical son of the sun-god, divine worship was essentially a royal family cult, the mysterious power shared by gods and kings being passed on

[1] Blackman, *E.R.E.*, x., pp. 293 ff.
[2] Blackman, *Journal of Egyptian Archæology*, iii, 1916, pp. 16 ff.
[3] Erman, *Handbook of Egyptian Religion* (Lond., 1907), p. 72.
[4] *Op. cit.*, pp. 53 f.

by inheritance from one generation to another. But, nevertheless, the fact that royal priestly functions were exercised by virtue of the divine soul-substance temporarily resident in the living manifestation of the sun, or other divinity, and were capable of transmission to others within or without the family circle, implies that the ultimate source of sacerdotal power was external to its agent. Thus, in some communities it was considered possible for a king to lose his divinity through infirmity or old age, thereby showing that his mysterious potency was not his inalienable possession in his own right.

Moreover, if inheritance was the most natural way of transmitting the priestly office from one generation to the next, it was not the only method adopted. In Morocco, for example, the *baraka* of a saint may be passed on to one of his followers (*hdîm*) by spitting into his mouth, or eating food that the holy man has also partaken of,[1] but usually the process of transmission involves special intercourse with the gods or spirits, either by ecstatic communion, or through some material object or social institution directly associated with the celestial order.

When ceremonial initiation is resorted to the ritual is frequently of a secret and mysterious character, performed by certain persons belonging to a particular ruling group or sacred order. On the other hand, ecstatic dreams and visible signs of communion with a tutelary deity are required as a necessary qualification among the Eskimo and Algonquian tribes, and the exhibition of supernatural insight and miraculous

[1] Westermarck, *Ritual and Belief in Morocco*, i, p. 41.

powers is often regarded as sufficient evidence for admission to the shamanistic office. It is doubtful, however, whether shamanism represents a variation of the priesthood regarded as an aspect of the divine kingship, though the two offices not infrequently coexist and react upon one another.

Shamanism

The shaman is at once "priest," prophet and medicine-man, but he always exercises his powers by virtue of his intimate relations with and first-hand knowledge of the supernatural order. Unlike the divine king, he is not himself a manifestation of the gods, and his intercourse with spirits, and access to the spirit-world being direct, he is "called" to rather than installed in his vocation, though the process of initiation generally involves protracted training and instruction in occult methods. In some cases the office is hereditary, but everywhere the supernatural gift is an essential condition to becoming a shaman.[1] Thus, only a person who can show that he is *en rapport* with certain spirits, or has the right disposition, can hope to find a vocation, and where a hereditary system prevails, signs of abnormal qualities are sought in childhood in prospective candidates.

Among the Ostyaks the father chooses one of his sons according to his capacity, to whom he gives his knowledge, while the youth has to do everything in his power to foster a neurotic condition in himself.[2] The Buriat hereditary shaman must display the proper

[1] M. A. Czaplicka, *Aboriginal Siberia* (Oxford, 1914), pp. 169 ff.
[2] *Op. cit.*, p. 177.

symptoms called *Ug garbul,* which consist in fainting-fits, excitability, moroseness, love of solitude and similar indications of a nervous temperament.[1] No one, in fact, among these tribes becomes a shaman of his own free will ; it comes to him, as Miss Czaplicka says, *nolens volens,* like a hereditary disease.[2] The office, therefore, depends on the acquisition of super-natural qualifications regarded as a *sine qua non* in the performance of shamanistic functions.

Among the Transbaikalian Tunguses a man who wishes to enter the sacred profession explains that a certain deceased shaman has visited him in a dream and commanded him to be his successor. He then shows himself " weakly, as if dazed and nervous," and suddenly utters incoherent words, falls unconscious, runs through the forest, lives on the bark of trees, throws himself into fire and water, lays hold on weapons, wounds himself, and generally behaves in a crazy manner. Having thus revealed the necessary symptoms, an old shaman is summoned to instruct the candidate in the lore of the spirits, and acquaint him with the mode of invoking them.[3] Moreover, since tutelaries help him in his struggles with disease, and appear in various forms, sometimes as a man and sometimes as birds, to endow him with power and instruct him, part of the mental training consists in coming into contact with the right spirits (i.e. with those who are his guardians).[4]

[1] A. Bastian, in *Geographische und ethologische Bilder,* Jena, 1873, pp. 402, 406.
[2] *Op. cit.,* p. 178.
[3] V. M. Mikhaïlowsky, *J.A.I.,* xxiv, 1895, pp. 85 ff.
[4] W. Jochelson, *The Koryat, Jesup North Pacific Expedition,* vi, New York, 1905-8, p. 47.

Physical training is also necessary as he must learn to beat the sacred drum accurately, a task requiring considerable skill. He must sing in the approved manner, and dance the ceremonial dances. When all this has been duly accomplished, together with the prescribed fasting and discipline in the matter of diet, the candidate is ready for initiation. Among the Yakut the old shaman who had instructed the novice leads his pupil up a high mountain, or into the open fields, clothes him in shaman's robes, provides him with the tambourine and drumsticks, places on his right nine pure youths, and on his left nine pure maidens. Then he gives him his own robes, and standing behind him makes him repeat certain words, and promise faithful allegiance to his tutelary spirit for the rest of his life. Instruction follows concerning the whereabouts and powers of the various spirits, and the manner of propitiating them. Finally, the old shaman slays the animal selected for sacrifice, sprinkles the candidate's clothing with the blood, and closes the proceedings with a feast on the flesh, in which the spectators take part.[1]

Among the Buryats the rite of consecration begins with a libation, the water being taken from three springs, and fortified with sacred plants and the blood of a sacrificial victim. Then in a few days the first of the nine consecrations begins at a hut or *yurta* prepared for the ceremony. The candidate is smeared with the blood of a sacrificial goat, birched and further instructed before entering the *yurta*. He then takes in his hand horse-staves consecrated for the occasion, and chants adjurations to the lord of the pole-cat who

---

[1] Mikhaïlowsky, *op. cit.*, p. 86.

established shamanism in the tribe. Subsequently he climbs up two trees to symbolize, apparently, his progress towards the heavenly sphere as he advances in the various degrees of consecration. Each stage in the sacred office is marked by additions to the elaborate shamanistic costume and regalia.[1]

In this ritual can be detected something akin to a priestly hierarchy. The birch tree erected in the *yurta* and passing through the roof is supposed to represent the deity opening heaven to the shaman, and that outside is notched in the sides to enable the candidate to spring up from one incision to the next as he ascends from one degree to another. Each notch denotes a special heaven, and every heaven has its special deity with whom he is brought into union at his consecration. Thus the duly consecrated shaman owes his position to his special relationship with the spirits, a relationship which does not depend entirely upon his ordination since the soul-substance in the horse-staves, cut from a live birch tree in a forest where shamans are interred, enables the priest to gallop to heaven when occasion calls for " ghostly counsel and advice " in the execution of his office; or he may summon the spirits to his aid by his tambourine or other heavenly music. Thus equipped, he is ready for any eventuality, but only as the agent of the higher powers with whom he is in constant converse.

If the principal function of shamanism is prophetic in the sense of revealing the mind and will of the gods and spirits, it tends to assume a sacerdotal significance when the shaman is installed in the same manner as a

---

[1] D. Klementz, " Buriat," in *E.R.E.*, iii, pp. 15 f.

priest.   Consequently he may himself on occasions
offer sacrifice and preside at the tribal ceremonies, as,
for example, among the Altai, when at the great
sacrifice to the god Bai-Yulgan he waves a twig over
the horse selected to be the victim in order to drive its
soul to the gods accompanied by that of the man who
holds its head.   Having assembled the spirits in his
tambourine, he sits on the image of a goose in order
to pursue the soul of the horse upon it.   When he
captures it, he blesses it, and with the aid of assistants
slays the horse.   He and the company then solemnly
eat the flesh.   The next evening, after the purificatory
rites have been duly performed, he mounts the heavens
on the soul of the victim, or on the goose, to learn and
utter prophecies, discover whether the sacrifice has
been accepted, and ascertain certain future events, such
as the weather forecast and prospects of harvest,
together with the nature of the offerings which will
then be required.[1]   In recounting his experiences, and
the secrets learned during his visit to the spirit-world,
a dramatic ritual is employed, the shaman acting the
part of the deity, and other supernatural beings whose
voices he reproduces. Thus he combines the
functions of prophet and priest, being at once the
diviner, the possessed and the officiant.

Nevertheless, he is not a true priest in the sense of
being the representative of the divine king, and the
ordained minister of the public rituals.   He may on
occasions function in public ceremonials, but the
séance rather than the temple is his proper sphere of
action.   In Peru sometimes a room was provided for

[1] V. V. Radlov, *Aus Sibiren* (Leipzig, 1884), ii, pp. 20 ff., 49 ff.

this class of functionary within the precincts of the temple where those who so desired could consult him but there was no organized class of prophets, seers, healers and tricksters comparable with and complementary to the political scheme, as in the case of the sacerdotal institution. The priestly office definitely controlled the social order with a carefully prescribed ritual, often of a calendrical character, upon which the well-being of the community depended. If the priesthood ceased, the whole complex ritual pattern would be thrown into confusion. Not so in the case of shamanism. As Clark Wissler has said, " the fact that the shaman lagged behind and shared but little in this elaboration would seem further basis for the assumption that the chief formative factors in priestcraft and ritualism are not found in shamanism." [1]

It is possible that the use of narcotics such as kava, Soma, and Avestan Haoma, and ambrosia, in installation and sacrificial rites constitutes a connecting link between priesthood and shamanism. Thus in Fiji the drinking of kava was the central feature in the installation of a chief, and it was also used in ordination to the priesthood. The purpose of this ceremony as described by Hocart was to possess the initiate by watersprites in the same way as in the Vedic ritual Soma was drunk sacrificially in order to gain immortality by ascending spiritually to heaven and so becoming one with the gods.[2] In both cases an intoxicating plant was employed to induce an ecstatic condition, the narcotic in India and Persia being regarded as itself a

[1] C. Wissler, *The American Indian* (New York, 1922), pp. 203 ff.
[2] *Kingship*, pp. 59 f. ; cf. *Rig Veda*, viii, 48. 3.

royal god. Therefore it was only drunk by the gods and priests as a religious ceremony for the purpose of raising those who partook thereof to the divine order. "We have drunk Soma, we have become immortal, we have entered into the light, we have known the gods." [1] Hence its introduction into the coronation and ordination ritual as a means of imparting to the initiate the divine life which he in turn communicates to the society over which he rules, or in which he functions, by virtue of his divinity. Moreover, since the sacred drink is itself none other than the " real presence " of the god, a sacrificial significance is accorded to the act of crushing the plant comparable with that of the Fraction in the Mass,[2] just as in both rites immortality is conferred through the life-giving elements (cf. St. John vi. 53 f.).

The soma-sacrifice, however, contains a shamanistic as well as a sacerdotal aspect since the priest, unlike the divine king, may become possessed and exercise prophetic and ecstatic functions when stimulated by the divine plant. In the process of becoming immortal signs of divinity may become manifest in occult phenomena, and it is not improbable that stimulation by intoxicating plants has played a prominent part in bringing together the two offices through a common method of initiation, as each began to disintegrate and react on one another.

Divination and Prophetism

Closely allied to shamanism is the practice of divination and prophetism, which again has definite points

---

[1] *Rig Veda,* viii, 48. 3.   [2] Cf. Chap. VI, p. 181.

of contact with the priesthood. Thus, Aztec priests living in the vicinity of the temples declared oracles, and the history of the Delphic oracle shows how the office of diviner can become part of the sacerdotal administration when it is given a social significance. In Babylonia the term *barû*, or soothsayer, meaning " to inspect," was applied to a class of priests whose duty it was to divine the will of the deity by the inspection of the liver, as the seat of the soul-substance of the sheep to be sacrificed.[1] Since the victim was in vital union with the god to whom it was offered, the future could be determined by reading the divine mind as reflected in the soul-substance of the sacrificial animal. Therefore, it was the duty of this class of priest to study the liver and gall-bladder with great care to detect signs which might give a clue to forthcoming events, a custom which led to every part of the organ being noted and interpreted with the minutest care.[2]

A similar practice seems to have prevailed in pre-Exilic Israel where the Hebrew *Kōhēn*, or " seer," was engaged in divining by various devices. Twice in the Old Testament the liver is mentioned as a life-centre (Lam. ii. 11, Prov. vii. 23) possessed of the power of divination by its convulsive motions when taken from a sacrificial victim. In Tobit vi. 4–16, viii. 2, the liver of a fish is referred to in connexion with exorcisms, and in Ezekiel xxi. 21 Nebuchadnezzar is

---

[1] Jastrow, *Religious Beliefs in Babylonia and Assyria* (New York, 1911), p. 149. Since the liver contains about one-sixth of the blood of the human body it would readily become a centre of soul-substance.

[2] Jastrow, *Die Religion Babyloniens und Assyriens* (Giessen, 1912), ii, pp. 210 f.

said to have looked into the animal's liver to divine the road he should take when he stood " at the parting of the ways " leading to Jerusalem, and " Rabbah of the children of Ammon." It would seem, then, that hepatoscopy was not unknown in Israel, though it was not in vogue apparently to the same extent as in Babylonia. Possibly the practice was introduced with the submission of Judah to Tiglath-Pileser since in 2 Kings xvi. 15 it is stated that Ahaz used an old altar for " inquiry," and divination by entrails is the only type which *needs* an altar.

The numinous object *par excellence* in Hebrew tradition in which divination centred was the sacred ark of the covenant. So great was its potency, in fact, that after its recovery and removal to Jerusalem, its sanctuary continued to be the chief home of worship down to the time of the destruction of the city in 585 B.C., while sacrifices were offered there for some time after that event (Jer. xli. 5). As the earthly home of Yahweh it was charged with his personality, or soul-substance, as a kind of miasma clinging to the " mercy seat " which was overlaid with gold, just as gold was built into the altar in the Brahmana ritual to render it immortal.[1] There is reason to think that this metal has played a prominent part as a life-giving agent in the history of religion,[2] and there can be little doubt that it had a similar significance originally in Israel.

Doubtless the details of the construction and contents of the ark were elaborated in the later priestly narrative (Ex. xxv. 10–22, xxxvii. 1–9), but there is

[1] *Satapatha Brahmana*, x, 1, 3, 7.

[2] Moret, *Ann. du Musée Guimet,* Bibl. d'Études, 20, 1902, p. 48. Elliot Smith, *Evolution of the Dragon*, pp. 221 f. Perry, *Children of the Sun*, pp. 388 ff.

reason to think that in a much earlier period the prosperity of the community was bound up with this sacred emblem as the centre of supernatural power, comparable with the Fire-Altar in Vedic India, around which the life-story of Prajapati, the father and creator of gods, was re-enacted. Thus, the ark was alleged to contain stones taken from the sacred mountain and inscribed with the very finger of Yahweh, together with a pot of manna, the heavenly food, and the rod of Aaron. So great was its power that to touch it even by accident proved fatal (2 Sam. vi. 6 f.), and when it was carried to an alien territory it wrought havoc among gods and men alike (1 Sam. v. 3 ff.). It was able to direct its own way home when liberated on the new cart prepared for it, and the two cows responsible for its safe return were immediately sacrificed in its honour (1 Sam. vi. 7 ff.). In short, the ark and Yahweh were practically synonymous terms, both sharing the same divine life, so that on the two occasions when it was not taken to battle Israel was defeated (Num. xiv. 44; Jos. vii. 4), and when it was ultimately captured the glory was said to have departed altogether from the nation (1 Sam. iv. 22). Moreover, it was around this object that the priesthood is represented as having developed.

Here, however, an important question arises. What was the nature of this priesthood that centred in the ark? According to Hebrew tradition it was attended by Moses and Aaron through all the wanderings in the desert (Ex. xviii. 15, xxxiii. 7–11), and when Joshua was appointed he departed not out of " the tent of meeting " (Ex. xxxiii. 11). Nevertheless, only in one instance (Ps. xcix. 8) is Moses actually *entitled* priest, and this passage belongs to the post-Exilic literature. Elsewhere he is essentially the vehicle of revelation—the law-giver and prophet—or, according to P, the human instrument employed in instituting the Aaronic priesthood (Ex. xxviii., Lev. viii.). It was he, in the opinion of this school (P), who initiated the sacrificial system at the newly-erected altar, and for a week exercised sacerdotal functions at it, but only during the ceremonial installation of Aaron and his sons. This accomplished, he ceased to usurp priestly rights.

It is highly improbable that this account preserves the actual historical circumstances under which the Levitical order came into being. In tracing the origin of the post-Exilic system to the great Law-giver and " culture hero " of Israel, the priestly writer was merely following a well-established custom in ancient society, and this is not the only similar practice that was assigned to Moses in Hebrew tradition. Thus snake worship was attributed to him, and possibly at one time he was held to be the author of the bull cult at Dan and Bethel (2 Kings xviii. 4). Outside the Priestly narrative, however, there are few allusions to a Mosaic priesthood, and none to an exclusive Aaronic order, though Moses is represented as the son-in-law of Jethro, the priest of Midian (Ex. ii. 16ff.), and he is also regarded as the ancestor of the Danite succession (Jud. xvii. 7 ff., xviii).

The fact that he is said to have " hearkened to the voice of his father-in-law, and to have done all that he had said " (Ex. xviii. 24) suggests that he may have been initiated into his office by Jethro during his sojourn in Midian,[1] and in this case it is significant that the incident at the burning bush is alleged to have occurred while he was keeping the flocks of his teacher (Ex. iii. 2). Visionary experience of this nature is not an unusual accompaniment of the attainment of the prophetic office, and if Moses was the recipient of such a revelation it explains why his conception of the deity was incompatible with the Egyptian pattern based on the divine kingship. Hence the subsequent contention between the agricultural and nomadic sections of the community, and their varying attitudes to Yahweh worship.

The institution of sacrifice cannot be excluded from the pre-Exilic cultus, as has been demonstrated, and it is not improbable that Moses was initiated into this priestly ritual, but, nevertheless, he was essentially an organ of revelation just as the Hebrew *kōhēn*, like the Babylonian *barû*, was first and foremost a soothsayer and seer. There is no evidence in the Old Testament of ecstatic conditions on the part of the priests in pre-Exilic times, but oracular divination and prophetism apparently were their chief functions. Thus, when Micah required ministrations he established an ephod not an altar, and consecrated one of his sons to serve the shrine ; the priestly writer adding significantly, "in those days there was no king in Israel" (Jud. xvii. 5). In the person of Samuel (at least according to the compiler of the book of Samuel) priest and prophet were combined, but even so it was he who restored the "open vision" in Israel (1 Sam. iii. 1), and throughout the monarchy the cult of the

---

[1] G. B. Gray, *Sacrifice in the Old Testament*, p. 207.

visionary experience was highly developed, notably in connexion with the ark.

Between David and the Exile, however, the king exercised a sacerdotal ministry as the duly *anointed* servant of Yahweh, and he did not hesitate to offer sacrifice when occasion demanded (1 Sam. xv. ; 1 Kings ix. 25 ; 2 Kings xii. 33, xvi. 12, cf. Jer. xxx. 21 ; 2 Chron. xxvi. 16). Furthermore, at the coming of the ark to Shiloh David is described as wearing a linen ephod like Samuel (2 Sam. vi. 14, cf. 1 Sam. ii. 18), while the fact that his sons are said to have been priests suggests that the office was hereditary in the royal family.

As the community contracted and attempts were made to centralize worship at Jerusalem, the sacerdotal order was systematized, especially after the reformation of Josiah, if Deuteronomy [or part of it] is to be identified with the law-book discovered in Israel. Up to this time at any rate all Levites were priests, but there is no evidence that in pre-exilic Israel the guardians of the sanctuary and interpreters of the oracle were ever anointed to their office, though this method of initiation appears to have been adopted occasionally in the case of the prophets (1 Kings xix. 16). Nevertheless, some of the priests of the more important shrines enjoyed considerable prestige, those of Dan, and possibly also the house of Eli at Shiloh, tracing their descent to Moses.[1]

The transference of worship to Jerusalem, and the degradation of the priests who had ministered at the local shrines, gave the sons of Zadok precedence in the temple ritual. This prepared the way for the

[1] Cf. Gray, *Sacrifice in the Old Testament*, p. 209.

hierarchical system after the Exile to take the place of the monarchy as the ruling body, fully equipped with the high priest as the spiritual head of Israel embodying all the former royal glory of the nation, assisted by the family of Aaron, with the rest of the tribe of Levi as subordinates.

How Aaron came to replace Zadok in the post-Exilic community is not explained, but it is not improbable that the new name denotes a widening of the hereditary office.[1] Dr. Kennett has suggested that after the fall of Jerusalem the people who remained in Judæa, being deprived of their priests, appealed to the Bethelite or Aaronite priests to exchange Bethel for Jerusalem. Joshua the colleague of Zerubbabel, was one of these, and by a genealogical fiction this Bethelite (and Aaronite) priest was made son or grandson of Seraiah, the last of the Zadokite priests before the Exile.[2] This theory, however, involves placing Deuteronomy towards the end of the Exile instead of in its customary place a generation before. There are, therefore, serious critical difficulties in the way of accepting this ingenious hypothesis. Nevertheless, it is probably true that the extension of the priesthood began in Palestine during the Captivity.

The kingship survived in theory until after the return from Babylonia though it no longer had a sacerdotal significance (Ezek. xxxiv. 23 f., xxxvi. 24 f.). No mention of the office of high priest, however, is made by Ezekiel, and in the restored community in Palestine Zerubbabel the Davidic prince, and Joshua

---

[1] A. Kuenen, *The Religion of Israel* (Lond., 1875), Eng. trans., ii, pp. 203 ff.
[2] Kennett, *J.T.S.*, vi, 1905, pp. 161–86.

the priest, exercised dual control. But with the removal of the civil governor the royal line came to an end and the chief priest was left as the highest Jewish official in the land. It was then that he automatically occupied the position vacated by the royal occupant of the throne, and, like the king, he became the only anointed person in the nation (Num. xxxv. 25; Lev. xvi. 32; cf. Ex. xxix. 7; Lev. viii. 12), though later the rite was extended to all priests (Ex. xxx. 30; cf. 2 Macc. i. 10).

Thus duly installed and consecrated, and invested with his regalia, the high-priest, as "the *anointed*" representative of Yahweh (Lev. iv. 3, 5, 16; vi. 15), speedily assumed the attributes of the divine kingship in a modified form. Consequently his death was not without significance for the well-being of the community (Num. xxxv. 26), as in earlier society, and the hereditary character of his office was maintained till its dissolution. When after the expulsion of Jason by the Benjamite Menelaus (2 Macc. iv. 23 f.) the succession was temporarily broken, after the death of the usurper it was speedily restored in the Aaronic family of Alkimus (1 Macc. vii. 9; 2 Macc. xiv. 2; Josephus, *Ant.* xx. 103). So the priestly functions of the divine kingship were carried on from generation to generation within the hereditary line of Aaron in which the process of initiation occupied a position analogous to that in the royal succession.

The Altar and the Temple Worship

With the establishment of the new hierarchy after the Exile, the temple became the visible centre of

Israel as a hierocracy wherein the priests alone ministered in holy things, standing between the sacred
congregation on earth and its god in the heavenly
places. The dual conception of Yahweh as a
" sky god " who " dwelleth not in temples made
with hands " (1 Kings viii. 27), and yet worshipped on
earth with elaborate sacrificial ritual, found expression
in the fire-altar and its attendant rites. Now it has
been recently demonstrated by Miss Levin that
" throughout the whole of the Fire Altar ritual (in the
Brahmana texts) there runs one constant theme : the
attainment of immortality for the king." [1]   To this
ceremonial we have already referred in connexion with
the ark, and its significance in the interpretation of the
temple worship is equally apparent. The fire-altar in
India represents the sky-world, the place where the
making of the king into a god is consummated ; the
bricks used in its construction being the counterpart
of the body of Prajapati, whence the gold and fire were
obtained to make the structure immortal. By repeating the process adopted in giving immortality to
the father of the gods, the king sought to obtain the
same gift for himself. Furthermore, since the altar
fire symbolized the sun, the source of all life, whatever
was burnt in it shared in this life and became immortal.
Doubtless similar ideas lay behind the Jewish ritual,
and it is possible, as Professor Hooke has suggested,
that " the altar-steps, like the ladder of the coronation
ritual in the Ramesseum Papyrus, are the means of
ascent to heaven, to the sky-world." [2]   Hence the

[1] *Man*, xxx, 1930, pp. 44 ff.
[2] S. H. Hooke, *Journal Manchester Egyptian and Oriental Society*, xvi, 1931,
pp. 27 ff.

tabu in Ex. xx. 26, as in the case of the similar prohibition in the case of blood, to avoid confusion with
the former ritual.

The priestly description of the altar of burnt offering
and the altar of incense in Exodus xxvii, xxx can hardly
be accurate since a construction made of acacia wood
overlaid with bronze or gold would not stand the
heat of the fire. The altar of incense here mentioned
may have been fashioned in the likeness of that of
the earlier temple, but the burning of incense was not
confined to this structure even in later times. The
rite, however, would seem to have been a post-Exilic
introduction since it is not mentioned in the earlier
literature and was apparently unknown to Ezekiel.
Moreover, the use of incense was regarded by Jeremiah
as a foreign custom (Jer. vi. 20, xli. 5). In Egypt and
elsewhere it was extensively employed as a life-giving
agent in connexion with mummification, and the
present writer has produced evidence of smoke and
fire having been widely regarded as a means by which
immortality could be secured and soul-substance
transferred to the sky.[1] But if the body could be reanimated in this way and the soul made to ascend to
its celestial home in the smoke of its fleshly integument, a reason is forthcoming for the offering of life-
giving incense to revivify the gods, and for burning the
victim to convey its vitality to the sky to be consumed
by deities in need of such sustenance.

When we encounter these alien practices in post-
Exilic Israel, however, their significance has undergone
a profound change, though without any very marked

[1] James, *American Anthropologist*, xxx, 1928, pp. 231 ff,

alteration in ritual, except perhaps that two altars in the same sanctuary appear to be a peculiarity of the later Hebrew practice.[1] The ascending smoke and the sweet savour now became symbolic of ethical atonement (Ps. cxli. 2 ; cf. Rev. v. 8, viii. 3, 4). If a sacrificing priesthood was rigidly established (Num. xvi. 10), side by side with these regulations there arose a mystical reinterpretation of the ritual,[2] and an apocalyptic conception of a heavenly sacrificial worship modelled on the service of the temple on Zion. This notion was latent in Ex. xxv. 40 (cf. xxvi. 30), and in Ezekiel's vision of a temple to be built on earth according to a divine plan (Ez. xl. 4 ff.). In the later apocalyptic literature it found its ultimate expression, notably in the last book of the New Testament.[3]

It was doubtless this highly spiritualized theory of the ancient rite which enabled the institution of sacrifice to survive the destruction of the temple in A.D. 70, and in its Christian form to take on a new lease of life. So far as Judaism is concerned, the catastrophe put an end to the sacerdotal service at the altar, and reduced the specific functions of the priestly office to the blessings during public worship on festivals (Num. vi. 24 ff.). The high priesthood inevitably ceased, and cannot be revived till the altar is restored in Jerusalem, if that interesting event should ever occur. For practical purposes the priesthood is now inopera-

---

[1] But cf. Herodotus, i, 163, for a Babylonian parallel, though the two altars were of very different proportions.

[2] Philo, *De Victimis off.*, cf. *The Works of Philo Judaeus*, Eng. trans. by C. D. Yonge (Lond., 1855), iii, pp. 235 f.

[3] Gray, *Sacrifice in O.T.*, pp. 157 ff. ; Charles, *Studies in the Apocalypse* (Edin., 1913), pp. 161 ff., 172 f.

tive, and in place of the sacrifices of former times, appropriate citations from the Pentateuch and the Mishnah treating of the offerings are recited daily.[1]

The Christian Priesthood

The Church as the New Israel at a very early period looked back to the Jewish hierarchy as the pattern of its own ministry. Thus St. Clement of Rome connected the threefold order of High Priest, Priests and Levites with the Christian succession,[2] and if a formal hierarchy of Rulers, Presbyters and Deacons had not emerged in his day, evidently at Corinth, and probably at Rome, something very like it was coming into existence from the fluid Apostolic system of the first century. The vexed question of the origin of the Christian ministry is so obscure owing to the nature of the evidence that no useful purpose can be served by attempting to analyse it in the space at our disposal. Moreover, it really lies outside the scope of the present volume which makes no pretence to be a theological treatise.[3] Therefore, without entering upon a discussion of whether the Founder of Christianity did or did not intend to institute a priesthood in the sacrificial sense, it suffices to affirm that a society existed in the first days under the leadership of the Apostles, and those upon whom they conferred ministerial functions.

It is not until the second century that evidence occurs of a definite hierarchical organization based on

[1] Talmud, *Taanith*, 27b; *Menaḥoth*, 110a. Cf. *ibid.*, pp. 263 ff.
[2] *Ad Cor.*, xl, 2–5.
[3] For a recent, if somewhat hypothetical, investigation of the evidence, see B. H. Streeter, *The Primitive Church* (Lond., 1929).

Jewish precedents, though this, of course, is not to deny that a similar system may have been in vogue in apostolic times. The subordination of the diaconate as a kind of apprenticeship for the priesthood may owe its origin to the idea that the office was the Christian counterpart of the Jewish levite, just as the presbyterate corresponded to the priesthood, and the episcopate to the office of high priest. As the threefold system definitely emerged, the offering of the Eucharist became the chief and characteristic function of the *sacerdos*, the office of presbyter-bishops gradually separating into two orders according to the general plan of the post-Exilic hierarchy.[1]

Thus, no sooner had the altar ceased in the temple of Yahweh on Zion than its successor was raised up, perhaps first in the catacombs, but certainly in the new edifices that were erected as the earthly counterpart of the same apocalyptic heavenly worship centring now in the " Lamb as it had been slain." St. Paul's phrase τράπεζα (1 Cor. x. 21)[2] was frequently used by the Greek Fathers after the third century, and in Eastern liturgical documents, as a designation of the Christian altar, while in the Ignatian Letters the term θυσιαστήριον (1 Cor. ix. 13, x. 18) seems to be applied to the Eucharistic altar.[3] Irenæus refers to the sacrifice of bread and wine being offered on the altar,[4] and Eusebius mentions the altar (θυσιαστήριον) in the basilica

---

[1] Ignatius, *Rom.* iv, *Trall.* iii; Origen, *in Levit.*, v, 3; Cyprian, *Ep.* xl.; cf. Gore, *The Church and the Ministry* (Lond., 1919), New Ed. by C. H. Turner for further references.

[2] If the Eucharistic significance of Heb. xiii. 10 is open to question, some connexion between the Jewish and Christian priesthood and altar is implied.

[3] *Ad Philad.* 4.   [4] *Haer.* iv, 18. 6.

dedicated at Tyre in A.D. 314, together with the altars
(θυσιαστήριον) erected throughout the world when
the days of persecution ceased.[1] In his reply to Celsus,
who charged the Christians with being a secret society
because they had no altars, Origen admitted that the
"altars are the hearts of every Christian."[2] This,
however, and the similar passage in Lactantius,[3]
may be only a figurative statement emphasizing the
spiritual character of Christian worship analogous
to the notion of the heart as the temple of God,
an idea which does not disapprove the existence of
churches.

This evidence is sufficient to show that certainly
from the fourth century, and probably from 250 A.D.,
onwards the Christian ministry was *definitely* sacerdotal in character. Doubtless the struggle with
Gnosticism encouraged the growth of the hierarchy,[4]
and gave greater prominence to the Roman Church in
view of its political importance. Thus Irenæus in
opposing Gnosticism looked to Rome as the most
efficiently organized stronghold of orthodox Christianity,[5] though he does not indicate that its bishop then
exercised sovereign rights. As the Church in the
West became more and more legalized and dominated
by its central community, the primacy of Rome
developed into an autocratic jurisdiction exercised by

---

[1] *Historia Ecclesiastica*, x, 444.

[2] *Cel.* viii, 17.   His view of the whole Christian life and worship being a
sacrifice goes with his teaching about the altar in heaven, cf. *Let. han.*,
7. 2, *Jud. han.*, 7. 2.

[3] *De origine erroris* ii, 2 ; cf. Minucius Felix, *Octavius,* x ; Arnobius, *Adv.
Gent.*, vii, 3.

[4] Cf. R. Sohm, *Outlines of Church History* (Lond., 1895), p. 31.

[5] *Adv. Haer.*, iii, 3.

divine right.[1] This doctrine gained considerably by the removal of the Imperial Court to the new capital, thereby leaving the bishop in possession at Rome to develop his social and ecclesiastical prestige and authority.

In 451, as the twenty-fifth Canon of the Council of Chalcedon records, ecclesiastical privileges granted to Old Rome because it was the Imperial city, were extended to "the most holy throne of New Rome," because "the city which is honoured with the Sovereignty and the Senate, and enjoys equal privileges with the Old Imperial Rome, should, in ecclesiastical matters, also be magnified as she is and rank next after her." This decree was repudiated by Leo I (440–461) because he disputed the right of Constantinople to rank with the " Apostolic See." To consolidate the position of the Papacy he set to work to establish the Church in Rome on the foundations of the declining secular authority, and boldly proclaimed himself the successor of St. Peter, and as such the vicegerent of Christ on earth.

Already in Pagan Rome sacerdotal functions were exercised by the king-magistrate, and in the last century of the Republic divine worship had been offered to Metellus Pius [2] and Marius Gratidanus. [3] After the victory of Munda in 45 B.C. the image of Cæsar had been carried in procession and a similar statue set among the gods in the temple of Quirinus. The appearance of a comet in the year following the murder of Julius (43 B.C.) was interpreted as the dead Cæsar's

[1] Jerome, *Ep.* 15, *Ad Damasum* ; Migne, *Patr. Lat.* xxii, p. 356.
[2] Macrobius, *Sat.*, iii, 13. 7.
[3] Seneca, *De Ira*, iii, 18 ; Cicero, *De Officiis*, iii, 80.

spirit raised to heaven,[1] and on the first of January, 42 B.C., he was officially deified by the Senate.[2] A temple was erected on the spot where his mangled remains were shown to the people, though, owing to various delays, it was not till 29 B.C. that the *ædes Divi Julii in foro* was consecrated by Augustus and equipped with a *dies natalis*, a flamen and a general staff. The successor of the new god, Sextus Pompeius, who performed the consecration, claimed to be son of Neptune, and in 27 B.C. he accepted the title Augustus, which connoted a sacredness not far removed from divinity.[3]

Most significant is the coin inscription *Caesari Augusto*, inscribed FOR(tunae) RE(duci) suggesting that the return and triumph of Augustus brought back to Rome the dual goddess Prosperity (Fortuna Victrix and Fortuna Felix).[4] This phrase was repeated by his successors, and as the custom spread of identifying the Emperor and the Imperial family with one of the old gods, Apollo, Mercury, Jupiter, etc., it was given an appropriate meaning.[5] True, it was only the worst monarchs, such as Nero, Caligula, Domitian and Commodus, who claimed divine honours during their lifetime, but the practice became established when the need for backing up the Roman autocracy with the Oriental conception of divine kingship arose with the decline of the Empire. Thus Aurelius (A.D. 270–275) took the title *dominus et deus*,

---

[1] Pliny, *Historia Naturalis*, ii, 94.
[2] *Corpus Inscrip. Latinarum*, i, 626 ; ix, 26, 28.
[3] Dio. Cass., liii, 16 ; Ovid, *Fasti* i, 609.
[4] Grueber, *Coins of the Roman Republic in the British Museum,* 1910, vol. ii, p. 77.
[5] A. E. Bevan, *E.R.E.*, iv, p. 530b.

and Diocletian (284–303) assumed the names Jovius and Herculius both for himself and his colleagues.

Thus the stage was set for the transference of the divine kingship to the spiritual head of the Church, as in post-Exilic Israel. Actually, however, the monarchy did not cease to exist, as in the Jewish community, when the Bishop of Rome assumed a royal high priesthood, and eventually adopted the title *Pontifex Maximus*, conferred on Augustus in 13 B.C.[1] Throughout the Middle Ages kings continued to rule by divine right, and if they owed their crown virtually to the ecclesiastical authority, they in their turn claimed sacerdotal powers ; an aspect of the royal office which still survives in the regalia and the coronation ceremony. Actually, however, the priest-king, though combined in the Papacy, has now become differentiated, the occupant of each office exercising his functions in his appropriate sphere.

[1] This title, which became a regular designation of the Pope from the eleventh century, seems to have been applied to earlier occupants of the Holy See, though it is not clear whether it was adopted by Leo I.

CHAPTER IX

THE INSTITUTION OF SACRIFICE

FROM the foregoing analysis of the complex ritual pattern in which the institution of sacrifice and its associated rites and beliefs are woven, it has become apparent that in each and every design the dominant feature is a particular attitude to the perplexing concept of life and of reality. As a recent writer has pointed out in another connexion, " every religion embodies an attitude of life and a conception of reality, and any change in these brings with it a change in the whole character of the culture, as we see in the case of the transformation of ancient civilization by Christianity, or the transformation of the society of Pagan Arabia by Islam." [1]

It is around the life-process that ritual has collected as the great dynamic in social activity, while its associated myth has become the highest social ideal of the moment, " a narrative resurrection of a primeval reality told in satisfaction of deep religious wants, moral cravings, social submissions, assertions, even practical requirements."[2] But enshrined in the thought-forms of a long-forgotten past are the reactions of former generations to the ever-present life interest, the will to live manifesting itself in a life-giving and a life-getting ceremonial which at an early

---

[1] C. Dawson, *The Age of the Gods* (Lond., 1928), p. xx.
[2] Malinowski, *Myth in Primitive Psychology* (Lond., 1927), p. 23.

255

period conformed to a general pattern centred in the king and his functions in securing the prosperity of the community over which he ruled as the embodiment of the gods.

The main strands of the pattern, at any rate so far as the sacrificial design is concerned, are found in the earliest records of the thought of Neoanthropic man, but it was not until these elements were brought together that sacrifice as an organized institution can be said to have become established as a means of controlling the unpredictable aspect of human experience, and securing a renewal of vitality, often by a re-enactment of the original situation out of which the civilization of the community came into existence—a reproduction of the life-theme in a concrete ritual upon which gods and men alike depended for their continuance.

The fundamental principle throughout is the same ; the giving of life to promote or preserve life, death being merely a means of liberating vitality. Consequently, the destruction of the victim, to which many writers have given a central position in the rite, assumes a position of secondary importance in comparison with the transmission of the soul-substance to the supernatural being to whom it is offered. This may be done simply by applying the blood to a sacred stone, or pouring it out at its base. Or an altar may be erected and a priest employed to make the presentation according to certain prescribed rites in association with subsidiary ceremonies.

In all the manifold variations of the ritual the underlying significance consists in the setting free of life for one or more of the following reasons : (*a*) to augment the power of the god or spirit approached to enable him to perform his beneficent functions on earth ; (*b*) to meet the forces of death and destruction by a fresh outpouring of vital potency, and so to strengthen the worshipper against malign influences, and to " cover " or " wipe out " the transgression ; (*c*) to establish or re-establish a bond of union or covenant with the benevolent powers in order to maintain a vital relationship between the worshipper and the object of worship, and so to gain free communication between the natural and supernatural order.

From these primary considerations secondary motives have arisen, such as the notion of securing the favour of an offended deity by offerings which are in the nature of fines rather than of efficacious oblations like the application of the blood of the victim to the altar and the penitent. The collection of ancient Hebrew laws known as *The Book of the Covenant*, incorporated in the E document of Exodus (xx. 22–xxiii. 33), belonging probably to the period of the Conquest of Palestine, seem to reflect a time when Yahweh was thought to claim the first-born sons (Ex. xxii. 29). While this conclusion is confirmed by the injunctions in the J narrative (xiii. 12 f., xxxiv. 19 f.), a definite modification of the rule is introduced. The presentation of the first-born is no longer demanded as an efficacious offering, but instead a sum of money is ordered to be paid by way of redemption, though the price is not yet fixed, except in the case of the ass, which, being an unclean animal, must be replaced by a lamb or goat, unless its neck is broken.

In the story of the offering of Isaac (Gen. xxii. 1–

19), probably an eighth-century B.C. prophetic Midrash, the substitution of an animal as the redemptive price of the human victim is emphasized, and in the Deuteronomic legislation the sacrifice of the first-born of man is described as an " abomination " of the surrounding Semitic tribes (Deut. xii. 31, xviii. 10). But all the firstlings of the herd and of the flock, if free from blemish, are still to be regarded as belonging to Yahweh, and consequently to be set apart for a sacrificial meal (Deut. xv. 19 ff.). In the later Priestly legislation the practice of redemption is systematized, a fixed sum of five shekels per head being definitely established as the price due to Yahweh to be paid to the priests (Num. xviii. 15–18 ; Lev. xxvii. 27 ; Ezek. xliv. 30).

This custom of commuting sacrifices into money, which is significant of the later Hebrew ritual, shows how completely the original purpose of the offerings had disappeared. With the rise of ethical monotheism it became preposterous to the mono-Yahwists to suppose that the all-righteous Judge of all the earth could require revivification through the blood of bulls and goats, to say nothing of the life of a human victim (cf. Ps. xl. 6 ; l. 8–13). It is at this point that a fundamental change in the original pattern becomes apparent. Hitherto it has displayed a purely ritual situation in a series of ceremonials embodying a primitive theory of life and death, and good and evil. With the establishment of ethical and spiritual ideas, and a new moral conception of deity, the institution must either cease or alter completely its character and significance.

The Hebrew prophets of the eighth century seem to

have favoured the abandonment of the ritual as the only way to dissociate the higher ethical worship from its agricultural counterpart. It was not enough, in their opinion, to make a stand against the enthronement of Yahweh as the new lord of the local shrines, or, like Elijah and the Rechabites, to have nothing to do with a vegetation cultus. So long as the indigenous "high places" survived, the syncretistic movement was bound to go on. If Hezekiah wrought havoc among the local sanctuaries, and broke in pieces the brazen serpent, Manasseh speedily set to work to undo his reforms and introduced fresh "abominations" in the form of child sacrifices in the valley of Hinnom in honour of Moloch. The centralization of worship at Jerusalem in the days of Josiah proved ineffectual as an antidote, and in sheer despair Jeremiah was led to denounce the institution of sacrifice altogether, and to deny its divine origin. "I spake not unto your fathers, nor commanded them in the day that I brought them out of the land of Egypt, concerning burnt-offerings or sacrifices; but this thing I commanded them, saying, Hearken unto my voice" (Jer. vii. 21).

To the great spiritual leaders of the seventh and eighth centuries B.C., Yahweh was essentially ethical in his demands as in his nature. Therefore to associate him with the syncretistic cultus of an agricultural deity was nothing short of blasphemy. To go to Bethel was to transgress, and to visit Gilgal was to multiply transgression, while even to bring sacrifices every morning and tithes every three days, and thanksgiving or free-will offerings was to engage in a wilfully devised worship (Amos iv. 4).[1] Thus Amos, who had been brought up in the pastoral culture of Tekoa in complete detachment from the agricultural community, does not hesitate to cry in the name of Yahweh, " I hate, I despise your feasts, I will take no delight in your solemn assemblies. Yea, though ye offer me your burnt-offerings, and meal-offerings, I will not accept them; neither will I regard the peace-offerings of your fat beasts " (v. 21). For him it was social justice that mattered most, and this was completely lacking in Israel, while to his successor from the north, Hosea, the syncretistic cult of Yahweh appeared as nothing less than the rejection of a love bestowed on a faithless nation. Finally, to Isaiah Israel appeared as the nation set apart and called to reflect the ethical holiness of its righteous god.

How far the pre-Exilic prophets realized the implications of their teaching it is difficult to say, but in any case it was not until the disaster they foretold had become an accomplished fact that the seeds they had sown sprang up and bore fruit. Once Jerusalem was captured, the Temple destroyed, and the nation driven from its natural home, the old territorial view of Yahweh became impossible. Either the tribal and localized conception of deity must be abandoned, or terms must be made with the victorious gods of Babylonia, Marduk and his pantheon. It was this situation which Ezekiel had to face (Ez. xiv. 1–11), and it is clear that there was a grave danger of a return

---

[1] It would seem that at this time the earlier purely vegetation significance of sacrifice as a life-giving ritual had taken over the later notion of paying dues to the god of the land as a sort of rent or tribute in recognition of his ownership.

to the new syncretistic worship in which the Babylonian deities would take the place of the Palestinian vegetation divinities in relation to Yahweh. On the other hand, those who refused to have anything to do with the allurements of the temples of the conquerors were inclined to relapse into a negative pessimism (Ps. cxxxvii.), hanging up their harps in despair in their inability to sing the Lord's song in a strange land.

Between these two attitudes Ezekiel sought a solution of the problem, and in his case the drastic discipline of the Exile proved to be a unique spiritual experience which was calculated to have far-reaching effects on the subsequent history of religion. Out of it emerged the conception of the transcendant greatness and holiness of God who demands from every individual a life of active and beneficent virtue (Ez. i. 26–28 ; xviii. 1–18). The recent catastrophe he interpreted as the just punishment of a righteous God on a sinful nation, but he looked forward with confidence to the time of restoration when the exiles would be gathered again like the resurrection to life of an army that had been slain. Then would the promise of Yahweh be fulfilled : " A new heart also will I give you, and I will take away the stony heart out of your flesh, and I will give you an heart of flesh. And I will put my spirit within you, and cause you to walk in my statutes " (Ezek. xxxvi. 16 ff., 26 f. ; xxxvii. 1–15). Thus the Exile is represented as a process of regeneration to bring about an internal spiritual change both in the individual and in the nation.

It is to this context that the vision of the restored

Temple belongs, in which the revival of the sacrificial system is set forth with great elaboration modelled in the characteristic manner on its heavenly counterpart (xl.–xlviii.). The new ritual order, according to this scheme, includes expiatory offerings and a ceremonial law, but the ethical righteousness of Yahweh demands above all things and side by side with objective worship, rightness of conduct. No attempt is made to harmonize the two theories of salvation, but nevertheless the work of the priest-prophet Ezekiel marks a turning-point in the institution of sacrifice. Henceforth the ritual in Israel was invested with an ethical and spiritual content, the central conception of the sacrificial approach to the deity being made to cover all that was meant by his righteousness. The former notion of a non-moral holiness no longer sufficed, and therefore when the Temple and its worship were restored it was a deeper sense of sin which found expression in and characterized the elaborate system of post-Exilic *'āshām* (guilt-offerings) and *ḥaṭṭāth* (sin-offerings).

The Deutero-Isaiah, as a result of the experience of the Exile, carried the ethical teaching of Ezekiel to its final conclusion in the enunciation of Yahweh as the only all-righteous Lord and Ruler of the universe (Isa. xl. 12 ff. ; xli. 24 ; xliii. 12 f.) ; it was impossible to return to the former modes of sacrificial ritual, and yet if the Temple was to be rebuilt Yahweh must be worshipped objectively. This was the dilemma which confronted the priestly school when the people were allowed to return to Jerusalem, and the piacular system constitutes the answer. Thus the work of

Ezra and his successors was really only the application and elaboration of the principles laid by Ezekiel, the purpose of all the sacrifices having been already defined as that of reconciliation (Ez. xlv. 15, 17), and their atoning efficacy that of divine forgiveness. The old symbolism of the blood as the life remained (Lev. xvii. 11), but it was re-evaluated in terms of ethical concepts.

The sin-offerings, for example, which originally was an outpouring of blood to revivify and augment the power of the god, or drive forth the forces of evil, became a compensation for injury (cf. 2 Kings xii.17), and a symbol of an inward cleansing by true repentance, typified by the phrase " the sacrifices of God are a broken spirit " (Ps. li. 16f.). On this new hypothesis, it was not the mere outward oblation that counted but the spirit of penitence and contrition in which it was made (Ps. iv. 5, 7, 14, 18). Again, the peace-offering, which was frequently an accompaniment of the sin-offering, from being a sacred meal became essentially an act of thanksgiving ; i.e. a sacrifice offered in a thankful spirit (Ps. iv. 14)—so that the ceremonial banquet on life-giving substances came to assume a eucharistic character before it was associated with the theology of the " bread of life " as a divine gift of spiritual renewal.

This process of symbolical interpretation gained a new impetus at the beginning of our era by the destruction of the Temple, which necessarily brought the sacrificial system to an end in Israel as an accomplished fact. Yet, as Dr. Gaster has pointed out, in theory it was only temporarily suspended until a new

Jerusalem and a new Temple should be re-established.[1] The hope still survives among orthodox Jews, but, nevertheless, in the meantime the devout are thrown back on substitutes for the actual offerings. Thus in the Rabbinical literature the " broken-heart " is declared to take the place of the sin-offering,[2] while he who studies the precepts concerning the daily oblation (Ex. xxix 38–42 ; Num. xxviii. 1–8) is regarded as having offered the sacrifices.[3]

Of all the various substitutes allowed by the Rabbis, prayer occupies the chief place, and is even described as " better than sacrifice," though the revival of the former worship is also earnestly desired.[4] In the additional *'amidah* for sabbaths, new moon, and festivals, this is explained in the following petition :

" Sovereign of the universe ! thou didst command us to offer the daily sacrifice in its appointed time and that the priests should officiate in their service and the Levites at their stand and the Israelites by their delegates. But, at present, on account of our sins, the temple is laid waste, and the daily sacrifice hath ceased ; for we have neither an officiating priest, nor a Levite at his stand, nor an Israelite as delegate. But thou hast said that the prayers of our lips shall be as the offering of bulls (Hos. xiv. 2). Therefore let it be thy will, O Lord our God, and the God of our fathers, that the prayers of our lips may be accounted, accepted, and esteemed before thee, as if we had offered the daily sacrifice at its appointed time, and had been represented by our delegation." [5]

---

[1] *E.R.E.*, xi, p. 24b.　　　　[2] *Pes.*, 158b.
[3] *Pes.*, 60 b.　　　　[4] *Ber.*, 32 b ; *Midr. Shamuel*, i. 7.
[5] M. Gaster, *The Prayer Book and Order of Service* of the Spanish and Portuguese Jews (Lond., 1901), i, p. 11.

At the hours, and on the festivals corresponding to those prescribed in the Temple worship, appropriate portions of the law are read—a practice that may go back to the time of the *ma'amadoth* before the destruction of the Temple,[1] and is regarded as the equivalent of a sacrifice.[2] Fasting, again, is considered to take the place of a sin-offering, just as the Indian lays great stress on this asceticism as a means of union with the divine, and in preparation for sacrificial worship. For the Jews, however, it is only " in the present distress " that the substitution is allowed, as is shown by the prayer of the Rabbi Sheshet :

" Lord of the world, when the Temple was standing one who sinned offered a sacrifice, of which only the fat and the blood were taken, and thereby his sins were forgiven. I have fasted to-day, and through this fasting my blood and my fat have been decreased. Deign to look upon the part of my blood and my fat which I have lost through my fasting as if I had offered it to Thee, and forgive my sins in return." [3]

Although there is by no means general agreement now among Jews concerning the revival of the sacrificial system should this possibility become practicable, there can be little doubt that the original idea was the provision of substitutes to preserve the essential elements of the ritual until the institution should be restored. From the days of Maimonides there have been those who refused to follow the symbolists in their attempt to keep alive in theory the ancient rite, maintaining that the sacrificial service is not the primary

[1] Gaster, *E.R.E.*, xi, p. 26.   [2] *Menahoth*, 110 a ; *Ta'an*, 27 b.
[3] *Ber.*, 17 a.

object of the law.[1] But this was not the view of the Mishnā. Thus in the *'amidah*, which is required to be repeated three times daily by all the devout, the petition occurs, " mayest thou bring back the sacrifice to thy holy house, and the fire offerings, as well as their prayers receive with favour."

The position, therefore, in the Tannaitic period was not very different from the attitude adopted by Ezekiel during the Exile. The people were looking for the return of the former worship, but the process of spiritualization begun by the prophets made it possible to adopt for the original institution non-sacrificial substitutes, such as prayer, the reading of the Law, and fasting. By so doing the ancient ritual underwent a fundamental change in character so that the concept of life-giving became that of self-giving, the offering of the broken heart and the contrite spirit, " the sacrifice of the lips instead of the calves " (Hos. xiv. 2).

With the rise of Christianity the ethical interpretation of the sacrificial approach to a righteous god as a means of advance in the way of personal holiness underwent a further change. The precise attitude of Christ to the institution is a matter of acute controversy among theologians, and it would require a separate volume to deal at all adequately with the problem. Moreover, as our purpose here is to determine the anthropological situation, the purely theological aspect of the problem lies outside the limits of our present discussion. Therefore, whatever may have been the significance of the teaching of Jesus

[1] Moreh, III, xxxvi, cf. xxxii.

in ultimate reality, as a historical phenomenon, His death, as we have seen, was interpreted by the Church as a sacrifice before the close of the first century A.D. (Ephes. v. 2 ; Heb. ix. 14). The offering of His blood was connected with the sin-offering in the former dispensation (Rom. iii. 25, viii. 3 ; 1 Cor. x. 16 ; Heb. xiii. 11), while He Himself was represented as the Paschal victim (1 Cor. v. 7), bearing the sins of the people in perfect obedience to the will of His Father (Heb. ix. 28, x. 8f.), and at the same time the high priest of the human race (Heb. ix. 11ff., 23).

From the Epistle to the Hebrews in might appear that in the mind of this writer the intention was to abolish the Hebrew ritual by fulfilling its spiritual purpose (Heb. x. 9)—" He taketh away the first that he may establish the second "—but against this view must be set the words, " I came not to destroy the law and the prophets but to fulfil " (Matt. v. 17). In any case, the Jewish sacrifices are represented as " expressing a need which they could not satisfy, but which Christ does, and embodying a faith which Christ justifies." [1] That is to say, the system is treated symbolically, and given a new and highly ethical evaluation.

This is clearly brought out in St. Paul's account of his own experience of Judaism. The blood of bulls and goats could not effect a satisfying expiation and redemption in terms of ethical righteousness. Therefore, he concludes, God sent forth His Son to be " an expiation, through faith, by his blood because of the passing over of the sins done aforetime." (Rom. iii. 25). Thus, he definitely affirms the death of Christ to have

---

[1] W. P. Paterson, *Dict. of the Bible* (Hastings), iv, p. 348 b.

been in some sense an atoning sacrifice, analogous to the post-Exilic piacular sacrifices (cf. Rom. v. 9), effected through a perfect act of self-surrender.

As a Pharisee he was prepared to admit that the sacrificial system had failed to attain its true object, regarded from the highest ethical standpoint. In his opinion, no atonement, in fact, from the human side can be ultimately efficacious. The mystery of Calvary succeeds, however, on his hypothesis, because " God was in Christ, reconciling the world unto himself " (2 Cor. v. 19). Having emptied Himself and become of no account in order to enter into the experience of human life, the Incarnate Son offered Himself in complete surrender and obedience to the will of the Father, pouring out sacrificially before God His life-giving blood of the new covenant. This in a word is the Pauline interpretation of the sacrifice of Christ and its significance in the history of religion and of the human race. In this highly metaphysical form the inward surrender of the will is combined with the ritual offering of the life of the victim, who is none other than in literal fact the Lamb of God, " a symbol," as Hocart says, " expressing a sum of innocence, purity, gentleness, self-sacrifice, redemption and divinity which no form of words could express with such forceful appeal." [1]

If this evaluation of the institution is to be complete, however, it carries with it the significance of the poured-out blood representing the life of the victim. Death is merely incidental to the offering of the life, for it is this which gives efficacy to the rite. Conse-

[1] *Kingship*, p. 243.

quently, in an age saturated with sacrificial ideas, the interpretation of the death of Christ as a sacrifice involved the oblation of the blood, which normally would be poured out partly on the altar and partly on the penitent, to reunite the worshipper with his god in a covenant relationship. Subjectively this might be spiritualized in the form of a heavenly offering made accessible by faith instead of by ritual, but it very soon found objective expression in a eucharistic theology in which the ceremonial representation of the drama of creation and redemption was re-enacted as in former practice. The elements employed in the sacred banquet would suggest to the Jewish mind the *minhah*, or vegetation offerings, by which a new covenant was to be inaugurated, just as baptism (and its Eucharistic counterpart, the *asperges*) was interpreted as an initiation ceremony symbolizing the new birth in union with the risen Christ. Finally, the sacrificial action culminated in the symbolical re-enactment of the death of the victim offered for the redemption of the world.

The ancient ritual order in this way received a new lease of life by incorporation in a metaphysical scheme —a new " vision of reality "—which was destined to play a determining part in the development of modern civilization. In the process the institution of sacrifice underwent a still further transvaluation, while at the same time the purely ethical and spiritual approach to the deity became entangled in the meshes of the kingship culture complex. The original magico-religious situation was abandoned in favour of a highly spiritualized conception of divine life laid down in voluntary self-sacrifice made accessible to man sacramentally in order that incorporation in the quickening life permeating the ever self-extending organism of the Incarnate might be effected by participation in the symbols of sacrifice. By this entry of a new principle of divine vitality into the world the human race was thought to have been raised to a higher order in which the eternal and the temporal, the absolute and the finite, the supernatural and the natural, the supraspatial and the spatial, were brought into harmony, that " the divine grace in one even course, as it were, might uniformly extend through all creation, the lower nature being mingled with that which is above the world." [1]

It was in these terms that the Christian Faith, with its central doctrines of the incarnation, atonement and resurrection, was presented to the Græco-Roman world. Mystery ideas, as we have seen, already prevailed, and Dean Inge may be correct in his surmise that if Christ had not instituted Baptism and the Eucharist, the Church would have had to invent them.[2] In other words, a system of Christian sacrificial and sacramental symbolism was inevitable if the Church were ever to prevail in the Empire, so deeply rooted was the ritual in the Gentile as well as in the Jewish mind. Nevertheless, from the sixth century B.C. onwards protests were raised in Greece, as in Judæa, against the cruder primitive aspects of the institution.

The reaction against polytheism in higher Græco-Roman thought runs in two streams, the one practical

[1] *The Catechical Oration of St. Gregory of Nyssa*, Eng. trans. by J. H. Srawley (Lond., 1917), pp. 39 f.
[2] *Contentio Veritatis* (Lond., 1916), p. 279.

and popular, the other philosophical, which find their confluence in the mind of Plato, at once philosopher and poet, and derive from him through Aristotle to Cleanthes and the Stoics. In a few passages in Homeric literature θεός is used in the abstract as the equivalent of Zeus,[1] and while Æschylus recognizes a number of gods, in the *Prometheus* the central issue lies between God and man. A generation earlier Xenophanes, in the words of Aristotle, "throws his glance upon the whole heaven and says that God is unity."[2] For him God is one, uncreated, righteous, and without resemblance to man; the only prayer which may be addressed to him legitimately is for "power to do what is right." In this he is nearer to Hebrew and Christian monotheism than Heraclitus who places the Deity beyond good and evil. "To God all things are beautiful and good and right, but men consider some things wrong and other things right."[3] Bacchic ritual, purifications from blood, and the whole anthropomorphic system, are an abomination to Heraclitus, though he never came to grips with popular religion so closely as Xenophanes whose protest against the traditional conceptions of Deity was to receive classical expression a century later in the *Republic* of Plato.

Meanwhile philosophy was pursuing a path which prepared the way for the break-up of polytheism and the primitive notion of sacrifice for thoughtful men. The material unity—water, air, fire—proclaimed by the Ionian scientists, the logical unity asserted by Parmenides, the pupil of Xenophanes, the deistic unity asserted by Anaxagoras all alike attest an instinct

---

[1] *Il.*, xiii, 730. *Od.*, iv, 236.   [2] *Metaph.*, I, v.   [3] *Fragm.*, 61.

or innate disposition which could not rest content with pluralism, and either ignored the evidence of the many or else relegated it to the sphere of unreality and opinion. In this atmosphere we are, of course, far removed from the theology proper of the Olympian deities : the problem of Being has ousted the problem of the gods : even in Anaxagoras the Mind which ordered chaos in the beginning has no other *rôle* in things to play. Nevertheless, we cannot regard this development as without significance for Greek theology.

It was reserved for the genius of Plato to give expression, first in the *Republic* and its correlative dialogues, later, and with greater precision and critical analysis, in the *Timæus* and the *Laws*, to a thoroughly Greek monotheism, and to gather up into it all that the poetical imagination, moral earnestness and metaphysical subtlety of his predecessors had portended. Into the Platonic conception of God it is impossible here to enter ; nor can we trace the criticism of it through which Aristotle passed to his pregnant conception of the Unmoved Mover. Suffice it to say that in this philosophical conception of Deity the universe depends on, and, indeed, is made to exist in, an ultimate spiritual reality which gives it birth and maintains it.

In such an interpretation of theism there was no room for the ancient ritual order, but, nevertheless, the tendency of the later Greek ethical and metaphysical thought was to humanize and moralize sacrifice rather than to repudiate it. In fact, no serious attempt was made to reconcile philosophical speculation with popular religious practice, though the moral weaknesses of the cults were deplored. Thus Euripides denounced the Tauric immolation of a human victim, and he appears to have shared the sentiments of Theophrastos regarding bloodless sacrifice " without fire of all fruits of earth poured forth in abundance on the altar," being more acceptable to a merciful God than the life of an animal.[1] To Euripides nothing was sacred unless it had some ethical quality, and he affirmed that it was the piety behind the offering, and not its value, that alone could win salvation.[2] But the popular ritual tradition persisted, for despite all the efforts of the philosophical thinkers to give an ethical interpretation to the theory of sacrifice, the institution was " the ancient and best law "—νόμος δ' ἀρχαῖος ἄριστος—on which society depended for its assured well-being.

Far-reaching as the influence of Greek metaphysical thought has been on the subsequent higher developments of religion in the West, it had little effect on the sacrificial system compared with that of either Judaism or Christianity. The philosophers never felt as keenly as the Hebrew prophets the contradiction between popular polytheistic practice and ethical religion. Furthermore, the genial Hellenic spirit was incapable of understanding the profound mysteries of the moral life, for which the doctrine of the Atonement, even in forms which may be justly regarded as irreconcilable with certain of our moral convictions, has seemed to supply a solution, though for the majority of thinking

[1] Eur., *Frag.* cx. ; Porphyry, *De Abstin.*, ii. 29.

[2] Stob., *Flor.* (Meineke), iv, 264 ; cf. Farnell, *Cult of Greek States*, iv p. 210.

men the earlier jurisprudence has been abandoned. Furthermore, if the Greek ritual eliminated almost entirely the magical element which was liable to recur in the higher developments of the institution where the notion of compelling the deity, or controlling the course of nature, tended to survive, the establishment of mystery cults became prevalent to supply the needs satisfied in Judaism by the post-Exilic sacrificial system, and in Christianity by sacramental communion.

As a matter of fact, in the Græco-Roman world metaphysical and moral philosophy were divorced from practical religion until they were reunited in Neo-Platonism and Christianity. Whereas for the Hebrew and the Christian theologians and philosophers the personality of God was mainly a moral power, by Plato and Aristotle and the Neo-Platonists it tended to be expressed in intellectual terms, so that God could be defined as the supreme " Nous " or Mind of the universe, as Apollo was explained by Empedokles in the " Holy Thought " of the world.[1] The unification of the cosmic order introduced a higher reality which transcends all change and limitation, but it reduced the conception of Deity to a pantheistic metaphysical principle of pure Being, eternal and supreme Mind, that had so long held sway among Oriental mystics.

Indian philosophy, however, never broke away from religion. When the Brahmans became the recognized priesthood, and assumed the name that was identified with the Creator, sacrifice was given the first place in Hindu ritual. According to the *Vedas,*

[1] Farnell, *The Attributes of God* (Oxford, 1925), p. 219.

should the rite cease for an instant the gods would not send rain, or cause the sun to return at dawn to ripen the harvest, presumably because they would lack the power to perform their beneficent functions.[1] " By sacrifice," says the *Taittiriya Brahmana*, " the gods obtained heaven," and on earth the celestial offerings had their counterparts, so that the kindling of the sacred fire—" the shoot of *Rita*, born in the *Rita* "— was regarded as the agent and instrument for stimulating and maintaining the divine activities. The mystical identity of the order of nature and the order of sacrifice, whether on earth or in heaven, arises from the notion of the *Rita(rta)*, a term signifying the universal order cosmic, ritual and moral, and, therefore, used in the *Vedas* for both natural and moral law.[2] From the heaven and the earth the gods proceed, the Sun is " its clear and visible face," the year is its wheel, and along its ordered course all things move.

The gods, however, are not merely born of the *Rita*, but they follow it, practise it, and know it. The special guardian and foundation of the *Rita* is Varuna, a divine king who is righteous and the protector of morality, and therefore entitled " Lord of Law." He seems to have been also connected with the sun and the order of nature, while Agni, the sacrificial fire and fire-god, is *Rita*-born, and is declared to become Varuna when he strives for the *Rita*.[3] In his divine personification, Agni rises into cosmic significance as a pervading energy sustaining the world, but he never loses his physical and sacrificial character. Thus the

---

[1] A. Barth, *Religions of India* (Lond., 1882), p. 36.
[2] *Satapatha Brah.*, iv, 1. 4. 1 ff.   [3] *Rig-Veda*, X, viii, 5.

sacred fire is the means by which the offerings are carried to the sky by way of *Rita*, and at the same time the priest assures Agni that he invokes the gods without witchcraft, and offers his devotion with righteousness.[1] Fire is the earthly counterpart of the sun, and " Right is this Fire, Truth is yonder Sun ; or rather Right is yonder Sun, and Truth is this Fire." [2]

The conception of righteousness in the *Vedas*, therefore, finds expression in this complex term *Rita*, which denotes at once the cosmic order and the order of the moral law, on the one hand, and the institution of sacrifice, on the other. The earthly ritual being the counterpart of the celestial offerings of the " Fathers " in the heavenly sphere whose perfect performance of the law is the result of their having " grown according to the *Rita*," it becomes the highest form of morality attainable in this world, the equivalent of *satya*, truth, considered as correspondence with Reality. Heaven and earth are *satya*, and they are *ritavan*, faithful to the path, as is also a righteous man ; the same word being used to denote the holiness of the gods, the order of nature, human piety, and the institution of sacrifice. Therefore, all were but aspects of one fundamental conception, *Rita*.

Although this theology was later replaced by that of *Karma*, the doctrine of the Deed, and the *Atman*, or world-soul, it, nevertheless, had a profound influence on the subsequent religious and philosophical development of India. In the *Brahmanas* sacrifice remained the efficient cause of the order of nature, and the ultimate power behind the universe, though as the

[1] *Rig-Veda*, VII, xxiv, 8.   [2] *Sat. Br.*, v, 4.4.10.

idea of one god developed, or at any rate the notion of a divine essence diffused throughout the world under the name of Prajapati, it was the " Lord of Creatures " who underwent repeated offering in every sacrifice, " The sacrificer is the god Prajapati at his own sacrifice." [1] It was with this deity, as we have seen, that the Fire-Altar ritual was connected in which the king becomes immortal and divine, and Mr. Hocart has explained the Vedic theory of sacrifice as " an enacted series of equations." In the course of his consecration ceremonies the king makes an offering to Fire as Agni, " the face of the gods," and the general is " the face of the army." But the king is the embodiment of many gods with whom he becomes identified by sacrifice. It is suggested, therefore, that " the king makes an offering to the fire-god ; the offering is the fire-god ; the king becomes the fire-god ; but the general is the fire-god ; therefore the king becomes one with the general, and thus we can understand how the king by this offering gains power over the general and ' makes him his faithful follower.' " [2] In this ritual elaboration the ethical significance of the oblations becomes obscured, since Vedic ritualists were content to maintain a ceremonial order calculated to enable the gods and the king to fulfil their functions independent of the ethical good of the sacrificer. If truth was still regarded as a divine virtue, it was thought to be outside human capacity, and, therefore, it ceased to be inculcated as a serious duty.

Such moral duties as are enforced in the *Brahmanas*

---

[1] Sat. Br., v, 1.1.2 ; iii, 2.2.4.   [2] *Kingship*, p. 115.

were developed in the higher thought of the *Upani-sads* through many conflicting teachers, and many priestly schools between 700 and 500 B.C. The voice of Prajapati heard in the thunder is represented as a call to self-control, mercy and charity,[1] while asceticism, liberality, truth and straight dealing are among the virtues enumerated in the *Chhāndogya Upanisad*[2] as essential elements in the great sacrifice of life. Being concerned with an intellectual quest of the Absolute, the Vedanta abstracted the *Brahman* from the institution of sacrifice which became merely a symbolic representation of the higher reality.

Behind the cosmological process, and all being, according to this philosophy, is a Supreme Power (*Brahman*), of whom all the lesser deities were emanations, and who alone is real, the embodiment of joy and peace, truth and knowledge, but unconnected with holiness and righteousness. In this conception of Ultimate Reality, both sacrifice and morality are virtually excluded since *Brahman* is beyond ethics and ritual, true happiness being secured only by the union of this supreme principle—the *ātman* of the universe—with the individual *ātman*, the soul of man. Yet *ātman* is the embodiment of the gods and of the sacrificer—a kind of mystic soul-substance—which is united by sacrifice very much in the same way as in Christianity by an act of sacramental communion the faithful are made to dwell in Christ and Christ in them.[3] Thus the human soul is incorporated into the divine order—the *ātman* of the gods, or the mystical body of Christ,

---

[1] *Brhādaranyaka Upanisad*, v, 2.   [2] iii, 17.
[3] *Sat. Brahm.*, iv, 3.4.5 ; ix, 5.2.16.

and made to dwell in heavenly places. In this higher metaphysical thought, be it that of the *Upanisads* or of Christianity, the divine kingship ritual has become transformed into a philosophical symbolic representation of ultimate reality, behind which is the fundamental conception that all things take their origin in creative sacrifice uniting god and man and the universe in a conceptual identity.

In Persia higher religious thought moved in a rather different direction under the influence of Zarathustra. It is, in fact, possible to see in Zoroastrianism the first determined effort against the institution of sacrifice, both the *haoma* (i.e. *soma*)—offering of the sacred life-giving plant, and the animal sacrifice conflicted with Zarathustra's highly spiritual conception of God.[1] According to the Gathas, " as an offering Zarathustra brings the life of his own body, the choiceness of good thought, action and speech, unto Mazda " ; an action which Moulton compares with St. Paul's contention : " I beseech you . . . that you present your bodies a living sacrifice, holy, acceptable unto God." [2]

After the death of the prophet, however, the ancient sacrificial system was restored in Mazdean ritual, and with it came a return to a non-moral notion of sin and ceremonial uncleanness. Nevertheless, Asha, which retained an intimate connexion with the sacred fire, and remained the name of the supreme Deity, preserved a moral aspect, and became the personification of the divine righteousness. Morality and religion there-

[1] Moulton, *Early Zoroastrianism* (Lond., 1913), p. 395, n. 1.
[2] *Yasna*, 33.14 ; Moulton, *ib.*, p. 360.

fore were united in Zoroastrian dualism, and while the later official worship did not leave much room for the ethical ideals of Zarathustra, in the *Avesta* the sacrifices are frequently brought into relation to sin. But if behind the ritual there lay a high appreciation of moral purity and truth, the only provision for the expiation of evil was the accumulation of good works and vicarious sacrifices.

From a purely ethical point of view the Avestan ritual represents an advance on the Vedic and Brahmana systems, of which it constitutes a particular development. In fact, at one time it seemed likely to develop the purest monotheism in the history of religion. It proved, however, to be too deeply rooted in Aryan polytheism, and the ancient ritual order, to break away permanently from its original character, though it undoubtedly played an important part in the introduction of higher conceptions in the formative period of the ethical movement.

In was in the welter of Oriental philosophies and systems which characterise the religious thought of India and the surrounding nations from the sixth century B.C. onwards, that Gautama set to work to find a "way" through the maze of conflicting theories. Himself a twice-born Hindu of royal descent, and versed in the *Vedanta* teachings and the philosophy of the *Upanisads*, he evolved his "Noble Eightfold Path" to secure Enlightenment, Morality and Concentration, and ultimately to attain Nirvana. This new mystic ladder was complicated enough, but it was simpler than the intellectualism of the *Upanisads* and the philosophical schools, and it provided a moral aim and purpose in life by asserting the ethical element in the Vedic notion of *Rita*.

Starting from the general principles of the *Upanisads*, the Buddha evolved an ethical system around the " Four Noble Truths "[1] in which moral conduct is based on the cultivation of those tendencies and acts which produce or preserve the true values of life, and destroy life's evils. It has no reference, however, to an ethical conception of deity, as in Hebrew and Christian theology, or to a ritual holiness, as in the original culture pattern. If it is not strictly true to say that Buddhism is an agnostic moral philosophy, since it does not really deny the existence of the gods, it made no contribution to the spiritualization of the sacrificial system. Existence being an evil and therefore a thing to escape from at all costs, there is no room in this scheme for a sacrificial cultus, or, indeed, for any ritual order, especially as to become a god means to attain a lower state than that of Nirvana.

Nevertheless, even during the lifetime of the Buddha, or at any rate shortly after his death, the repetition of portions of the *Dhamma* became a kind of ritual, while the distribution of the cremated remains of his body among the faithful opened the way for a cult of relics and shrines. Out of pilgrimages to these sacred places, probably arose the first symbols of Buddhist veneration—the tree, the wheel and the stupa,[2] to which later was added the image of the Buddha. As shrines became temples, the statues of

---

[1] (1) All existence involves suffering ; (2) the cause of suffering ; (3) the cessation of suffering by the elimination of desire ; (4) the Noble Eightfold Path.

[2] Foucher, *Beginnings of Buddhist Art* (Paris, 1917), chap. i.

Gautama and the twenty-four mythical and previous Buddhas, set up originally as aids to meditation, were transformed into objects of worship, and offerings of fruit, flowers, incense and the usual accompaniments of Oriental sacrificial cultus made at them.

With this development of the cult, the Founder was given a cosmological significance as the latest of several divine emanations, and therefore a personal centre of faith, devotion and worship. As systems and philosophies increased, Buddhism began to resemble the Hinduism against which it had been the revolt. With the rise in the North of the school of Mahāyāna, or " Greater Vehicle," the ritualistic tendency developed towards a schism, since the Hīnayāna (Lesser Vehicle) sect claimed to preserve the original philosophical ideal against the later innovations. The new Buddhism (Mahāyāna), on the other hand, claimed to have evolved a more profound doctrine of salvation in the elaboration of a polytheistic theology with monarchical and devotional tendencies.

The fundamental conception of Buddhism, however, is atonement by good deeds which produce the necessary merit to counteract the evil committed by the individual, and if any balance remains it is made available for others. The stations on the road to the good life in the *Kutadanta Suttanta* are set forth as so many degrees of sacrifice (*yanna*), the term being employed apparently as a symbol of self-offering.[1] Moreover, the Brahmanical sacrifices conflicted with

---

[1] *Kutadanta Suttanta : Dialogues of the Buddha*, Eng. trans. by W. Rhys Davids (Oxford, 1899), i, pp. 173 f.

the deeply-rooted aversion to the taking of life, and thus blood-offerings were ruled out on this score.

> " Let Brahmins, Brahmins kill . . .
> We see no cattle asking to be slain
> That they a new and better life may gain.
> Rather they go unwilling to their death,
> And in vain struggles yield their latest breath.
> To veil the post, the victim and the blow,
> The Brahmins let their choicest rhetoric flow." [1]

Again, the actual offerings were regarded as ineffectual :

> " The sacrifices speak to us of things
> We see and hear, yea, taste, of men's desires
> And women. I have learnt to say of things
> That bring rebirth, ' Lo I it is canker.' Hence
> No more delight I take in sacrifice
> Nor in oblation." [2]

Therefore, the institution of sacrifice was foreign to the fundamental metaphysical philosophy of Buddhism, the whole of existence being reduced to purely ethical and spiritual concepts which limit the vision of reality to subjective intuition of the Absolute attained by renunciation. But, as Dean Inge says, " we cannot make our highest intuitions and experiences our own without translating them into symbolical or mythological forms. Myth and cultus seem to be the untransparent middle term between the spiritual and the temporal." [3] And the symbols that exert the greatest influence on men's lives and minds are those which belong to a venerable tradition. Consequently, it is

---

[1] *Jataka*, vi, No. 543.
[2] *Vinaya Texts : Sacred Books of the East*, xiii, 1881, 118–39.
[3] *Outspoken Essays* (Lond., 1923), ii, p. 254.

the ancient myths and rites that most readily lend themselves to interpretation as symbols of a higher reality, though they will always tend to retain their original significance for the unsophisticated. Thus, Buddhism was compelled to adopt the erotic imagery of Hinduism, which proved to be more human and satisfying to the popular mind than the loftier abstract speculations of Gautama and his earlier followers, till it finally collapsed in the land of its birth, and began its long pilgrimage eastwards to China, Korea and Japan.

Symbols, however, can seldom be transplanted to an alien culture without undergoing some change, and it was the very elasticity of Buddhism that fostered its progress in the Far East, and enabled it to adapt its philosophy to the needs of less mystically-minded people. Furthermore, in China both Lao-tse and Confucius had already given an ethical turn to the ritual pattern. Lao-tse recognized in the conception of *Tao* a metaphysical principle of transcendent existence, the indefinable ground of all things yet immanent in the universe and bringing to perfection individual entities. This ultimate essence and impulse of all definite things had an ethical significance as the " way " that men should follow, and therefore the highest virtue was to live in accordance with *Tao*. Lao-tse, however, made little impression on the popular religious practice, and the ethical movement in China owes more to Confucius than to any other teacher.

Without committing himself to any theological position beyond the recognition of the accepted religious duties, Confucius emphasized the moral implications of the traditional rites by which, he main-

284

tained, "the ancient kings sought to represent the ways of heaven and to regulate the feelings of men. Therefore he who neglects or violates them may be spoken of as dead, and he who observes them as alive."[1] They have their origin, that is to say, in the familiar ritual pattern in which the divine chief *shen*, who rules all things as the Supreme Emperor, is worshipped at the winter solstice by his earthly son, the head of the State, in one of the most elaborate sacrifices ever performed. By this action the beneficence of heaven is renewed, in the usual manner, and the ritual for all the State sacrifices is similar to that for Heaven, though the magnificence varies according to the rank of the gods.

In short, the State religion performed by the Son of Heaven as high priest, and his deputies, is thoroughly ritualistic and sacrificial, offering being made to secure the good working of the *Tao*, or universal order, on its *Yang*, or beneficent side, and so to frustrate the evil spirits who constitute the *Yin* cosmic soul. The exercise of this worship is the highest duty of the rulers because upon it depends the maintenance of the natural order, and the well-being of the community. Moreover, the worship of ancestors is regulated in the State ritual, and if the spirits of the departed are represented as partaking in the offerings in the ancestral temple, and at the altar on the grave, there is also a deeper significance in the ritual since the true sacrifice is the heart of the offerer without which the most elaborate ceremony would fail to secure the approval of the spirits.

For Confucius the ethical value of the system lay

---

[1] *Sacred Books of the East*, iii; *Lu-yun*, iv, 5, and i, 4.

in the conformity of the individual will to the common good, the promotion of the " Great Unity " by the merging of self in the universal order, and in the case of the ancestral sacrifices, the encouragement of filial piety. This, however, is not religion, and for practical purposes Taoism as a ritual cultus, and Buddhism in its Mahayana form, proved to be more attractive. Nevertheless, Confucianism played its part in investing the ritual order with an ethical significance, and strengthened the ties of family life around the common altar.

Throughout these developments the central conception underlying the institution of sacrifice—the giving of life to promote and conserve life—continued to find expression, but in a spiritualized and moralized form. Thus behind the Confucian State religion there was the ancient belief in the control of natural processes by a ritual organization. In association with the *Yang* and the *Yin*, as the positive and negative principles in heaven and earth responsible for the recurrence of the seasons and their phenomena, there arose a ritual worship of the gods to secure health and wealth and banish famine and barrenness. Out of these ideas a moral law of justice and ethical righteousness emerged, just as the Vedic ceremonial order was reinterpreted in terms of a metaphysical philosophy by Zarathustra, Gautama, and the writers of the *Upanisads*, as the vision of transcendent reality became the highest revelation of the ultimate meanings of life. But for the practical purposes of religion these lofty ethical conceptions of Ultimate Reality were too abstract and nebulous, so that it was not long before Hinduism, Buddhism and Mazdæism were back again where they started on the higher quest. In the Græco-Roman world metaphysical and moral philosophy were so completely separated from practical religion that they had little direct effect upon the institution of sacrifice. The religious duties demanded by the ancient ritual order were usually admitted by the philosophers, though not infrequently treated with some measure of contempt or ridicule, as, for example, in the conversation between Socrates and the Athenian soothsayer Euthyphro, who maintained that piety consists in learning how to please the gods by prayer and sacrifices. Whereupon Socrates inquired, " then sacrifice is giving to the gods, and prayer asking of the gods ? " On receiving from Euthyphro an answer in the affirmative, the Satirist was able to show that piety, on this hypothesis, is a business device between the gods and men.

Post-Exilic Judaism, on the other hand, was more successful in arriving at a solution of the problem by establishing a re-evaluation of the ancient law of sacrifice in terms of ethical monotheism as a new vision of reality vouchsafed through the spiritual experience of the Exile, and the prophetic movement. In Christianity the movement was further developed in a new world order, the earlier life ritual taking over a highly spiritualized significance in metaphysical concepts centring in the theology of a progressive re-creation and regeneration of the human race by which mankind is revivified and incorporated in a higher divine unity. The Oriental search for the Absolute transcending all finite modes of being, which virtually excludes all ritual expression of reality as a means of salvation, was abandoned in favour of the doctrine of an accessible personal Deity permanently united to man in so close a union that the natural and the supernatural are regarded as inter-penetrated in such a manner that " the self-offering of Christ reaches the utmost limit of externality through the presentation of material symbols, in order that souls in material bodies may have sensible assurance of Christ's coming to them from without, which their earthly condition craves, even while they cannot see Him come." [1] Thus, the ancient ritual order was transvaluated, and a link forged between the higher reality of ultimate concepts, and their symbolical representation.

Being founded upon the most fundamental concepts in human society, the institution of sacrifice is capable of becoming infused with a new spirit, and undergoing a complete ethical transformation. Nevertheless, it is essentially part of a culture pattern, and in consequence when the institution ceases to operate the associated religious order tends to disintegrate. Thus Buddhism broke up the old religion in India for a time just as the corresponding ethical movement in Europe in the days of the Reformation undermined historic Christianity in its institutional form. For a while, it is true, the sacrificial principle was maintained in Protestantism by shifting the centre from the Eucharist to the Atonement, from the altar to the cross. But in the majority of Protestant communities the idea of sacri-

[1] O. Quick, *The Christian Sacraments* (Lond., 1927), pp. 204 f.

fice has now almost lapsed except as a purely subjective offering of a pure heart, and vocal thanksgiving which is sometimes connected with the symbols of the death of Christ. With it has gone the old religious solidarity so that in every country where the Mass has been decentralized institutional religion is in process of collapse. There are, of course, other factors in the case, but it can hardly be denied that the break-up of the ritual order is one of the most important causes of the phenomena.

The history of ritual is the history of religion, and the vitality of sacrifice is shown by its remarkable power of survival when the ancient myths and rites become reinterpreted as symbols of metaphysical and ethical concepts. With the spiritualization of the conception of Deity has come a refinement of divine attributes and requirements. Offerings from being the means whereby the sacred order is maintained, and the gods enabled to fulfil their beneficent functions on earth, tend to be explained as gifts in the form of presents, or tributes paid by the creatures to the Creator. These may take the form of honorific free-will offerings in grateful recognition of the goodness of the deity—an honorarium rather than a necessity or a bribe. Or sacrifices may be made as an act of atonement for wrong-doing—piacular offerings of a life in expiation for sin. When this aspect of the institution finds its highest expression ethically in voluntary self-immolation, the destruction or surrender of something greatly valued or desired for a higher claim, such as duty or the welfare of others, comes to be spoken of as self-sacrifice. On a lower plane, any philanthropic endeavour involving loss in devotion to a worthy cause may be termed a " sacrifice," while in modern language the expression is frequently used to signify the disposal of an article at a greatly reduced value. At this stage the process of desacralization and disintegration is complete, the conception of sacrifice having entirely lost its age-long significance as an ancient ritual institution.

BIBLIOGRAPHY

INTRODUCTION

Bacon, B. W., *The Fourth Gospel in Research and Debate.* New Haven, U.S.A., 1918.

Barth, A., *The Religions of India.* London, 1882.

Bernard, J. H., *The Gospel according to St. John* (International Critical Commentary). Edinburgh, 1928.

Breasted, J. H., *Religion and Thought in Ancient Egypt.* London, 1912.

Carpenter, J. E., *The Johannine Writings.* London, 1927.

Davids, Mrs. C. A. F. Rhys, *Buddhist Psychology.* Second edition, London, 1924.

Davids, T. W. Rhys, *Buddhism.* London, 1904.

Driver, S. R., *An Introduction to the Literature of the Old Testament.* Edinburgh, 1913.

Eliot, Sir C. N. E., *Hinduism and Buddhism.* London, 1921.

Erman, A., *Handbook of Egyptian Religion.* London, 1907.

Harrison, J. E., *Ancient Art and Ritual.* London, 1913.

Harrison, P. N., *The Problem of the Pastoral Epistles.* Oxford, 1921.

Hobhouse, L. T., Wheeler, G. C., and Ginberg, M., *The Material Culture and Social Organization of the Simpler Peoples.* London, 1930.

James, E. O., *Primitive Ritual and Belief.* London, 1917.

Jones, M., *New Testament in the Twentieth Century.* London, 1914.

Keith, A. B., *Buddhist Philosophy.* Oxford, 1923.

Kent, C. F., *The Growth and Contents of the Old Testament.* London, 1926.

Langdon, S., *Sumerian Liturgical Texts.* Philadelphia, 1919. Oxford Editions of Cuneiform Texts. Vol. II : *The*

Weld-Blundell Collection. 1923; Vol. VII: *Pictographic Inscriptions from Jemdet Nair.* Oxford, 1928.

Macdonell, A. A., *History of Sanskrit Literature.* London, 1900.

Malinowski, B., *Myth in Primitive Psychology.* London, 1926. " Culture " in *Encyclopædia of the Social Sciences* (London, 1931). Vol. IV.

Marett, R. R., *The Threshold of Religion.* London, 1914.

McNeill, A. H., *Introduction to the Study of the New Testament.* Oxford, 1927.

Monier-Williams, M., *Religious Thought and Life in India.* London, 1883.

Nicholson, R. A., *Literary History of the Arabs.* Second edition, Cambridge, 1927.

Oldenberg, H., *Die Literatur des alten Indien.* Stuttgart, 1903.

    Sacred Books of the East: XIII, XVII, XX (Vinaya Texts). Edited by T. W. Rhys Davids and H. Oldenberg.

Sandy, W., *Oxford Studies in the Synoptic Problem.* Oxford, 1911.

Smith, S., *The Early History of Assyria to* 1000 *B.C.* London, 1928.

Streeter, B. H., *The Four Gospels.* London, 1926.

CHAPTER I

Batchelor, J., *The Ainu and their Folk-Lore.* London, 1901.

Bégouen, le Comte, *Comptes-rendus de l'Academie des Inscriptions et Belles-Lettres,* 1912.

    L'Anthropologie, XXIII, 1912.

    Revue Anthropologique, 1923.

Boule, M., *Les Hommes Fossiles.* Paris, 1921.

Bourke, J. G., "Notes on the Religion of the Apache Indians," *Folk-Lore,* II, 1891.

    " The Medicine-men of the Apache," 9*th Report Bureau American Ethnology.* Washington, 1892.

Burkitt, M. C., *Prehistory*. Second edition,Cambridge, 1925.
   Our Forerunners. London, 1924.
   South Africa's Past in Stone and Paint. Cambridge, 1928.
Cook, S. A., *The Study of Religions*. London, 1914.
   The Foundations of Religion. London, 1914.
Cushing, F. H., "Zuñi Fetishes" in *2nd R.B.A.E.*
   Washington, 1883.
Frazer, Sir J. G., *Totemism and Exogamy*. London, 1910.
Freud, S., *Totem and Tabu*. Eng. trans. by A. A. Brill.
   New York, 1918.
Hoffman, W. J., "The Midé'wiwin or Grand Medicine
   Society of the Ojibwa," in *7th R.B.A.E.* Wash-
   ington, 1891.
Howitt, A. W., *Native Tribes of South-East Australia*.
   London, 1904.
Hubert,H.,and Mauss, M., in *L'Année Sociologique*,ii, 1897–8.
Im Thurn, Sir E. F., *Among the Indians of Guiana*. London,
   1883.
James, E. O., *Primitive Ritual and Belief*. London, 1917.
   "Concept of Soul-substance in N. America," *Folk-
   lore*, xxxviii, 1927.
Jevons, F. B., *Introduction to the History of Religion*. London,
   1896.
King, I., *The Development of Religion*. New York, 1910.
Kruijt, A. C., "Indonesians" in *Encyclopædia of Religion and
   Ethics*, pt. vii, 1914.
Kühn, H., "Das Kuntsgewerbe der Eiszeit," in Bossert,
   Geschichte des Kunstgewerbes, Vol. I. Berlin, 1928.
   Kunst und Kultur der Vorzeit Europas. Das Paläolithi-
   kum. Berlin, 1929.
Luquet, G. H., *The Art and Religion of Fossil Man*. Transla-
   tion by J. T. Russell. New Haven, Yale Univ.
   Press, 1930.
Macalister, R. A. S., *Textbook of European Archæology*.
   Cambridge, 1921.
Mainage, Th., *Les Religions de la Préhistoire*. Paris, 1921.

Marett, R. R., *The Threshold of Religion*. London, 1914.

Money-Kyrle, A., *The Meaning of Sacrifice*. London, 1930.

Obermaier, H., and Kühn, H., *Bushman Art*. Oxford, 1930.

Rivers, W. H. R., " Concept of Soul-substance in New Guinea, etc.," *Folk-lore*, vol. xxxi, 1920.

Roheim, G., *Australian Totemism*. London, 1925.

Smith, G. Elliot, *The Evolution of the Dragon*. Manchester, 1919.

Smith, W. R., *The Religion of the Semites* (3rd ed. S. A. Cook). London, 1927.

Smyth, R. E., *The Aborigines of Victoria*. Melbourne, 1878.

Spencer, W. B., and Gillen, F. J., *Northern Tribes of Central Australia*. London, 1904. *Native Tribes of Central Australia*. London, 1898.

The Arunta. London, 1927.

Stow, G. W., *Rock-Paintings in South Africa*. Notes, etc., by D. F. Bleek. London, 1930.

Trumbull, H. C., *The Blood Covenant*. London, 1887.

Verneau, R., *Les Grottes de Grimaldi*. Monaco, 1906.

The Men of the Barma Grande. Menton, 1908.

CHAPTER II

Batchelor, J., *The Ainua and their Folk-lore*. London, 1901.

Blackman, A. M., *Récueil de Travaux*, vol. xxxix, 1, 2. Paris, 1920.

Zeitschrift für Ägyptische Sprache Altertumskunde, Bd. 50, 1912.

" Worship," in *E.R.E.*, vol. xii, 1921.

Breasted, J. H., *Development of Religion and Thought in Ancient Egypt*. London, 1912.

Brugsch, H., *Religion und Mythologie der Alten Aegypter*. Leipsic, 1885–8.

Budge, E. A. W., *Osiris and the Egyptian Resurrection*. London, 1911.

The Legends of the Gods. London, 1912.

Burkett, M. C., *Prehistory*. Second edition, Cambridge, 1925.

Cobo, B., *Historia del nuevo mundo*. Sevilla, 1895.

Cumont, F., *Les Religions Oriental dans le Paganisme Romaine*. Paris, 1909.

Dechelette, J., *Manuel d'archéologie préhistorique celtique et gallo-romaine*. Paris, 1908–14.

Erman, A., *Handbook of Egyptian Religion*. London, 1907.

Farnell, L. R., *The Cults of the Greek States*, ii. Oxford, 1896.

Foucart, G., " King " (Egyptian) in *E.R.E.*, vol. vii, 1914.

Frankfort, H., *Studies in Early Pottery in the Near East*. London, 1924.

Frazer, Sir J. G., *Golden Bough*. Pt. IV, " Adonis, Attis and Osiris," 2 vols. Pt. V, " Spirits of the Corn and of the Wild," 2 vols. Pt. VI, "Dying God," London, 1914.

Harrison, J. E., *Prolegomena to the Study of Greek Religion*. Cambridge, 1907.
Themis. Cambridge, 1912.

Hartland, S., *The Legend of Perseus*. London, 1894.

Hepding, H., *Attis, seine Mythen und sein Kult*. Giessen, 1903.

Hocart, A. M., *Kingship*. Oxford, 1927.

Jackson, J. W., *Shells as Evidence of the Migration of Early Culture*. Manchester, 1917.

Junker, H., *Die Stundenwachen in den Osirismysterien*. Wien, 1910.

Langdon, S. H., *Sumerian and Babylonian Psalms*. Paris, 1909.
Babylonian Liturgies. Paris, 1913.
Tammuz and Ishtar. Oxford, 1914.

MacCurdy, G. G., *Human Origins*, 2 vols. London, 1924.

Malinowski, B., " Magic, Science and Religion," in *Science, Religion and Reality*. London, 1926.

Mannhardt, W., *Ant-Wald-und Feldkulte*. Berlin, 1877.
Mythologische Forschungen. Strasburg, 1884.

Moret, A., *Kings and Gods of Egypt*. New York and London, 1912.

Annales du Musée Guimet, Du caractère religieux de la Royauté Pharaonique. Paris, 1902.

Murray, M. A., *The Osireion at Abydos*. London, 1904.

Newberry, P. E., "Egypt as a Field of Anthropological Research," in *Report of British Association*, 1923. London, 1924.

Nielsson, M. P., *Greek Religion*. London, 1925.

Obermaier, H., *Fossil Man in Spain*. New Haven, 1925 (Introd. H. F. Osborn).

Perry, W. J., *The Children of the Sun*. London, 1923.

Roberts, C., *Oidipus*. Berlin, 1915.

Sacred Books of the East. Edited by F. Max Müller. Translation by J. Eggeling. Vol. xli. Oxford, 1894.

Schaefer, H., *Mysterien des Osiris in Abydos*. Leipzig, 1904.

Schmidt, W., *The Origin and Growth of Religion*. Eng. trans. by H. J. Rose. London, 1931.

Seligman, C. G., *Cult of the Nyakang and the Divine Kings of the Shilluk*. Khartoum, 1911. (4th Report Wellcome Research Laboratories.)

"Dinka" in *Encyclopædia of Religion and Ethics*. Vol. IV, 1911.

Sethe, K., *Dramatische Texte zu Altægyptischen mysterienspielen*. Leipzig, 1928.

Smith, G. E. Elliot, *The Evolution of the Dragon*. Manchester, 1919.

Stow, G. W., *Native Races of South Africa*. London, 1905.

Wiedemann, A., *Religion of the Ancient Egyptians*. London, 1897.

CHAPTER III

Bancroft, H. H., *Native Races of the Pacific Coast*. San Francisco, 1882. Vols. ii, iii, v.

Brasseur de Bourbourg, Abbée, *Histoire des nations civilisées du Mexique et de l'Amérique-centrale.* Paris, 1857–9.
Popol Vuh. Paris, 1861.
Brinton, D. G., *Myths of the New World.* New York, 1868.
Campbell, J., *Wild Tribes of Kurdistan.* London, 1864.
Charnay, D., *Les Anciennes villes du Nouveau Monde.* Paris, 1888.
Cieza de Leon, P., *Travels.* English trans. by C. R. Markham. London, 1864.
Cobo, B., *Historia del nuevo mondo.* Vol. iv, Sevilla, 1896.
Förstemann, E. B., "Mexican and Central American Antiquities," *28th Bull. B.A.E.* Washington, 1904.
Frazer, J. G., *Golden Bough.* Pt. VII, "Spirits of the Corn and of the Wild." London, 1914. Pt. IX, "The Scapegoat." 1914.
Joyce, T. A., *Mexican Archæology.* London, 1914.
South American Archæology. London, 1912.
Macpherson, S. C., *Memorials of Service in India.* London, 1865.
Molina, C. de, *Relación de las fabulas y Ritos de los Ingas.* Lima, 1916.
Morley, S. G., "An Introduction to the Study of Maya Hieroglyphs," *57th R.B.A.E.* Washington, 1915.
The Inscriptions at Copan. Washington, 1920 (Carnegie Institution Publication No. 219).
Payne, E., *History of the New World called America.* 2 vols. Oxford, 1892.
Prescott, W. H., *The Conquest of Mexico.* 2 vols. London, 1922.
Ranking, J., *Conquest of Peru and Mexico.* London, 1827.
Sahagun, Le R. P. Fray Bernardino de, *Histoire générale des choses de la Nouvelle-Espagne,* par D. Jourdanet et R. Simeon. Paris, 1880.
Schoolcraft, H. R., *Indian Tribes of the United States.* Philadelphia, 1853–6.

BIBLIOGRAPHY

Seler, E., "Mexican Antiquities" in 28th *Bulletin Bureau American Ethnology.* Washington, 1904.

Altmexikanische Studien, vol. ii. Berlin, 1899.

Smet, J. de, in *Annales de la propagation de la foi.* Vol. xi (1838); vol. xv (1843).

Spence, L., *The Myths of Mexico and Peru.* London, 1913.

The Civilization of Ancient Mexico. Cambridge, 1912.

Spinden, H. J., *Memoirs Peabody Museum American Archæology and Ethnology,* vi, 1913.

Torquemada, J. de, *Monarquia Indiana.* Madrid, 1723.

Velasco, P. Juan de, *Histoire du Royaume de Quito.* Paris, 1840.

Westermarck, E., *Origin and Development of Moral Ideas.* Vol. i, London, 1906.

CHAPTER IV

Bastian, A., *Die Völker des Östlichen Asien.* Leipzig, 1866.

Baudesson, H., *Indo-China and its Primitive People.* London, 1919.

Best, E. J., *Journal of the Polynesian Society,* vol. xii, 1903.

Boas, F., "Reports of the N.W. Tribes of Canada," *Report of the British Association for the Advancement of Science,* 1890.

Bowdich, T. E., *Mission from Cape Coast Castle to Ashantee.* London, 1873.

Codrington, R. H., *The Melanesians and their Folk-lore.* Oxford, 1891.

Cross, E. B., "On the Karens," *Journal of American Oriental Society.* Vol. iv, 1854.

Ellis, W., *Polynesian Researches.* London, 1832–6.

Fox, C. E., *The Threshold of the Pacific.* London, 1924.

Frazer, Sir J. G., *Golden Bough.* Pt. I, "The Magic Art," vol. i. London, 1917.

Belief in Immortality, vol. i. London, 1913.

Furness, W. H., *Home-Life of Borneo Head-Hunters.* Philadelphia, 1902.

Haddon, A. C., *Journal of the Anthropological Institute,* XIX. 1890.

Hartland, S., *The Legend of Perseus*, vol. ii. London, 1895.

Hose, C., and McDougall, W., *The Pagan Tribes of Borneo*. London, 1912.

Hose, C., *Natural Man*. London, 1926.

Howitt, A. W., *Native Tribes of South-East Australia*. London, 1904.

Hutton, J. H., " The Significance of Head-Hunting in Assam," *Journal of the Royal Anthropological Institute*, vol. lviii, 1928.

James, E. O., " Concept of Soul-substance, etc.," *Folk-Lore*, vol. xxxviii, 1927.

" Cremation and Preservation of the Dead in N. America," *American Anthropologist*, new series, xxx, 1928.

Keating, W. H., *Narrative of an Expedition to the Source of the St. Peter River*. Philadelphia, 1824.

Marshall, H. I., *The Karen People of Burma*. Ohio, 1922.

Mills, J. P., *The Ao Naga*. London, 1926.

Nieuwenhuis, A. W., *Quer durch Borneo*. Leiden, 1907.

Nordenskiöld, E., *Indianerleben El Gran Chaco (Sudamerika)*. Leipzig, 1912.

Ratzel, F., *History of Mankind*. London, 1897.

Rivers, W. H. R., *History of Melanesian Society*. Vol. ii, Cambridge, 1914.

Roheim, G., *Australian Totemism*. London, 1925.

Scott, J. G., and Hardiman, J. P., *Gazetteer of Upper Burma and the Shan States*. Rangoon, 1900–1.

Talbot, A. M., *Some Nigerian Fertility Cults*. Oxford, 1927.

Tremearne, A. J. N., *Tailed Head-Hunters of Nigeria*. London, 1912.

Westermarck, E., *Origin and Development of Moral Ideas*, vol. i. London, 1906.

Whiffen, T. W., " The Indians of the Issá-Japurá District (S. America)," *Folk-Lore*, vol. xxiv, March, 1913.

Wilson, J. L., *Western Africa*. London, 1856.

CHAPTER V

Angus, S., *The Mystery Religions and Christianity*. London, 1925.

The Religious Quest of the Græco-Roman World. London, 1929.

Anrich, G., *Das antike Mysterienwesen*. Göttingen, 1894.

Baumeister, A., *Hymni Homerici*. Leipsic, 1860.

Casson, S., *Macedonia, Thrace and Illyria*. Oxford, 1926.

Cornford, F. M., *The Origin of Attic Comedy*. London, 1914.

Crawley, A. E., *The Mystic Rose*, New Edition by T. Besterman. London, 1929.

Cumont, F., *Textes et Monuments relatifs aux Mystères de Mithra*, 2 vols. Brussels, 1896–9.

Religions orientales dans le paganisme romain. 2nd Edition, Paris, 1909. English trans. by T. J. McCormack, 2nd Edition. Chicago, 1910.

Dieterich, A., *Eine Mithrasliturgie*. Leipzig, 1903.

Dill, S., *Roman Society from Nero to Marcus Aurelius*, 2nd Edition. London, 1905.

Dorsey, J. O., "Omaha Sociology," in *3rd R.B.A.E.* Washington, 1884.

"A Study in Siouan Cults," in *11th R.B.A.E.* Washington, 1894.

Durkheim, E. *The Elementary Forms of the Religious Life*, English trans. London, 1913.

Farnell, L. R., *Cults of the Greek States*, vol. iii. Oxford, 1906, vol. v, 1909.

"Sacrificial Communion in Greek Religion," *Hibbert Journal*. Vol. ii, No. 2, 1904.

Fison, L., "The Nanga, or Sacred Stone Enclosure, of Wainimala, Fiji," *Journal of the Royal Anthropological Institute*, vol. xiv, 1885.

Fletcher, A. C., "The Hako, A Pawnee Ceremony," in *R.B.A.E.*, vol. ii. Washington, 1904.

Foerster, R., *Der Raub und die Rückkehr der Persephone.* Stuttgart, 1874.

Foucart, M. P., *Les Grands mystères d'Eleusis.* Paris, 1900.

Fowler, W. W., *Religious Experience of the Roman People.* London, 1911.

Frazer, Sir J. G., *Golden Bough*, Pt. XI : " Balder the Beautiful," vol. ii, London, 1914. Pt. VII : " Spirits of the Corn and of the Wild," vol. i, London, 1914.

Belief in Immortality. London, 1913.

Totemism and Exogamy, vol. iii. London, 1910.

Gardner, P., " Mysteries (Greek) " in *E.R.E.*, vol. ix. Edinburgh, 1917.

The Religious Experience of St. Paul. London, 1911.

Grote, G., *History of Greece.* London, 1869.

Harrison, J., *Prolegomena to the Study of Greek Religion*, Third Edition. Cambridge, 1922.

Hepding, H., *Attis, Seine Mythen und sein Kult.* Giessen, 1903.

Hoffmann, W. J., " The Mide'wiwin or Grand Medicine Society of the Ojibwa," in *7th R.B.A.E.* Washington, 1891.

Howitt, A. W., *Native Tribes of South-East Australia.* London, 1904.

Jevons, F. B., *Introduction to the History of Religion.* London, 1902.

Koch-Grunberg, *Zwei Jahre unter den Indianern.* Berlin, 1909–10.

Lang, A., *Myth Ritual and Religion.* London, 1887.

Lobeck, C. A., *Aglaophamus sive de theologie mysticæ Græcorum causis.* Konigsberg, 1829.

Perry, W. J., " The Drama of Death and Resurrection," *Hibbert Journal.* January, 1927.

Radin, P., " Ritual and Significance of the Winnebago Medicine Dance," in *Journal of the American Folk-lore Society*, vol. xxiv, 1911.

Reitzenstein, R., *Griechish-agyptischen und fruh christlichen Literatur*. Leipzig, 1904.
Die hellenistischen Mysterienreligionen. Leipzig, 1910.

Rohde, E., *Psyche*. Eng. trans. by W. B. Hollis. London, 1925.

Routledge, W. S. and K., *With a Prehistoric People, the Akikuyu of British East Africa*. London, 1910.

Schoolcraft, H. R. S., *Indian Tribes of the United States*. Philadelphia, 1853, vol. iii; 1856, vol. v.

Scott, W., in *Proceedings of the Society of Historical Theology*. Oxford, 1917–18.

Showerman, G., "The Great Mother of the Gods," in *Bulletin of the University of Wisconsin*, vol. xlviii. Madison, 1901.

Vetter, K., *Nachrichten über Kaiser Wilhelms-land und den Bismarck-Archipel*, 1897. Berlin.

Webster, H., *Primitive Secret Societies*. New York, 1908.

CHAPTER VI

Abrahams, I., *Studies in Pharisaism and the Gospels*. First Series. Cambridge, 1917. Second Series, 1924.
"How did the Jews Baptize?" *J.T.S.*, vol. xii, No. 48, July 1911, pp. 609–12.

Angus, S., *The Mystery Religions and Christianity*. London, 1925.
The Religious Quest of the Græco-Roman World. London, 1929.

Bacon, B. W., *Jesus and Paul*. London, 1921.

Bartlet, J. V., and Carlyle, A. J., *Christianity in History*, Pt. ii. London, 1917.

Batiffol, P., *Études d'histoire et de Théologie Positive*. Paris, 1905.

Brandt, W., *Die judischen Baptismen*. Giessen, 1910.

Branscomb, B. H., *Jesus and the Law of Moses*. London, 1930.

Büchler, A., " The Levitical Impurity of the Gentile in Palestine before the year 70," *The Jewish Quarterly Review*, vol. xvii, No. 1, July 1926.

Burckjardt, J., *Die Zeit Constantin's des Grossen*. Bale, 1857.

Burkitt, F. C., *The Eucharistic Sacrifice*. Cambridge, 1921.

Clow, W. M., *The Church and the Sacraments*. London, 1923.

Cumont, F., *Les Religions orientales dans le paganisme romain*. Paris, 1909.

Dalman, G., *Jesus-Jeshua*. Leipzig, 1922.

Edersheim, A., *The Life and Times of Jesus the Messiah*, vol. ii. London, 1887.

Gardner, P., *The Religious Experience of St. Paul*. London, 1921.

Gavin, F., *The Jewish Antecedents of the Christian Sacraments*. London, 1928.

Glover, T. R., *The Conflict of Religions in the Early Roman Empire*. London, 1909.

Harnack, *History of Dogma*, vols. v, vi (Eng. trans.). London, 1894–9.

Headlam, A. C., *Life and Teaching of Jesus Christ*. London, 1923.

Hicks, F. C. N., *The Fullness of Sacrifice*. London, 1930.

Hölscher, G., *Geschichte der israelitischen und jüdischen Religion*. Leipzig, 1922.

Hüfling, J. W. W., *Das Sacrament der Taufe*. Erlangen, 1848.

Kennedy, H. A. A., *St. Paul and the Mystery Religion*. London, 1913.

Kennett, R. H., *The Last Supper : Its Significance in the Upper Room*. Cambridge, 1921.

Kidd, B. J., *The Later Mediæval Doctrine of the Eucharistic Sacrifice*. London, 1898.

Knox, W. L. *St. Paul and the Church of Jerusalem*. Cambridge, 1925.

Kohler, K., *Jewish Encyclopædia*, " Essenes," vol. v (1903).

Krauss, S., *Talmudische Archäologieä*, Bd. iii. Leipzig, 1910.

Lake, K., *The Earlier Epistles of St. Paul.* London, 1911.

Lambert, J. C., *The Sacraments in the New Testament.* Edinburgh, 1903.

Lietzmann, H., *Messe und Herrenmahl, eine studie zur geschicte der Liturgie.* Bonn, 1926.

Loewe, H., " Demons and Spirits (Jewish) " in *E.R.E.*, vol. iv. Edinburgh, 1911.

Loisy, A. F., *Les Mystères païens et le mystère Chrétien.* Paris, 1914.

Moore, G. F., *Judaism.* Cambridge, 1927.

Nock, A. D., " Early Gentile Christianity and its Hellenistic Background," in *Essays on the Trinity and the Incarnation.* Edited by A. E. J. Rawlinson. London, 1928.

Oesterley, W. O. E., and Box, G. H., *The Religion and Worship of the Synagogue.* London, 1911.

    The Jewish Background of the Christian Liturgy. Oxford, 1925.

Reitzenstein, R., *Die Hellenistischen Mysteriereligionen.* Leipzig, 1910.

Rogers, C., *J.T.S.*, vol. xii, April 1911.

Schechlter, S., *Documents of Jewish Sectaries. Fragments of a Zadokite Work.* Cambridge, 1910.

Schürer, E., *History of the Jewish People.* Edinburgh, 1890. Eng. trans. of *Geschichte des Judischen Volkes.* Leipzig, 1886.

Schweitzer, A., *The Mysticism of Paul the Apostle.* London, 1931.

    Quest of the Historical Jesus, Eng. trans. London, 1910.

Scott, E. F., *The First Age of Christianity.* New York, 1926.

Scott, W., *Proceedings of the Society of Historical Theology.* Oxford, 1917-8.

Singer, S., *Authorised Daily Prayer Book of the Hebrew Congregations.* London, 1922.

Stone, D., *A History of the Doctrine of the Eucharist.* London, 1909.

Streeter, B. H., *The Four Gospels*. London, 1926.
  The Primitive Church. London, 1929.
Thackeray, H. St. J., " Josephus," in Hastings' *Dictionary of Bible*, Extra Volume. Edinburgh, 1904.
Wendland, P., Die Hellenistisch-Romische, Tübingen, 1912; cf. Lietzmann, *Handbuch zum Neuen Testament*, vol. i, Bd. 2.

CHAPTER VII

Anselm, St., *Cur Deus Homo*. Translation in Ancient and Modern Library. London, 1889.
Bückler, A., *Studies in Sin and Atonement*. Oxford, 1928.
Burney, C. F., *The Old Testament Conception of Atonement fulfilled by Christ*. Oxford, 1921.
Charles, R. H., *The Apocrypha and pseudigrapha of the Old Testament*. Oxford, 1913.
Curtiss, S. I., *Primitive Semitic Religion To-day*. Chicago, 1902.
Dale, R. W., *The Atonement*. London, 1875.
Dillman, A., *Handbuch der Altestamentlichen Theologie*. Leipzig, 1895.
Dimock, N., *The Doctrine of the Death of Christ*. London, 1903.
Driver, S. R. and Neubauer, A., *The 53rd Chapter of Isaiah according to Jewish Interpretation*. Oxford, 1877.
Farnell, L. R., *Greece and Babylonia*. London, 1911.
Foakes Jackson, F. J., and Kirsopp Lake, *The Beginnings of Christianity*, vol. i. London, 1920.
Frazer, Sir J. G., *G.B.* Pt. I : " The Magic Art." London, 1918. Pt. ix : " The Scapegoat." London, 1914.
Gayford, S. C., *Sacrifice and Priesthood*. London, 1924.
Glover, T. R., *Jesus in the Experience of Men*. London, 1921.
Gray, G. B., *Sacrifice in the Old Testament*. Oxford, 1925.
Grensted, L. W., *A Short History of the Doctrine of the Atonement*. Manchester, 1920.

Hubert, H, and Mauss, M., *Mélanges d'histoire des religions.* Paris, 1909.

Jastrow, J., *Religious Belief in Babylonia and Assyria.* New York, 1911.

The Religion of Babylonia and Assyria. Boston, 1898.

Kennett, R. H., *Old Testament Essays.* Cambridge, 1928.

King, L. W., *The Seven Tablets of Creation*, vol. i. London, 1902.

Kostlin, J., *The Theology of Luther*, Eng. trans. by E. Hay. Philadelphia, 1883.

Langdon, S. H., " The Hebrew Word for ' Atone,' " in *The Expository Times*, vol. xxii, 1911.

" The Scapegoat in Babylonian Religion," in *The Expository Times*, vol. xxiv, 1912.

" Expiation and Atonement," in *E.R.E.*, vol. v. Edinburgh, 1912.

Sumerian and Babylonian Psalms. Paris, 1909.

Babylonian Penitential Psalms. Paris, 1927. Oxford edition of Cuneiform Texts, vol. vi.

McLeod Campbell, J., *The Nature of the Atonement.* London, 1886.

Moberly, R. C., *Atonement and Personality.* London, 1901.

Montefiore, C. G., " Rabbinic Conceptions of Repentance," in *The Jewish Quarterly Review*, vol. xvi, January 1904.

Rabbinic Literature and Gospel Teachings. London, 1930.

Morgenstein, J., *The Doctrine of Sin in the Babylonian Religion.* Berlin, 1905.

Mozley, J. K., *The Doctrine of the Atonement.* London, 1915.

Oxenham, H. N., *The Catholic Doctrine of the Atonement.* London, 1869.

Rashdall, H., *The Idea of Atonement in Christian Theology.* London, 1920.

Rawlinson, A. E. J., *The New Testament Doctrine of the Christ.* London, 1926.

Rawlinson, W. H., *The Cuneiform Inscriptions of Western Asia*, vol. iv. London, 1880–4.

Schweitzer, A., *The Quest of the Historical Jesus*. London, 1919. Eng. trans.

Thompson, R. C., *Devils and Evil Spirits of Babylonia*. London, 1904.

Tylor, E. B., *Primitive Culture*, vol. ii. 5th Edition. London, 1913.

Weiss, J., *Die Predigt Jesu vom Reiche Gottes*. Göttingen, 1892.

Westermarck, E., *The Origin and Development of Moral Ideas*, vol. i. London, 1906.

Zimmern, H., *Babylonische Busspsalmen*, vol. iv. Leipzig, 1885.

Beiträge zur Kenntnis der Babylonischen Religion. Leipzig, 1899.

CHAPTER VIII

Bevan, E. R., " Deification," in *E.R.E.*, vol. iv, 1911.

Blackman, A. M., " Priest " (Egyptian), in *E.R.E.*, vol. x, 1920.

Büchler, A., *Die Priester und der Cultus*. Wien, 1895.

Charles, R. H., *Studies in the Apocalypse*. Edinburgh, 1913.

Cheyne, T. K., " Ark of the Covenant," in *Encyclopædia Biblica*, vol. i, 1899.

Codrington, R. H., *The Melanesians and their Folk-lore*. Oxford ,1891.

Curtiss, S. I., *Primitive Semitic Religion To-day*. London, 1902.

Czaplicka, M. A., *Aboriginal Siberia*. Oxford, 1914.

Delahaye, H., *Les origines du culte des martyrs*. Bruxelles, 1912.

Duchesne, L., *Christian Worship : Its Origin and Evolution*, fifth edition, Eng. trans. by M. L. McClure. London, 1919.

Edersheim, A., *The Temple : its Ministry and Services as they were at the time of Jesus Christ*. London, 1874.

Fowler, W. Warde, *The Religious Experience of the Roman People*. London, 1911.
Roman Ideas of Deity. London, 1914.
Frazer, Sir J. G., *The Early History of Kingship*. London, 1905.
Gray, G. B., *Sacrifice in the Old Testament*. Oxford, 1925.
Hocart, A. M., " Mana," in *Man*, 1914, No. 46.
Kingship. Oxford, 1927.
Hooke, S. H., *Journal of the Manchester Egyptian and Oriental Society*, vol. xvi, 1931.
Jastrow, M., *Religious Beliefs in Babylonia and Assyria*. New York, 1911.
Die Religion Babyloniens und Assyriens. Giessen, 1912.
Journal of Biblical Literature, vol. xxviii, 1909.
Jochelson, W., " The Koryak," *Jesup North Pacific Expedition*, vol. vi, New York, 1905-8.
Klementz, D., " Buriat," in *E.R.E.*, vol. iii, 1910.
Kuenen, A., *The Religion of Israel*, vol. ii. Eng. trans. London, 1875.
Landtman, G., *The Origin of Priesthood*. Ekenaes, 1905.
Levin, M., " Mummification and Cremation in India," in *Man*, vol. xxx, Nos. 18, 32, 48, 1930.
Malinowski, B., " Magic, Science and Religion," in *Science, Religion and Reality*. London, 1926.
Marett, R. R., *The Threshold of Religion*. London, 1914.
" Magic," in *E.R.E.*, vol. viii, 1915.
Martin, R., *Die Inlandstämme der Malayischen Halbinsel*. Jena, 1905.
Mikhaïlowsky, V. M., "Shamanism in Siberia and European Russia." Eng. trans. by O. Wardrop, in *J.R.A.I.*, vol. xxiv, 1895.
Oesterreich, T. K., *Possession, Demoniacal and Other*. London, 1930. Eng. trans. by D. Ibberson.
Perry, W. J., *The Children of the Sun*. London, 1923.
Radlov, V. V., *Aus Sibiren*. Leipzig, 1884.

Rivers, W. H. R., *The History of Melanesian Society*. Cambridge, 1914.

Seligman, C. G., "Dinka," in *E.R.E.*, vol. iv, 1911.

Sellin, E., *Tell Ta'anek*. Dinkschriften der kaiserlichen Akademie der wissenschaftern. Wien, 1904.

Smith, W. R., *Religion of the Semites*. 3rd Edition, edited by S. A. Cook. London, 1927.

Sohn, R., *Outlines of Church History*. London, 1895.

Stevenson, S. M., "Fors Fortuna," *Dictionary of Roman Coins*. London, 1889.

Streeter, B. H., *The Primitive Church*. London, 1929.

Westermarck, E., *Ritual and Belief in Morocco*. London, 1926.

Origin and Development of Moral Ideas, vol. ii. London, 1908.

INDEX

A

Adonis, the Greek cult of, 65, 133

Agape, the, and its connexion with the Eucharist, 174–5

Agriculture, its discovery and connexion with the maternal functions of the soil, 52–6

  seasonal rituals and human sacrifices connected with, 53–73, 77, 84–100, 103–8, 119, 191

  potency of the human head in, 102–8

Animals, their mystic relation to man, 34–42

  employment of as sacrificial substitutes, 186, 189, 196–8, 203–5

Atonement, primitive idea of, 184–8

  and the semitic ritual of the scapegoat, 196–205

  origin and significance of the Jewish Day of, 201–5

  the Mishnaic conception of, 205–6

  the Christian notion of, 207–8

  the Pauline doctrine of, 212–13

  Christian transactional doctrine of, 213–14

  the Anselmic and penal theories of, 214–15

Attis, the Greek cult of, 65, 120–1, 133–5

Aztecs, sun worship of the, 80–1, 91–3

  human sacrifice as practised by the, 80–93, 99, 109–10

B

Babylonia, ancient literary sources of, 6–7

  New Year festival in, 61–2

  the cult of Tammuz and Ishtar in, 62–4, 73, 193, 196–9

  divination by the priests of, 238

Baptism, origins of Christian, 142–64

  Pauline theology of, 142–3, 160

  Jewish, 143–7, 153–4

  as instituted by John the Baptist, 147–9, 150–1

  of Jesus, Messianic significance of, 157–8

Baraka, the conception of in Morocco, 227–30

Batiffol, P., 175

Bezzant, Rev. J. S., ix

Blackman, Dr. A. M., viii, 68, 72

Blood, significance and vitalizing power of, 21–4, 26–33

  atonement by, in the Hebrew ritual, 199

Blood-covenant, significance of the, 33–4, 111

Blood-offering, as the origin of sacrifice, 48, 177

Box, Dr. G. H., viii

Breasted, Dr. J. H., 6

Büchler, Dr. A., 205

Budge, Sir E. Wallis, 66

Burckhardt, J., 143

C

Campbell, J. McLeod, 215

Cannibalism, prompted by desire to imbibe the soul-substance, 108–12

Chambers, Prof., 178–9

Christianity, ancient literary sources of, 10–14

  sacrament and sacrifice in, 142–83, 266–70, 288

  as a mystery religion, 142, 164

  origins of baptism in, 142–64

  as an outcome of Galilean Judaism, 154–7

  effect of Pauline theology upon, 159–64

  development of as a spiritualized mystery religion, 163

  and the ideas of mediation and atonement, 206–8, 210–20

  development of the priesthood of, 249–54

  and the struggle with Gnosticism, 251

Circumcision, as a sign of covenant among the Jews, 117, 145, 146, 153

Codrington, R. H., 226

Confucius, the teachings of, 284–6

310

INDEX